T0368904

THE HATE FACTORY

David Leslie has worked for the *News of the World* since 1970. He is also the author of the bestselling *Crimelord*, about Tam McGraw, as well as *The Happy Dust Gang, The Gangster's Wife* and *Mummy, Take Me Home*. He lives in Glasgow.

THE HATE FACTORY

THIRTY YEARS INSIDE WITH THE UK'S MOST NOTORIOUS VILLAINS

DAVID LESLIE

MAINSTREAM
PUBLISHING

EDINBURGH AND LONDON

First published in Great Britain in 2010 by
MAINSTREAM PUBLISHING COMPANY
(EDINBURGH) LTD
7 Albany Street
Edinburgh EH1 3UG

ISBN 9781845966195

A catalogue record for this book is available
from the British Library

Typeset in Bauhaus and Stone Informal

1 3 5 7 9 10 8 6 4 2

Penguin Random House is committed to a sustainable future for
our business, our readers and our planet. This book is made from
Forest Stewardship Council® certified paper.

Printed and bound in Great Britain by Clays Ltd, Elcograf S.p.A.

ACKNOWLEDGEMENTS

During a trip to meet Eileen Glover in 2000, Billy Ferris told me a series of stories about prison life. I suggested he should consider being involved in a book about his experiences. Following his reunion with Paul, he agreed to the suggestion. It was the start of a long and sometimes uphill journey, one fuelled by Billy's enthusiasm and the encouragement of his family and friends. Despite losing his liberty in 2005, he insisted the project should carry on. At that time, it would have been easy and understandable for him to have given up, but he never considered it.

Strong as has been Billy's determination to see his story in print, it has been matched by that of his friend Harry Young. Harry's faith has never wavered, nor has his support, and without him this account might never have come to fruition. Paul Ferris gave me invaluable memories. I was privileged to meet and listen to Jenny Ferris, a remarkable lady. Billy's wife Carol-Anne opened her heart about their life together. Lorraine Casey was happy to talk candidly about being with Billy when he was on the run, while her brother Steve Sinclair kindly gave help. To all, and to the many others who prefer to remain anonymous, I am sincerely grateful. My thanks also to everyone at Mainstream and to my colleagues George Wright, Gary Jamieson and, in particular, Brian Anderson, who allowed me use of his superb photographs taken at the reunion of Billy and Paul.

David Leslie

CONTENTS

FOREWORD

Having an older brother whom I have always wanted to get to know has proved very difficult, especially when that brother was hundreds of miles away from me in an English prison. Try to come to terms with that when you're a ten-year-old boy and being bullied mercilessly by a group of brothers known as the Welshes. Each of the Welshes had a brother at hand at all times; although I had a brother too, he couldn't help me escape from what I was forced to endure at the hands of the bullies. It was a situation that never failed to anger me, yet it gave me strength and the determination that one day I would get the opportunity to tell my brother that he was always with me in mind and in spirit, that he never left me.

My first-ever conviction resulted in a sentence of three months' hard graft, military style, which I served in the detention centre at Glenochil. Knowing that my brother had already spent several years in prison helped me to fight the demons that plagued me daily. Keeping my brother in my mind was a real comfort and helped me get through my own incarceration. Had we been raised in a different environment, I might well have had the opportunity to get to know my brother better. But even on the occasions when we were in the same prison together, the authorities still kept us apart most of the time, which seems like a never-ending theme to this day.

I eventually caught up with Billy when I became a free man on 22 January 2002, having served seven years for gunrunning. We began to forge a strong bond over the months that followed, and that first year left me feeling I had been reunited with a long-lost friend. Sadly, our bond was to be broken once again when dark forces descended upon Billy. A young boy was tragically killed and my brother was subsequently charged with and convicted of a crime that he did not commit. My brother is prepared to continue to fight to clear his name. Despite several attempts having been made already, the appeal courts don't appear particularly keen to listen to any further evidence. The authorities are no doubt satisfied that that have already secured their piece of flesh with the conviction of my brother. It may well take years to secure Billy's freedom without having to prove the guilt of someone else. We don't work that way and we never will; Billy did not implicate anyone else during his trial. However, an old friend of the family once said to me, 'Paul, it's not the size of the dog that's in the fight, it's the size of the fight that's in the dog that counts.' Billy and I, as brothers, will continue to fight on until the day comes when we can be together, free again and free at last!

Paul J. Ferris

Prologue

· · · · · · · · · · · ·

REUNION

FOR THE FIRST TIME IN A quarter of a century, the brothers were at liberty to embrace. There had been an all-too-brief occasion years earlier when they had held one another and laughed. But the circumstances of that meeting – Billy had been on the run from prison – had been such that neither they nor anyone else present felt comfortable remembering it. They had been together during the past 25 years, but only for brief visiting periods or for short spells when they were held in the same institution. Now, in a hotel in Glasgow, they were free to hug and celebrate the end of the years of enforced separation. Gone was the fear that an intruder might infiltrate the privacy of this moment and cause it to be abruptly ended. And while there were many who rued their reunion, and who would actively seek to end the joint freedom of the brothers, for now they could relax and enjoy the day. It was Monday, 22 January 2002.

At seven o'clock that morning, the gates of Frankland jail – an escape-proof showpiece of the English prison system a few miles from the city of Durham – had opened to release a handful of high-risk inmates whose long years of incarceration were finally over – at least for the time being, as the standard parting joke of their custodians informed them. Among them was a slight figure in a neatly fitting dark suit and sober tie, clutching a few belongings and a bag filled with legal documents.

Paul Ferris walked into the glare of television lights. While flash cameras caused those who had waited for him in the chill, dark air under the razor-wire-decorated walls and orange floodlights to blink, he made a short statement. Passing guards, seemingly reluctant to head for homes where wives waited for their help in getting children out of bed and off to school, stopped to listen, curious to know the reason for such interest in a man who had been a model of good behaviour, a friend to most and intent only on gaining the maximum remission in order to secure early release and go back home to Scotland. If anyone had anticipated a tirade of complaint and abuse about his treatment inside, or threats to get even with enemies, then they were disappointed. He said simply, 'I would like to thank my family and friends for standing by me and all the support they have given me,' and then disappeared into the gloom.

There were many, 200 miles to the north, who were waiting to hear or read his words with great interest. The name of Paul Ferris was as familiar in Scotland as that of any sportsman or politician, if not more so. He had been a leading player in the vicious, bloody Glasgow underworld, accused, but acquitted, of one of the most sensational shootings of the previous decade. Just four years earlier, overworked police in the 'Dear Green Place' had breathed sighs of relief when he had begun a ten-year sentence (reduced to seven on appeal) after being convicted at the Old Bailey of gunrunning. He was caught partly because of information passed by Strathclyde Police but also, it was suspected, as a consequence of betrayal by a spy, someone his family had trusted.

Now, he climbed into a luxurious green Mercedes limousine to be driven back to Scotland, where he knew he would be watched over by police officers some of whom had privately made it plain to contacts in the underworld and media that they were confident their man would soon be back behind bars.

Paul was widely regarded in Scotland as a high-profile gangster. In contrast, his brother Billy had remained in the shadows, almost a forgotten figure, rating only the occasional mention in the highly sensational stories about Paul's exploits in dangerous Glasgow crimeland. Yet within the prison system, it was Billy, the elder by 13 years, who was the better known. He had seen the inside of dozens of jails in England and Scotland, and, more significantly, he had met many hundreds of inmates, often men with near-celebrity status. His list of acquaintances was akin to a newspaper library packed with files containing the names of hordes of murderers, robbers, fraudsters and drug dealers. Over the years, he had lived alongside men who had shopped their families and friends in return for favours, those who were mad or bad, the cowardly and the courageous, crooks and cannibals, monsters who had slaughtered for money, others who had killed because of a cross word or on a mere hunch, wannabe martyrs who had used bombs to maim the innocent, bank robbers who had stolen millions and others who had got away with just a few miserly pounds, slimeballs posing as human beings who had crawled out of dark places to molest and kill children, thugs who had mutilated women.

Billy Ferris had served his punishment. 'If you can't do the time, don't do the crime' was the traditional advice of the old lags who listened without feeling or sympathy to new inmates, known in jail slang as 'fresh fish', who thought they were hard men until the first night the cell door slammed on them. Well, Billy could not have foreseen that an innocuous night out would end in a *crime passionnel*, but he had done his time. More than a third of a biblical lifetime for a moment of horror that had left another man dead and Billy in the dock for murder. He had survived his years of incarceration, retaining his sanity and, most importantly in the fight against petty authority, his sense of humour. For a man who had gone through so much, it was strange that now, as he waited for his brother in a lavish suite in a city-centre hotel, a drink in his hand, he felt nervous, his mouth dry, his words coming out in a rush, barely hearing conversations around him. He too was worried how the police would react to the brothers walking the streets together.

'I had wanted to travel to Frankland, but in the end I decided to wait for Paul's call to say he was out and meet him in Glasgow. I had been up all night worrying in case the police found some excuse to serve Paul with a warrant and arrest him as he stepped through the gates to freedom.

'On more than one occasion, Paul had told me, "We are hotter than Madras curry. When we're together the police will be watching your every move."

'I remember joking with him, "Our every move, you mean. But thank fuck for that. I've been away from Glasgow for so long I've lost my way a few times now. It's comforting to know there'll be a policeman around to ask if I need directions."

'We were in the visiting room at Frankland and Paul looked at me, glaring over the top of his glasses as if to ask, "Are you daft?" Then he told me, "I'm not kidding, Billy."

'I returned his stare with an equally questioning look and said, "I'm only kidding. Loosen up."

'At that, Paul blurted out, "You're unbelievable," and we both burst out laughing, bringing curious looks from others visiting.

'Now, I wanted to cuddle him after reassuring myself it was true we were finally together and this was no dream. But whenever I had told Paul I loved him in the past, it had always seemed to embarrass him, as though he wondered if this might be the last time we would meet.

'As we'd grown older, we stopped sharing the closeness we'd enjoyed when he was a boy, a child dependent on me. Once I went to prison, our roles had been reversed. He did everything for me, always thought of me, always found an excuse for me when I'd fuck up and say something daft. I know there were often times when I should have been more diplomatic instead of having an in-your-face attitude. That was a result of having jail conversations that were a blink away from intensive care should the merest intonation suggest weakness. Of course, you didn't adopt that kind of attitude lightly, but in jail it was bite or be bitten. Better to choke on a big chunk of somebody else than have them nibble away at you.

'As the minutes ticked on, I was getting excited waiting for Paul to walk through the door. I loved a brandy and despite almost murdering a bottle at the hotel waiting for him, I still felt sober, unable to get either drunk or high. I smoked a few pipes of hash but I think my nerves were cancelling it out. It proved something I'd always known – that love of a brother is stronger than any drug.'

There was an irony in the fact that it was Billy who had to wait for his brother's release. Paul had been a schoolboy when the older sibling had gone to prison for what would stretch to 23 years. It had been Paul who had travelled to grim, sparsely furnished waiting rooms in jails throughout England and Scotland, sitting amid squabbling children and their love-starved mothers for his name to be called for a miserable half-hour reunion. One trip to Maidstone in Kent had entailed a draining 20-hour, 900-mile round trip by train and car.

His loyalty to Billy had never wavered, nor had that of the rest of the Ferris family. But then they were from an area to the east of Glasgow, Blackhill, where families stayed close, often notoriously so, in the face of what they saw as a constant war against officialdom, which targeted them simply because they came from that East End suburb. Outsiders, on the other hand, sometimes found talk of that spirit of camaraderie difficult to believe, especially when newspapers spouted headlines such as 'The Day the In-laws Became the Outlaws', reporting on a particularly lively Blackhill wedding reception in 1970 that left 12 guests in hospital, a man with his nose severed and the wedding cake flushed down the lavatory. It had all broken out because the bride's aunt had begun singing the famous old Scottish favourite that goes, 'And it's oh! but I'm longing for my ain folk.' Blackhill families, it was true, preferred the company of their own, and the Ferrises were no different.

Billy never doubted they would stand by him. He had finally got out in June 1999, 11 months after the Old Bailey beak had jailed Paul. So it had become his turn to visit, instead of being visited as had so often been the case. He had driven south from his new home in Irvine, Ayrshire, to meet Paul in Frankland, the two even having a photograph taken together, the first either could remember, certainly since childhood. They had talked of their plans for the future. Billy had what he hoped would be a highly promising contract with a mutual friend of the brothers, businessman Seyed Mohammad Benham Nodjoumi Qajar Alagha, who, happily for his acquaintances, preferred simply to be known as 'Ben' or 'Dr Ben'. The work involved extensive travel and appeared to be above board – a crucial factor bearing in mind that when Billy had been jailed for life, the sentence meant just that – life – and freedom was a privilege that could be withdrawn for the slightest indiscretion.

All lifers dread the prospect of a brush with the law, an argument with a neighbour, a suggestion of even minor involvement with drugs or just a suspicion that among a group of friends is another criminal. These minor gaffes, however accidental, are liable to see a man or woman hauled back to jail, often to complete the full term of the original sentence, a particularly feared consequence for anyone given life. A common nightmare is that police, not happy with having an old and troublesome client back on their patch, will use the suspicion of mingling with undesirables as an excuse for the authorities to revoke a licence. So Billy had these worries with which to contend, and Paul had left no doubt about his own concerns. As he waited for his release, he had issued a statement saying: 'No doubt I have my enemies in Glasgow, including some rogue police and their criminal partners. They would love something unsavoury to happen to me.'

Paul, who had a family of his own, had also made plain and public his intention, shared by Billy, to go straight. Throughout his imprisonment, he had kept in touch with his most trusted allies, planning a series of challenging business ventures. Billy, whose punishment had cost him his first family, now had another, and he had vowed to his pretty new wife, Carol-Anne, whom he had married 15 months after his release, that his past was just that: past, over, done with.

And she never doubted his promise. Not even when she experienced for the first time what it was like to be a victim of terrible violence. Billy had not even been present when it happened, and an indication of her love for him was that she tried shielding him from involvement. Carol-Anne knew the identity of her attacker but realised that if anything then happened to him, the finger of blame would immediately point to her husband. And with his past, who would believe him if he said he had done nothing?

So she didn't tell him who had inflicted the dreadful wounds, although, just as any loving husband would, Billy wanted to know his name. The incident, which took place five months before Paul's release, would have a devastating effect on Billy and his wife. Paul had been told of it, but it was a family matter, a private hurt that was not to be spoken of on that of all days, and certainly not with strangers present, however welcome they were to share in the happiness of reunion.

As he waited for Paul with journalists from the *News of the World*, the newspaper that had arranged the reunion, Billy admitted:

> It feels as if I'm the one being set free. I've waited a lifetime
> of lifetimes for this moment. It's as though my sentence

won't be finished until he's out. I haven't been able to feel properly free while Paul is in jail. Now we're both out, we're going to stay that way. There can be no going back. The past is past and our lives begin from now. We start writing our stories at the top of a clean, new sheet. We may not have been able to grow up and live like normal brothers, but I've never lost my love for Paul, nor he his love for me.

The love of one brother for another can overcome anything. If he is right, he's right, and if he's wrong, he's right. As my brother, he can do no wrong. He knows I am always there for him.

Paul's first action on arriving in Glasgow was an obligatory report to his probation officer. Then he was free to seek out his brother. 'At last, Paul was there. "Here he is," I remember telling myself, and then I was holding him. So many emotions charged through me. I felt breathless. It was as if my heart was being squeezed tight in my chest. There was so much I wanted to say, but the only words that came from my lips were, "I love you, brother." Tears burst from deep inside me, choking me, soaking my face. For the first time in nearly 30 years, I cried and was not ashamed to be seen doing so. Big boys don't cry, they only bawl their eyes out, and I know I did that on that special day.'

As glasses clinked and stories about prison life and cellmates flowed, that day should have marked the end of the brothers' story. Billy and Paul Ferris had no doubts about their determination to stay trouble free. Each had his own motives. Billy was desperate to avoid revocation of his licence and the prospect of being locked up for many more bleak years. Paul had made plain his fears that police might use the flimsiest of pretexts to send him back to jail or even remove him permanently. It was his belief that if he was merely seen through the window of his home holding a television remote control, it might be interpreted as his having a gun in his hands.

Watchers of the Glasgow crime scene spoke not of if Paul would infringe but when, regarding Billy as an also-ran in the race back into custody. Newspapers quoted anonymous police insiders as asserting that 'notoriety is a drug for someone like [Paul] Ferris' and 'the prison service is already warming up a cell for Paul Ferris'. Privately, among criminals with a line into conversations in the innermost sanctums of police headquarters, there was a suspicion that a permanent watch had been ordered on the younger brother, and probably Billy also. Surprisingly, it was the older brother who was destined to make headlines.

The calendar moved forward by barely a tick in time to December the following year, a mere 23 months. Much had happened in the meantime. Now, just as Billy had anticipated news of his brother's return to freedom, it was Paul's turn to wait. In 2002, a meeting had been guaranteed because both were legally free and no obstacles stood in the way. This time there could be no certainty of a reunion.

The scene was the High Court in Edinburgh, and for a second time Billy was in the dock facing a charge of murder, his future depending on the deliberations of a jury. He had first stood in the dock on a capital charge in 1976 at Northampton. Unlike in that appearance, this time he was not alone. Beside him sat 36-year-old Lance McGuiness, also known as Lance Goudie. Both were accused of murdering Jason Hutchison, aged 15, who, like them, lived in Irvine. Each denied being responsible. In February 2003, the youngster had been stabbed to death and the Hutchison home set on fire. It had been a terrible incident arousing strong feelings. The prosecution alleged that Ferris and McGuiness were responsible.

Paul had worked assiduously behind the scenes to gather information to be used in his brother's defence. He had travelled each day to the capital to be near the scene of the trial. But much as he wanted to show support for his brother, he had remained on the outside of the courtroom, fearing his reputation might adversely affect Billy's chances of an acquittal. And those chances were thought to be good. He was represented by Donald Findlay QC, the eminent criminal advocate who had successfully won Paul's acquittal 11 years earlier, in 1992, when he had been accused of shooting dead Arthur 'Fatboy' Thompson, son of the legendary Glasgow Godfather. The Ferris camp was confident that the lawyer was doing his customary skilful and impressive job.

The lead-up to the tragedy had left another innocent victim: Carol-Anne Ferris. Two years previously, in July 2001, she had been on the receiving end of a brutal assault that left her disfigured and needing to undergo emergency surgery to massive facial wounds that would require medication for the rest of her life. After the beating, Carol-Anne had been rushed to hospital and, because it was obvious she had been the victim of a brutal attack, doctors had to make a report to the police. In a small community such as Irvine, it was inevitable that the attack became the subject of widespread chatter, and soon gossips were whispering a name into the ear of the local bobbies. Detectives' enquiries centred on Jason's brother, David Hutchison, then aged 18, who, shortly after the incident, had gone off to Tenerife. He had been encouraged to do so by his parents, who had been told that Billy was demanding to know from his friends where he lived. He remained on the island for many months. The police naturally wondered why Hutchison had gone off and stayed away so long.

In February 2003, Jason was murdered, and a month later Billy and McGuiness were arrested. The police case was that their intended target had been David Hutchison, in retaliation for the attack on Carol-Anne. But in order to substantiate that motive, it was first necessary to show that he had in fact inflicted the terrible injuries on her. So Hutchison was arrested and charged with being responsible. In August 2003, he was tried at Kilmarnock Sheriff Court in Ayrshire. Newspapers were banned from reporting the case at the time, for fear it might prejudice Billy's forthcoming murder trial. Hutchison admitted he had struck Carol-Anne after she refused to let him into an all-girl party but claimed she had first hit him with a wine bottle and that he had been acting in self-defence. In court, she could not identify him as her attacker and said she remembered nothing of the assault on her. The result was a not proven verdict, allowing the accused man to walk free. That outcome may have raised doubts about the suggestion that Billy had good reason to want revenge on Hutchison, deprived the Crown of a motive for murder, but it did not prevent the prosecution of him and McGuiness.

The High Court in Edinburgh has been the scene of many thousands of murder trials, dating back to the days when at the conclusion of some a square of black cloth was laid on the head of the judge, he pronounced the death sentence and within a few weeks a hangman arrived to finalise the proceedings. But it is relatively rare for a man who has spent many years behind bars for one murder to be accused of a second. Such an event attracts widespread interest, and the fact that in this case one of the accused bore the name of Ferris was a guaranteed crowd puller.

The case lasted a month and had many distressing features, not least the photographs of the dead teenager that jurors were shown. Firefighter James McKinnon told how Jason's body had been found on a bed in the bedroom after firemen received an emergency call to say the Hutchison home was on fire. He said there seemed to be a slash wound on the boy's face. The hushed courtroom heard from Christine Bracey, who said that her boyfriend, McGuiness, had told her about the killing. She claimed McGuiness said he was in the Hutchison house with Billy Ferris at the time Jason was murdered but that he had been in another room when the assault on the schoolboy began. She alleged that Billy was the culprit. She admitted that after the murder she and McGuiness had fled to England. Billy's defence team gave a different version, telling the jury that he was never in the house and had been elsewhere in Irvine at the time.

In deciding how to present their case, Billy's defence team were forced to make a difficult decision. It was in regard to a peculiar twist, which, after considerable discussion, remained undisclosed. In 1992, Paul had been held in Glasgow's giant Barlinnie jail while he awaited his trial for the killing of Arty Thompson. He had been placed in a segregation area known as 'the Wendy House', where he was joined by a stranger who introduced himself as Dennis Woodman. It would later emerge that Woodman was an infamous supergrass, regularly claiming that other prisoners had made highly incriminating confessions to him. Several of these unfortunates were serving lengthy sentences in jails in England as a consequence. During the Thompson trial, Woodman, who had been promised a new identity when he eventually left prison, had claimed that Paul had made damaging admissions while they played chess in the Wendy House. This evidence could have proved the crucial nail in the Ferris coffin until it emerged that Woodman had been lying.

Now, more than a decade later, Woodman, who occasionally used the aliases Wilkinson and Smith, was back in prison, this time at Saughton in Edinburgh, facing a burglary charge. He would later be convicted and jailed for two years. One of his fellow inmates was McGuiness. Woodman's usefulness as a police informer and teller of tales was long gone; too many convicts had rumbled him, and other prisoners did their best to stay clear. But, according to Woodman, another prisoner, Alexander Ness, claimed to have overheard statements by McGuiness that could have added weight to Billy's version of events. Ness had nothing to gain by coming forward to offer help. He was not aiding the Crown and so could expect no relaxation of his 11-year sentence. While the defence felt that his story had considerable credibility, his own background and the nature of the crime that had led to him being in prison – the killing of his 11-week-old son – would lay him open to criticism that would detract from the value of his evidence. So what he had to say remained untold.

During the trial, Carol-Anne Ferris had wanted to be in court to show solidarity with her husband, but because she had been told she might be called as a witness she had been forced to sit outside the courtroom. Paul had arranged accommodation for her in Edinburgh, but as the ordeal drew to a close she went back home to Irvine, sure Billy would soon be joining her. Her confidence was boosted not only by the encouragement of the defence team. There were those in Irvine who felt great sympathy for her because of the injuries she had suffered, and even some friends of the Hutchison family had expressed misgivings over the prosecution of her husband and told her that they doubted he would be found guilty.

As he waited for the jury to reach verdicts, Billy was helpless to influence his future. 'McGuiness was seated almost next to the jury, with escorts either side of him. I was about 15 ft away at the other end of the bench in the dock. He couldn't look me in the eye. But my legal team and I had never had a bad day, and we were confident.'

It is said that a dying man sees his entire past scroll by in the seconds before his journey to another world. Such a sensation is not unlike that experienced while waiting to be on the receiving end of a jury verdict, even when the charge is for a relatively minor offence. Men and women who have faced that ordeal say that every minute feels long enough to relate the story of an entire lifetime. And as Billy Ferris waited, he saw images of the 53 years that had made up his life thus far, and remembered . . .

1

PAUL

HIS PLAYMATES WANTED TRAIN SETS and roller skates; they listened to Paul Anka and Elvis Presley, watched wide-eyed the exploits of John Wayne and Charlton Heston and fantasised about being up-and-coming football stars like Denis Law and Jim Baxter. But young Billy Ferris wanted only a brother.

The family home was a flat in a four-storey tenement building in Royston, a district in the north of the city that many of the population, largely made up of the descendants of Irish Catholic immigrants, still persisted in calling Garngad. Appropriately enough, the name Garngad derives from the Gaelic word meaning 'rough', a term that might have been disdainfully applied by strangers from more salubrious parts of Glasgow to its bottle-littered streets and graffiti-strewn closes.

Three floors up at 168 Millburn Street, Billy sometimes went for weeks hearing only female chatter. As a Merchant Navy seaman, dad Willie frequently spent long spells away from home, leaving the schoolboy with mum Jenny and three younger sisters, Janet, Carol and Catherine. To help support the growing family, Jenny worked as a machinist, meaning her son was sometimes left with the girls. On weekdays, he enjoyed meeting up with other boys at St Roch's Primary School, but when it came to holidays and weekends Billy could usually be found in the next-door block, in the home of his grandparents, Jenny's parents Thomas and Jenny McGinty.

These formative years gave no hint of the dramas that would overshadow the Ferris family. In the classroom, Billy was a bright, well-liked youngster but one who preferred discussing high-speed cars to history and arithmetic. When lessons were over, he met up with other kids who were fellow members of the Shamrock Boys, also known as the Royston Catholic Shamrock, a gang that had sprung up among the younger residents of the area. They banded together largely for reasons of security, reasoning that there was safety in numbers.

Glasgow was famous the world over for its gangs. Each area of the city had its groups, with exotic names such as Calton Tongs, Blackhill Toi, Norman Conks, San Toi and, possibly the best known, the Billy Boys. The origins of these bizarre titles were usually obscure and often the subject of argument. It was beyond doubt that the Tongs originated in the Calton, a tough district to the east of the city centre near the Gorbals. The term seems to have emerged from a 1960s cult movie, *Terror of the Tongs*, about a sinister and violent Chinese secret society running amok in gold-rush USA; it was said that during a showing of the film in the Calton a member of the audience shrieked 'Tongs ya bass', which became the war cry of the local gang ('Toi' was generally thought to have been a derivative of 'Tong'). Some suggested 'bass' was a shortened version of 'bastard', while others pointed out it was also close to a Gaelic word meaning 'battle'. In any case, etymological concerns were unlikely to have been uppermost in the minds of those who formed the Calton Tongs, which developed offshoots including 'Tiny Tongs' and 'She Tongs'.

While membership of such gangs was voluntary, boys were expected to join whichever local group predominated. The gangs defended their territories with vigour. A rival straying over a boundary, even for the most innocent of reasons, could find him or herself on the end of a savage beating. As boys grew into men, they often graduated into adult versions of the gangs. While the violence in the 1950s and '60s might not have been as severe as that meted out by the Glasgow razor gangs of earlier decades, it could be savage all the same.

Billy enjoyed the fierce and often physically robust comradeship of others of his age and gender. 'Membership of the gangs only meant anything in the scheme in which you stayed. Outside your area, you were on your own. That's how things were. Being tough and proud was all crap. If you needed help from a couple of pals, you didn't hesitate to ask and they gave it without thinking, without hesitation. You knew you would probably be battered if you went alone into the area of another gang, so taking along a couple of pals reduced your chances of being chibbed. Notoriety ruled.'

Billy's recollections of his early family life remain vivid. 'My memories of my parents are of their love for each other and their love for us children. Time flies when you're a child. Because my da was in the Merchant Navy, it meant his being away from home for long periods. To make up for his absences, everyone tried to be extra kind, so I always seemed to be getting presents and having parties at our house or my gran's. My da loved my gran and granda McGinty and they loved him just as much in return. My granda was a great man. It seemed to me there was nothing he couldn't do or make or didn't know about. I suppose because he was always there for me I didn't miss my da so much, but I loved them equally. Gran and granda would slip me beer at parties – that's the way things were done in those days. Having a big, warm family around us and with food always on the table meant I was luckier than many of my friends. And da being away meant I was the man of the house. Gran made me feel the same at her home until I'd annoy my sisters; then granda would give me a slap. But a minute later he'd say, "Come on, William," and it was down to the garden shed with a cup of tea, a piece and jam, and a biscuit in each pocket. We'd go together to get away from moaning women.'

One thing that Billy always felt was missing was a brother. 'I was forever picking on my sisters, as I thought they were somehow to blame for my not having a brother. I would tell my ma, "All my pals have brothers. Some of them have three or four. How come I'm different?" She would just smile and tell me, "Maybe one of these days if you behave, but not while you annoy your sisters."

'Once, I got a slap from my ma for nipping one of them after she teased and annoyed me. Ma told me, "Billy, you don't hit girls." No matter who was in the house at the time, it only took a yelp from any of the sisters for me to get the blame and a wallop. It made me learn at a very early age that sisters weren't as hard as brothers, and that just made me want a brother even more. They soon worked out that they could easily get me into trouble over the slightest thing. When we went next door to my grandparents, at mealtimes, for a laugh I would make faces, and my sisters would all chorus, "Granny, he's pulling funny faces." I knew what was coming next. Whack – a belt around the ear. Then it was my turn to yelp and they would all laugh. Looking back, I must have been a pest of a brother to them, a pain in the bum at times, but it often felt that while they had one another, because I didn't have a brother I was on my own.'

In the late '50s, families in Millburn Street were told by their council landlords that it was not financially viable to bring the old tenements up to decent standards and that the time had come to demolish them. The vast majority of tenants were glad, even if it meant having to uproot themselves. Jenny and Willie were especially delighted with the news, because their growing family had only one living room in which to eat and socialise, and meals had to be prepared in a tiny kitchen.

In 1959, Jenny and Thomas McGinty packed up their belongings and moved just under three miles away to Greenside Street in Provanmill, to be followed soon afterwards by the Ferris family, who had been allocated a home at Hogganfield Street in Blackhill. They were still close, just a short bus ride apart, but nine-year-old Billy was shattered because he loved the McGintys and, whereas he was used to being able to see them by just popping into the next close, now they seemed a million miles off. And the change of address promised further trauma. His new home was out of the catchment area for St Roch's, where his friends were pupils. Billy should have started lessons at St Philomena's, a short walk from Hogganfield Street, but his parents took pity, heeding his pleas, and arranged for him to remain at St Roch's.

Blackhill, in the north-east of Glasgow, had first been developed as a giant housing scheme in the 1930s. Planners had made no secret of their desire to build houses on the cheap and shunt the city's poorer families – many from Garngad – into them. Some of the new tenants at least had the consolation of being able to move out of tenements into homes that had a front and back door and a garden. But at the same time, the term 'poorer' was often unfairly interpreted by officialdom as a synonym for 'troublesome', with the result that the city police took an especial interest in Blackhill and tended to assume that young people in particular with addresses there were probably potential recruits to the criminal classes. The younger generation often felt the police were confrontational; as a result, they were sometimes distrustful and resentful, determined to show their refusal to submit to what they regarded as bullying by breaking the law.

Billy quickly came to love Blackhill, with its strong community spirit. He had old friends from Royston, where he continued his affiliation with the Shamrock Boys, while at the same time making new mates not only from around his new home but also from the streets around his grandparents'. 'I could well have had problems moving to Blackhill and calling on my grandparents in Provanmill, but my friends in Royston had cousins living in Blackhill and as a result I was soon accepted there and able to join the Blackhill Toi.'

Jenny Ferris was thrilled by her new surroundings. 'Moving into Hogganfield Street was like living in a mansion. We were in a block of four, two up and two down, and although we were "up" and still had stairs to climb, it was nothing compared with what we had been used to. And we all had gardens. Those at the front belonged to the two families living on the ground floor, while ours was at the side of the block. Billy loved the garden, and my parents now had a garden too, an even bigger one, and he loved going up to their home and listening to his grandpa telling him about plants and how to grow them.'

For a youngster of nine, the change of environment felt like a move to another planet. 'We didn't care, then,' remembers Billy, 'that Blackhill, or at least the people living there, had such a bad reputation, one that was generally not deserved. While it's true there were troublemakers, most families were just delighted to be out of the tenements. The change from high stone buildings to trees, fields and countryside was unbelievable and those were great days for me and my pals. Tom Sawyer would have been in his element. We'd climb a fence into a graveyard and hide among the stones, play football on a rubbish dump or go to what was known as "the Rhubarb Field" because it was overgrown with giant wild rhubarb plants. There we would break off these huge stems, sometimes 5 ft long, and fight with them, pretending to be knights on horseback or gallant swordsmen. Then Hogganfield Loch, a lake in the middle of a huge park, was just a few minutes away and we would spend hours there chasing one another around it or scrounging scraps to feed to swans.' Hogganfield Loch would later come to have a major significance for Paul. It was said to be the spot where his close friends Bobby Glover and Joe Hanlon were murdered in 1991.

When he was aged 13, Billy went off camping with a school party. He had known something was afoot within the family home; his mum was pregnant and Willie had quit the navy to help look after the children and with housework. The camping trip should have lasted a week, but teachers took advantage of an opportunity to extend it by a further seven days when the party that should have followed the youngsters from Royston called off. By the time Billy eventually returned to Blackhill, he discovered his long-held wish had been granted: he had a brother.

Jenny remembers his reaction. 'Billy had hated his sisters. If you said, "That's your dinner," and one of the sisters had sat in the chair in front of the meal first, he would say, "I'm not having that dinner – she touched it first." He couldn't stand them and if something went wrong, no matter what it was, Billy blamed them. He did his best to make their lives a misery because he wanted a brother and they were not brothers. He used to make stink bombs out of film negatives, light them and smell the house out just to annoy them. And he terrified the life out of one of them by teasing her with spiders and flies. As a result, she's still scared of them to this day. It was devilment, boys' stuff, and he thought he could get away with it because he was doing it to lassies. He never meant to actually do them any harm.

'He just wanted a brother and when one came along, Paul was given treatment the exact opposite to that Billy dished out to his sisters. He worshipped Paul. Grandma McGinty asked Billy, "What do you think of my wee boy?" and Billy told her, "He's all right." But when a neighbour asked him, "What do you think of your wee brother?" he told her, "It's not mine, it's my granny's," because she'd called him "my wee boy"! But Billy idolised him from the very first day he saw Paul.'

Willie took on work as a driver, steering a huge removal van around the East End streets before switching employment to drive a coach. It was a job he enjoyed, especially because it gave him the chance to meet and chat with passengers. There were sometimes tips and, like many others, he was not concerned about the complexities of income tax and National Insurance. Many employers simply handed over an envelope containing cash at the end of the week. That some of the recipients were already claiming state handouts – or, as most put it, were 'on the broo' – was a minor incidental and not a matter that was discussed or reported to the authorities. Blackhill was a community that preferred the police to stay away, settling its own disputes and bringing down wrath on anyone telling tales on neighbours or even enemies. Logic dictated that if one person was reported for 'dole fiddling' then investigators would begin peering into the affairs of others, so the commonly held attitude was 'live and let live and mind your own business'.

Paul was referred to in the family as 'the wee man', and by the time the wee man was about ten months old, Billy was taking him everywhere. In those days of innocence, it became a familiar sight in the streets around Hogganfield to see Billy carrying the tot in his arms or on his back, or pushing him in his buggy. Paul was usually kitted out in a blue jumpsuit that had two wide straps, and soon Billy resolved the problem of what to do with his young charge when it came to climbing over fences. He would hang Paul by the straps from a post until he was over, then he'd reach up, unhook him and haul him over the top. During a game of football, Paul was left sitting on a pile of jackets and jumpers that marked one of the goalposts, but after a few narrow misses, when the ball had whizzed close to the youngster's head, Billy hit on an alternative of where to place him in safety. After that, he simply hooked him onto a fence during football matches, and often the teams would hear squeals of delight coming from the bundle in blue.

Apart from the simple joy of having a brother to take around at long last, Billy discovered another advantage to having Paul with him. Adolescent girls experiencing budding motherly instincts delighted in holding and gently rocking the baby, who had a magnetic attraction for them. Suddenly, the elder brother found himself a target for not unattractive females, whose motive might have been the chance to play mother but who realised that in order to achieve that they needed first to charm the baby's keeper. And so Billy, by now aged 14, found himself the envy of his pals.

The graveyard, with its wide avenues of headstones, was an ideal spot in which to tempt a girl with Paul, but it was also one that had potential perils in the form of gravediggers who blamed unwelcome young visitors for trampling neatly trimmed verges and even knocking over the stones, some of which were ancient. One day, Billy had lifted Paul onto the fence while he climbed into the hallowed ground when he heard a screech of 'the polis', an expression regarded with dread. 'My pals ran off in different directions, leaving me with the wee man, who was hanging from a post by the hood of his blue jumpsuit. I saw a couple of bobbies in the distance and panicked, running after my friends and abandoning him there. He thought this was a game and all we could hear was him laughing and shouting. Other kids might have cried at being left on their own, but not Paul, who hung there on his own, an enormous smile over his face. I loved him so much that I doubled back, unhooked him and carried him off home. The police must have realised they'd scared us off; they were nowhere in sight. On reflection, I suppose running away sounds a cruel thing to do, but I never, ever deliberately did anything to hurt the wee man. Not intentionally.'

Similar behaviour in these current times, were it to reach the ears of social workers, would doubtless have resulted in both brothers being taken into care and their parents chastised. But social workers then were thin on the ground and few families in Blackhill had contact with them. It was different when it came to the police, but despite his forays into forbidden territory, this was Billy's first encounter with Glasgow's finest. While his brother had found it funny, the incident scared Billy because prior to then nobody in his family had ever been in trouble with the police. One of the tragedies for the Ferrises was that here was a normal, loving family, smothering the youngest with love, with no inkling of the troubles that were to come upon them. But already another brush with the emergency services was on its way.

2
CRASH, BANG, WALLOP

ONE NIGHT WHEN THE TOT was aged two, his brother had taken him to visit the McGintys while his parents had a rare night out at the cinema, watching Stan Laurel and Oliver Hardy in *Way Out West*. Although it had been made in 1937, the movie was still a favourite and Cumbrian-born Stan's death in 1965 had rekindled interest. It was mostly downhill from the McGintys' home to the Ferrises'. The family are clear and united in their memory of that night, with the exception of the mode of transport involved. Some remember Paul having a small tricycle; as he sat on the little seat, Billy stood on the rear, leaning over his brother to guide the handlebars. Paul himself has a different recall of the mode of transport that led to the disaster: 'I'm sure Billy had converted an old pram into what we used to call a "bogie", a "guidie", and we definitely went downhill at speed.'

Eyewitnesses would tell Jenny and Willie that Paul had been 'screaming with joy as they freewheeled downhill'. As the tricycle gathered speed, Billy found steering increasingly difficult and the result was that the front wheel crashed into a rock. The collision brought the machine to a near-instant stop, causing Billy to fly over the handlebars and land half on the pavement, half in the road, to be followed a fraction of a second later by Paul, who crashed into him, his face scraping along the rough tarmac.

When the brothers reached home, Paul's badly grazed face brought screams from his sisters. The eldest, Janet, shaken and scared, went for help from a neighbour, who on arriving first looked at the scratched and bloodied face of Paul and then walloped Billy around the head. There was worse to come.

'When we saw Paul's face, I went, "Oh God," and we waved down the first motor that chanced to be passing,' says Jenny. 'It happened to be a newspaper delivery van. We persuaded the driver to take us to Glasgow Royal Infirmary. We got hell from the staff there for letting it happen. They gave Paul a thorough check-up and assured us there were no broken bones, that he was only grazed and bruised and would be OK in a few days.' His parents signalled their relief by giving the culprit another hiding when they got back to the house. The message got home and from that day Billy was ultra-protective towards the wee man.

'I sat at home shitting myself as I waited for everybody to come back from the hospital. "I'm going to get the mammy and daddy of fucking doings," I kept repeating in my head. "I'm in for it now. What if he's dead? My da will murder me and then my ma will murder me as well. Aw, fuck, then my gran and granda will murder me too." And so I fell asleep worrying. I was woken by a violent shake. I woke up in that state where you wonder where you are, but I soon came to life. Bending over me was Da and I'd never seen him so angry. He was growling into my face demanding to know, "How did that happen?" Then, whack, whack, and he ranted on while I dodged but was caught with more slaps than missed. Da thought he was hurting me, but any pain vanished as soon as I saw Paul in Ma's arms, bruised and grazed but alive. The wee soul smiled at me and I cried with relief. I hadn't killed my wee brother after all and remember sinking to the floor sobbing and choking.'

The incident and what followed gave Billy the first real scare in his life. It was true he had suffered minor blows because of skirmishes with his sisters, but these were serious beatings, the first he'd ever received, and he believed his recklessness had deserved them. He'd never meant to cause Paul harm, but now he was aware that in future he had to take greater care. From that day, whenever he took the wee man out to play he was given a stern reminder of the tricycle incident, and while he listened to his parents' urgings to be careful, he needed no telling. Billy felt he had let Paul down and became conscious that even his sisters no longer seemed to trust him to be able to protect his brother. But worst of all were his feelings of guilt, knowing he could have killed the brother for whom he had wished for so long.

The near catastrophe is, in fact, Paul's earliest memory of Billy, but he admits, 'Because I was so young, it is a vague recollection. However, something I'm not likely to ever forget is that it involved a head injury. I ended up in hospital, with my mum crying.'

Jenny offers an example of the protective instinct the accident brought out in Billy. 'William was in his mid-teens when he announced he was going to fence in our side garden so Paul could play in safety. Further up the road from our home, workmen had been demolishing houses, and Billy removed the coach from Paul's pram to make a bogie, went up and got big sleepers and floorboards, huge lengths of wood, from the demolition site and carted them home. Our neighbours would watch as he hammered in huge long nails. Sometimes one gave him a hand by straightening out nails. Billy hammered and battered at this fence until it was finished. It was waist high and mighty impressive. That fence was up for years and he would put his little brother inside the enclosure. He even built a small roof over one corner to give him shelter. They would play in there often, imagining it was a tent, a house, even a fortress. Everybody thought it was great. While it might not have looked brilliant, it was safe and nobody was allowed in except him and his wee brother. I think, if he had had the means to do so, he would have built Paul a house.' There is in hindsight an irony in Billy sealing Paul in an enclosure, because in years to come society would do likewise to the brothers.

As all good things inevitably come to an end, so did Billy's schooldays, and the time came in 1965 for him to join the adult world and look for his first job. Teenagers then were, in comparison with those now, lucky in that jobs, often in the form of apprenticeships lasting five or even seven or more years, were relatively abundant. It was not so much a case of 'Will I get a job?' but 'What job do I want?' Coach driver Willie encouraged his son to train as a mechanic, using his contacts with garages and in the motor trade to secure an opening. Billy was offered an apprenticeship with a garage in Glasgow. It was a good opportunity, but the young man would never complete the course.

He mingled well with the other apprentices who, during lunch breaks, taught him how to drive, and he soon discovered that he preferred driving cars, vans, trucks and coaches to repairing them. He also learned how to hot-wire a vehicle – joining ignition wires in order to start an engine without the use of a key, a method normally associated with car thieves. At the age of 16, he quickly became car mad, passionate about motors and speed.

The apprenticeship involved getting experience of meeting customers by working in the garage's reception office one day a week. He would meet clients, talk to them about the problems they had with their vehicles, book motors in for repairs and pass the details to the other mechanics, who would then do any necessary work. It was an easy enough role and he soon learned what to do by listening to others in the office. By watching the more experienced mechanics, he also learned an aspect to the work that was not on the syllabus. It was a lesson leading to a long trail of self-destruction.

3

A BRUSH WITH MURDER

HE WAS JUST 16, BUT Billy knew a good fiddle when he spotted one. Staring out of the window of the reception office, he noted how on Fridays older apprentices 'borrowed' cars from the spray shop or vans from the waiting area. These were vehicles not due to be collected by their owners until the coming Monday, and any miles clocked up over the weekend could easily be explained away as having accrued during road testing to ensure the repair had been successful. He saw no reason why he too should not benefit from free weekend transport. A few of his friends had the stylish and increasingly popular Lambretta scooters, others little Vespas, but he quickly developed a taste for the speed and comfort of four wheels. If customers didn't know their motors were being borrowed, what was the harm in it? The practice might be illegal, but the others told him it was commonplace and he suspected that was true. He also learned how to take short cuts in the servicing process, using a paintbrush and paraffin to wash clean the engine oil filter, plug leads and brake adjusters to give the impression they had either been fully checked or were new.

The sight of a young man driving around Blackhill at weekends in what seemed to be an endless supply of motors did not go unnoticed, especially by older criminals. As a result, Billy found himself popular with these men. They would pass him in the street, acknowledging him with a pleasantry, or happen to appear on the scene as he was parking. A conversation would start up, usually beginning with an enquiry as to how his apprentice course was coming along, and at some stage Billy would be asked to demonstrate how to hot-wire a motor. 'No problem,' would be his reply. His pupils would then want to try it for themselves, but frequently clumsiness led to their burning the wiring system, resulting in the vehicle going on fire or the engine cutting out at a crucial moment and causing a smash. Despite a sometimes not inconsiderable age gap, these men developed a respect for the talents of the younger man, who seemed to have a natural affinity with engines and motors. They soon saw a use for these attributes.

Blackhill might not be completely a no-go area for the police, but the district did not have a police station and officers were reluctant to enter unless they were in numbers or had considerable backup. It wasn't only policemen and women who preferred staying away; taxi drivers too had concerns. While they would be happy to drive a fare to the outskirts, to Provanmill for instance, going further was another matter and would probably be met with a claim along the lines of 'Go in there and I'll be robbed, and you as well if you're a stranger'. In the eyes of outsiders, Blackhill was wild, akin to a Dodge City or Tombstone of the Old West. It was a haven, a place of sanctuary from the law for crooks – and Billy was about to find himself among them.

At the garage, he was occasionally given a five-gallon jerrycan by an older apprentice or mechanic and told to siphon fuel into it from cars and vans belonging to customers. The garage owners were unaware of this, and when Billy asked, 'Isn't this stealing?' he was told, 'Naw, Billy, it's just a wee fiddle.' Apprentices were paid around three pounds and ten shillings (£3.50) a week and could easily come close to doubling this through their scams, which included disconnecting new or nearly new batteries and spare tyres and replacing them with well-used models.

Billy admits he had reservations. 'I dreaded Da finding out about my fiddles, but the sight of the money going into my pockets soon calmed any nerves.' After around two years of undertaking these schemes on behalf of his colleagues, Billy decided it was time to branch out for himself. In addition to his Friday duties in reception, he was required to spend one day a week in the garage stores, where he could get his hands on hundreds of accessories. He soon came to look on this as a virtual licence to print money and set about fiddling with such enthusiasm that in a short time he was earning more than fully qualified mechanics. The money meant he was able to buy a second-hand Mini Cooper from a workmate. He loved the little car, with its throaty exhaust. Like the other vehicles he had 'borrowed', he had to park it in the street where the McGintys lived rather than outside his parents' house, terrified that Willie would discover his son had a motor he should not have been able to afford and begin asking awkward questions. When he first began leaving cars at their home, he explained that he felt they would be safer there, and his grandparents never challenged his reasoning.

Billy was no angel, and his parents knew that. While he did his utmost to prevent Willie discovering his misdemeanours, it was almost inevitable that Jenny would get to hear of them. 'He was doing really well at the garage,' she remembers, 'and had a boss who took a particular interest in his work. Billy had a special job that involved using a lot of grease, and frequently he came home with his face blackened with grease looking like an Apache Indian. One day, he turned up at the normal time with a dirty face and I told him, "You weren't at work today," and he said, "Yes I was," and I said, "Listen, you didn't bother to blacken your face enough. I know you weren't at work because your boss came around saying you'd been missing and he was worried about you. You blacked your face to make us think you'd been there. Your gaffer also told us you've been feeding your pieces to the swans. You're not getting any more pieces."

'Another time he arrived back intending to have a quick bite and change before going off out again. I asked him, "How did you get here so fast?" It turned out he'd borrowed a lorry from work, but he hadn't realised his dad was already in the house and when he heard Willie's voice he jumped back in the lorry, turned around so fast the motor must have been on two wheels and headed back to the garage. Billy never did anything bad, but he was mischievous. Most of what he got up to was just devilment.'

But while he did his utmost to leave his father in ignorance of his illicit enterprises, some of his seniors at work hadn't failed to notice what was happening. They became dismayed and jealous when long-established back-door customers of their own began asking for Billy by name. They discovered their junior was trading on his own and closed ranks. One afternoon, he returned from his weekly day release to Anniesland College to find himself sacked on suspicion of theft. Billy was not totally surprised, but he was angry that the man who fired him was the same individual who had assured him, 'It's just a wee fiddle.' Now he discovered that fiddle became theft when old customers began deserting to him.

But there was a worse punishment than finding himself on the dole. 'Da felt I had let him down, which I had, of course, and to this day I still regret it.' Willie was furious when his son broke the news. Billy had not seen his father so angry since the night of Paul's accident. Then, the worried father had used his hands to teach his son a lesson. Now his weapon was silence. For months, he did not speak to his eldest child.

So, without a job, Billy turned to his friends for companionship. Virtually all of them had already spent time in approved schools, detention centres or borstal while he had been grafting in the garage. It was almost inevitable that he would drift down the same path. His skill with motors made him a sought-after asset to criminals, and he quickly found himself used as a getaway driver. His friends stole carpets, refrigerators, televisions – whatever they could lay hands on and often to order. In the criminal rankings, it was minor stuff, but a more sinister category of crime was about to touch Billy's world as it spun ever more out of control, and that was murder.

One weekend, Billy went with a group of pals to watch their team, Celtic, at Parkhead. It was customary to enjoy a beer or two before the game, but on this day Billy's indulgence in German lager got the better of him and he became too drunk to continue. So, while the others went off to the game, he was packed into a taxi and sent back to Provanmill. He managed to stagger home and into bed, where, the following day, he awoke to find himself staring at police officers and his parents, angry with him for having disgraced the neighbourhood by bringing the hated bobbies to their door.

He was ordered to dress and told he was suspected of being involved in a brutal murder the previous day. Despite his protestations that he knew nothing and denials that he had taken part in any violence, he was hauled off to be questioned. 'I was hungover and, when the police began questioning me as to what I knew of the fight, confused.' His interrogators told him that a young man had been savagely killed. Two of the men Billy had intended going to the football with had witnessed the murder. They had not only grassed on one of Billy's friends but also said that Billy had been with them. It was only when the taxi driver who had taken him to Provanmill was traced and he confirmed the identity of the drunken passenger that Billy was released without charge. But the incident left a bitter taste in his mouth.

He knew the mother of the victim and told anyone who would listen, 'She's a good woman and her son a good boy.' His hurt was compounded by the thought that had he stayed sober, he would in all probability have been able to prevent the killing, and by the realisation that he had brought shame on his family. The atmosphere at home became even more difficult. 'Da had every right to bawl me out. I had betrayed and embarrassed him by getting sacked, because he had got me the job originally. Now I'd brought the police to the door. He was a proud man and I knew I had let him down badly.' Although his father had finally resumed speaking to him, it was mostly to shout at him, and he would storm from the house to pick a fight or simply cause trouble. Following one of these rows at home, he climbed into his Mini Cooper, drove off at speed and promptly smashed into two other cars. He was arrested and given three months' detention. It was his first experience of losing his freedom, but at the time he lamented even more that his beloved Mini was a wreck. 'It's not the only thing that's a write-off,' his father told him as his son was dragged off in handcuffs to Glenochil detention centre in Clackmannanshire.

This unit was run along the lines of a modern-day boot camp, the intention being to use harsh discipline of the type experienced in military prison. Inmates would first be broken of any spirit of defiance or mutiny and then gradually be built into better citizens, capable of accepting authority. That, at least, was the aim. Billy, constantly at odds with his father and classed as rebellious, took to it like a duck to water. Others cut their wrists or deliberately broke their legs or arms on metal bed frames, so desperate were they to escape the dreadful physical training. Billy found himself loving the physical side of the regime, while the barking of the instructors, which the other miscreants found so terrifying, was as nothing when compared with the censures delivered by Willie Ferris.

There were gang fights galore. Billy discovered among his fellow inmates at least 30 gang members of the Shamrock Boys and the Blackhill Toi. He had a foot in both camps and allies on both sides. Lined up against them were the Govan Tongs. Rivalry was bitter, and Billy often took revenge on a Tongs devotee who had beaten up a Toi or Shamrock Boy.

Bullying by staff was rife. He found himself on the receiving end of beatings for fighting, although the rumbles were often deliberately orchestrated by staff, who would move a troublesome member of one gang into a section controlled by another, theorising that a severe hiding would dampen any further enthusiasm for agitation. Violence was the inevitable outcome, giving staff the excuse to then move in and inflict further punishment of their own.

One penalty for infringing the strict code of behaviour was for teams of four rebels to be forced to run flat out the length of a football field carrying a ten-foot-long wooden batten on their shoulders. Billy soon found that stationing himself behind someone taller meant he barely felt any weight.

While this brutal regime did leave some cowering and pleading for a second chance, and others suicidal, it merely instilled in most a hardened defiance to authority. And it left Billy fitter than at any other time in his life.

After ten weeks and five days, he awoke to the realisation that following a final breakfast he would be on his way home to Glasgow. But not before he had wreaked havoc. Each section was issued with identification badges that had to be affixed at all times to detention-centre-issue jackets. Losing a badge meant extra physical training and being deprived of desperately longed-for canteen privileges such as buying sweets and tobacco. With a fellow conspirator, Billy stole 30 badges from a rival section, wrapped them individually in toilet paper and flushed them one by one down a toilet. Happy at the thought of the trouble in store for the 30 unfortunates, he marched from breakfast to reception for his discharge. On the way, he could hear the angry shouts of the Tongs and members of other gangs baying for his blood. He tried not to admit his guilt by laughing and hid his smirks.

Then agony suddenly hit him as a tremendous blow, delivered by an instructor regarded as the worst of the bullies, battered into his kidneys. The attacker was in charge of the section Billy and his companion had raided. Now, instead of climbing onto a bus heading west, he was marched off and dumped into a cell, still gasping for breath and clutching his back. When he recovered, the beating began again. But the harder the blows fell, the more he forced himself to laugh. His tormentor screamed, 'You are going nowhere, Ferris, until I get those badges back,' but the only reply was, 'Fucking Rent-a-Rod the plumber is the only cunt likely to see them again.' The cell door was slammed shut, leaving him on the floor in fits of laughter. He resigned himself to losing what remission he had earned and serving the full three-month term. But, as lunchtime approached, he was hauled out, ordered to change into his own clothing and pushed out of the gates of Glenochil.

Back in Glasgow, his sisters chatted amiably to him as though nothing had happened, while four-year-old Paul was overjoyed at his return. Willie, however, still felt let down, disappointed by his firstborn's stupidity. There was tension between them, not helped by the fact that the beatings and threats he had endured at Glenochil had hardened Billy against emotion.

His pride in the family, though, remained. When, around six months after his release, he returned drunk from a night out with a group of pals and young women, he saw, even though no one said it, how let down his mother and father felt. The next day, he walked into the Army Careers Office in Renfield Street and told an immaculately outfitted sergeant, 'I want to join the Royal Marines.' A chat was followed by form filling and the promise of a call within days to summon him for a medical examination. He felt elated on the journey home and told Willie, 'Da, I'm joining the Marines.' The pride on the face of his father was unmistakable and although he replied simply, 'Good on you, son,' the words meant much to Billy. It was as close as he and his father had been for many a day. A week later, a Marines doctor failed him, telling him the sight in one eye was not up to standard. 'You can always join the army,' said the officer, but Billy said nothing, stood up and walked out. He had built his hopes on starting afresh with a career in the Royal Marines, and now they were shattered.

Drink provided some consolation, but the atmosphere at home soured even further. 'My da's disappointment in me must have felt like the bitter blow I took when I was told I was not getting into the Marines. He had been really proud at the prospect of my joining that great and famous regiment, then it had all crumbled.'

When friends invited him on a trip to Manchester, he agreed to join them. It was 1968. Their problem was a lack of money. Then one of the group, whom we shall call Ron, came up with a possible solution: stealing from the Tennent's brewery in Wellpark Street, Glasgow. 'If I could drive, I'd get us a lorryload of beer to sell,' he said, and instantly found himself the centre of interest. Ron explained how the heist could be pulled off and immediately had a volunteer driver in Billy, who, however, still didn't have a licence.

While three pals waited on the other side of the road from the brewery entrance, Ron and Billy merely strolled into the loading bay, where vans and lorries were waiting laden with deliveries, keys in ignitions. Billy climbed into the cab of one vehicle packed with crates of bottled beer, reversed, drove through the gates, waving casually to security staff, and stopped to collect the waiting members of the gang. 'Security in those days was almost non-existent. Because we were young and knew a lot of people who ran pubs or shops, we had no difficulty selling the load in Blackhill and Royston. Then I dumped the lorry, went home, packed a bag and left without a word to anybody.

'That night, we took a train from Glasgow Central station. As we pulled away from the city where I had grown up, I thought, "Manchester has to be better." But my head was packed with regrets at leaving home. I just couldn't feel excited – only anxiety about what lay ahead in England. I drowned my fears by getting drunk on the way and woke up at Manchester Piccadilly. It seemed a new start awaited all of us.'

4

ESCAPE

SOON AFTER ARRIVING IN MANCHESTER, Billy was to meet for the first time a young Scot named Rab Carruthers. Friends in Glasgow had offered to put Billy in touch with him and encouraged a meeting, as Carruthers knew the city well and had contacts there. He was fresh-faced, but looks were deceptive. Carruthers was ruthless and fearless. A couple of years older than Billy, he too was Glasgow-born and a member of a gang, in his case the notorious Cadder Young Team. The boys' fathers were friends, and through that family friendship Carruthers knew of Billy and Paul. A keen bodybuilder, he had made friends with many of the leading figures in the Glasgow crime scene at an early age. During a trip to Manchester in the late '60s, at that time a city with a reputation for vibrant and exciting nightlife, he had taken a liking to the area and the men who ran clubland. In the years that followed, he became trusted as someone who would do favours without asking for rewards, all the time building up a network of contacts that he knew would come in useful.

Those contacts would come to his rescue in the mid-'70s when he was suspected of an underworld murder in Glasgow. Carruthers fled south, where he was given a home and an alibi. He spent most of the remainder of his life in and around Manchester, although he continued to visit his family in Glasgow frequently. At the time he shook hands with Billy, Carruthers was relatively unknown, but he soon had a reputation as a young man who was not to be messed with. He became a prolific supplier of drugs to the underworld in Scotland and north-west England and was jailed for 15 years in 1995 after a drug bust at a Manchester hotel.

Billy always remembered Carruthers for the welcome he provided and his kindness in helping him and his pals find a rented flat in the Cheetham Hill area of the city. There, the cash the gang had made from selling the stolen beer soon ran out, and in desperation Billy turned to crime. When in the spring of 1968 he was offered a job as getaway driver for a robbery at a shop on the outskirts of Manchester, he felt he had little alternative but to accept and stole a car. But when the alarm sounded during the robbery, the motor was no match for the pursuing posse of police cars, their blue lights flashing and sirens blaring. It crashed, his two companions fled and Billy was arrested and charged with robbery and car theft.

He awaited his trial in the young offenders wing of Strangeways prison, Manchester, a grim hellhole opened a century earlier and the scene of 100 executions, the last of which had taken place as recently as 1964. It had a dank, ghostly air about it, and as far as Billy was concerned, his trial and move to another jail could not come soon enough. Back in Glasgow, his family had been told of his downfall. They were saddened, not least Paul, who missed his big brother. But, despite the awkwardness of his having left without saying goodbye, Billy knew he had their support. 'When they wrote asking about my surroundings, I told them, "This place is mental. The only work allocated to young prisoners is painting toys that are being given away free in packets of Kellogg's Corn Flakes. There are a few other Scots here, and we all get on well together, but I can't wait to be moved out of here. Anywhere else will do. No matter where it is, it cannot be worse." I was glad to get my trial over with because it meant being moved from Strangeways. But the judge gave me two years' borstal, and that sounded like an eternity. When you're young, two years is a very long time, because there's so much growing up and learning to do.'

Billy was transferred to a semi-open borstal, Wetherby young offenders institution in West Yorkshire. Wetherby is a pleasant market town, listed in the Domesday Book and close to the A1 road, now upgraded to a motorway. Its principal resource is the local racecourse, which the young men in the borstal could see from the windows of their dormitories. After race meetings some of the lads would be taken out to the track to flatten the turf kicked up by horses, clean up muck left by the animals and collect litter. It could be dirty work, but at least it meant they were out among trees and fields. Being surrounded by countryside reminded Billy of Hogganfield Loch and happy days spent there with Paul and his friends. The memory of those not so distant times made him homesick and unhappy, and the fact that security was so minimal as to be practically non-existent made the temptation to return to Glasgow all the stronger.

Adding to his misery was the news, given to him by a borstal official, that his grandfather Thomas McGinty had died. The words of genuine condolence were ringing in his ears as Billy returned to his room, but by the time he reached it he had made up his mind. It was time to go home. Three weeks after arriving at the establishment, he walked out. Why? 'I had only one thought: to escape so I could get to Glasgow and see my gran and pay my respects to all the family. It might sound a dream, but when I set off I was convinced I'd make it home.'

No one saw or stopped him. He simply waited until lights out at 10 p.m. and in the darkness climbed through his window. Nearby he could see the lights of cars and trucks on the main road and some of them, he knew, would be heading to Scotland. For the time being, however, trying to hitch a lift was out of the question. He was dressed in standard garments issued to all prison and borstal inmates: blue striped shirt, grey V-neck jumper, grey trousers and black bomber jacket. He felt like an extra from a film about prison life and was sure that if he tried thumbing down a car or lorry, the driver was likely to suspect he was on the run. And so, staying close to the main road, he began trudging through fields in the direction of home, 200 miles off. How he would get there, he did not know. His instinct told him to keep moving.

5

HOME AND AWAY

ON 29 OCTOBER 1968, WHILE Billy was doing his best to put as much distance as possible between himself and Wetherby, another crook was about to join him in the great outdoors. Londoner John McVicar's success as an armed robber in the 1960s earned him the title of 'Public Enemy Number One' from the Metropolitan Police Flying Squad – glamorised in the television series *The Sweeney* starring the late John Thaw – and a generous reward was offered for information leading to his recapture. Privately some detectives told their informants they simply wanted McVicar off the streets, dead or alive. Eventually captured, he was jailed for 23 years but embarrassed the prison authorities by escaping from a bus taking him to Parkhurst prison on the Isle of Wight in 1966. Unauthorised excursions into freedom by him and others incurred the wrath of politicians, and just as the German war machine had put prisoners of war regarded as escape risks in Colditz Castle, so the Home Office decided to move problem escapers to the formidable Durham jail. A special wing – E Wing – was created within the old stone building and pronounced escape proof.

Four months after running off from the coach, McVicar was recaptured and immediately transferred to E Wing. It was not long before he discovered that the bricks in the shower room crumbled easily. Using a makeshift blade, he began chipping away, replacing bricks with papier mâché replicas as he removed them. At the time Billy was creeping from Wetherby, McVicar and two fellow cons were hauling themselves through the hole in the shower room wall, into a ventilation shaft, out into the yard and over the wall via a roof. His co-conspirators never made it to freedom, but McVicar was quickly and quietly sneaking through the narrow Durham streets. He twice swam the River Wear, and by morning was in the same countryside that Billy Ferris was heading towards. Both men were travelling in the same direction – north. McVicar was following first the Wear, before it turned off towards Sunderland and the coast, and then the London to Edinburgh rail link; Billy was using the same railway line and the motorway as a guide.

In Durham prison, the escape alarms had screeched from first light. Within minutes, the prison was surrounded by police, and armed officers were being drafted in from outside forces to help in the search for McVicar. It was assumed, because he was from London, that he would head south, but by going in the opposite direction, he had fooled his pursuers. Further south, at Wetherby, Billy's disappearance had been noted and the local police informed. But he was not looked on as dangerous or a threat and young men fairly regularly absconded, the vast majority handing themselves back in after a reunion with family or a girlfriend. However, as Billy plodded north, he was unaware that a growing contingent of police officers was moving towards him.

A description of McVicar had been widely circulated, together with a photograph showing a short, dark-haired, fit young man. He was similar in appearance to Billy and wearing almost identical prison-issue clothing. Eventually, McVicar reached the town of Chester-le-Street, midway between Durham and Newcastle upon Tyne. There he found a phone box, made a reverse charge call to a friend in London asking him to come and pick him up, broke into a deserted lock-up garage and went to sleep in a car to wait, oblivious to the manhunt.

There was no such comfort for Billy. 'I thought that if I could get far enough away, I could ring one of my pals and ask him to come to collect me. But first I had to find somewhere safe to hide. Throughout the night, I waded through marshes and crossed fields, still seeing the occasional light from a lorry or car. The easy thing to do would have been to step out and wave someone down, but what would a driver think if he was suddenly confronted by a stranger appearing at the side of the road out of nowhere asking for a lift? It was cold and damp, and with the morning came a mist that just became thicker and thicker. It was so thick that, crossing a field, I literally bumped into a grazing horse. That gave me the fright of my life, because in the mist it seemed as though smoke was coming from its nostrils. It was so cold I could see my breath.

'The horse just lifted its head as if to ask, "What the fuck is this mud-covered thing disturbing me?" I could only say, "Hello, boy," and at that the horse started ambling away. I was exhausted; my legs felt like lead from trudging through boggy ground and standing water, and I was wet through. It was as if somebody was keeping an eye on me and had sent the horse along to help. I thought, "What the fuck," and decided to have a go at riding it even though it had no reins or saddle, and the nearest I'd been to a horse before that was walking past the nag that pulled the rag-and-bone man's cart around our scheme in Blackhill.

'When you're desperate, you clutch at any straw, and I reckoned that if redskins in movies could ride horses bareback and without reins, there was no reason why I shouldn't be able to do the same. It looked easy in the films, but actually being able to do it was a different story. When I tried grabbing its mane, the animal just turned its head away. I said, "Easy, boy," then made a grab and managed to hang on, even though it was like clutching wet grass. My bomber jacket was soaked through and weighed a ton. "Bronco Billy," I thought as I tried pulling myself up, first slipping back then falling over the other side. The horse never moved as I tried again and again. The problem, I decided, was that the damp had made the animal slippery, so I took off my bomber jacket and jumper and tied the jumper around its neck.

'I led it around the field looking for a boulder on which I could stand to mount. When no stone emerged, I began looking for a gate, talking all the time to the horse as if I'd discovered a new friend. Finding a gate, I opened it, climbed on top and was able to get astride the horse. But staying on board the greasy back was a nightmare. I was leaning forward, holding on to its mane and clutching my jumper, which was still around the horse's neck. The horse was stinking and I was slipping from side to side and trying to hang on for dear life. If a bystander had spotted us, it would have looked as though I'd been shot and was unconscious, with my horse taking me home.

'It was clearly not used to taking instructions, at least not from strangers, because each time I told it to "gee up, gee up" it just turned its head, looked at me and ambled back into the field. The movement brought shivers of pain to my backside. It sauntered across the field and I thought, "At last, we're making progress," until we came to another field, separated off by a two-foot-wide ditch. That horse had made up its mind not to cross, and when I dug my heels into its flanks in an attempt to spur it over, it threw back its head, kicked up its back legs, threw me off and trotted off like a Grand National winner.

'It was game, set and match to the horse, and I lay there cold, soaked and laughing. Then I spotted a tractor coming over a field towards me, so I got up and disappeared into the cover of the mist. A couple of hours later, I crossed a railway line, unaware that a manned signal box was only a few yards to my left. When I looked up and saw it, the signalman had opened his window to get a better look at who was going over the line. He maybe thought I was a vandal. He didn't take his eyes off me and then I saw him reaching for a telephone. That was my signal to go, and I bolted off into a valley with a forest ahead. The man must have made the call, because half an hour later I saw a line of policemen, some holding the leads of dogs.

'When I climbed a tree to look for a way out, there seemed to be police everywhere. I was still up in the tree when suddenly a voice bellowed in a broad Geordie accent, "The bastard's up there. Come down, you bastard, or we'll shoot you down." I almost crapped myself. I was hanging on to a branch for dear life, petrified I was going to slip off and break my neck, but things were even worse when I looked down and saw men in uniform, some holding guns, surrounding the tree. I was terrified sitting up there with guns waving at me. I tried joking with them, asking, "Is this the special branch?" but they had no sense of humour and when I climbed down I was manhandled to the ground, soaking and shivering and stinking of stale marsh water. The police searched me and it was obvious they weren't in a good mood.

'I was dragged to my feet and the officer who seemed to be in charge shouted into my face, "Who the fuck are you?" Because I was shaking with shock and cold, when I looked around at all these guys who had been chasing me and who were pointing guns at me, I could only say, "I'm Billy Ferr . . ." The officer yelled, "Who?" and this time I managed to tell him, "Billy Ferris." My name was rasped into a radio and moments later I heard the reply, "He's a fucking borstal boy. It's not John McVicar." I thought, "Who the fuck is John McVicar?"'

While Britain's most wanted had been peacefully asleep, warm and dry, across the seats of a car parked in a garage on the outskirts of Chester-le-Street, the police, alerted first by the farmer whose horse Billy had tried to ride off into the distance and then by the signalman, had reasoned that their quarry was south of Durham. Thinking they now had him in their sights, they'd diverted their resources to the area in which Billy had been seen.

The Scot felt miffed that he could have been shot dead because of a man he had never met or even heard of and persisted in asking, 'Well, who the fuck is this John McVicar?' He was told, 'Shut the fuck up. How long have you been hiding in the woods? If you haven't heard of him, you must have been asleep in a hole for the last 24 hours.' But he would not be put off. 'Who is he?' he continued to ask.

As walkie-talkies crackled around Billy, one of the armed searchers took pity and passed on the news that a man classed as extremely dangerous had staged a daring escape from the top-security wing of Durham jail the previous night. And he added, 'Just your luck, Jock. You've been reported twice in the area where he's probably hiding out, and you're even wearing the same clothing. We were convinced when we spotted you up the tree you were him, and if you'd moved a muscle or tried to do a runner, you would have been shot.' Another officer, water dripping from his cap, eyeballed their captive and told him, 'We've wasted all this fucking manpower on a fucking borstal boy.'

At that, he was hauled off by two huge policemen and dragged through the forest towards a line of police vehicles, their blue lights flashing through the mist. He was driven to a local police station and pushed into a cold, bare cell. Despite his miserable, stinking state, he was offered neither a hot drink nor a change of clothing, and when he asked permission to wash, it was refused. One of his captors told him, 'You've caused no end of bother and now the top brass are asking questions about how a borstal boy managed to wander through a cordon that was supposed to be tight enough to prevent a rat escaping. You've fucked up the whole search. If McVicar gets away, they'll throw the book at you. The gaffers want to teach you a lesson by banging you up in the place that McVicar just left.'

Hours later, Billy's cell door opened. Two screws from Wetherby stood with a police sergeant, who told them, 'There's the little cunt who's caused us a lot of bother. He's all yours and you're welcome to him.' Billy was handcuffed and taken back to Wetherby.

On the return journey, his feelings see-sawed between realising how unlucky he had been to have picked the same time to escape as the most wanted man in Britain and how lucky he had been to have avoided being shot. He told himself, 'OK, I've been caught, but at least I tried.' At Wetherby, he was stripped, allowed to wash, given clean clothing and fed. Warm at last, he even felt glad to be back in a cell with a bed. He remembers he told one of his fellow inmates who brought him food, 'I can't take credit for John McVicar getting away, but I like to think my own effort helped him. The cops who found me wanted to shoot me.'

The following day, he appeared in front of an official for punishment. To his surprise, the man was laughing. 'You're quite a celebrity, young man. Quite a fuss you've caused in Geordie country. However, I'll have to remand you until the police find out how many cars you stole to get as far as you did.' Billy protested, 'But I never stole any cars,' and the smirking reply was, 'That's what they all say.' The official ordered him to be taken back to the borstal punishment block.

As the steel door was clashing behind Billy, John McVicar was pulling open the door of a car. The driver was tired. He had motored through the night, taking a roundabout route to avoid the cordon of police who had resumed their search for the fugitive. Both were unaware that a young Scot of whom they had never heard had inadvertently sabotaged the manhunt and made it easier for McVicar to lay low and ultimately get away. That evening, the car pulled into a quiet London street and the driver awoke his passenger, who silently disappeared inside a house. He remained at large for two years before an underworld informant passed details of his hiding place to police. Armed again with guns, they made no mistake and McVicar was dragged back to prison, his sentence increased to 26 years. His and Billy's paths would cross again, and next time the pair would find themselves considerably closer to one another.

At Wetherby, two weeks after his own recapture, Billy was called again before a senior officer and told that police had submitted a report confirming no cars had been reported stolen and no property damaged during his brief spell of freedom. A farmer, however, had reported that his horse had been removed from one field and left in an adjacent one, and the description of the culprit matched that of William Ferris. The report added, 'The farmer is not pursuing this and as far as the police are concerned we are content to allow you to deal with the matter.' The officer read the report aloud and wanted to know about the horse. 'Is that true?' he asked. He was told it was. Asked, 'Well, why did you do a runner?' Billy said, 'Because I was upset at the death of my granda.' The reply was, 'Well, you got quite a distance, young man. Had you stolen any cars or broken into any property, I would have moved you to a closed borstal unit. However, I won't do that unless it is what you want. Are you prepared to settle down and give your word you won't try this again?'

Billy thought his ears were deceiving him. It would be as if the episode had never taken place. He was quick to promise to behave. The news was not all good, though. 'You're fortunate not to be charged with horse stealing,' said the officer, laughing, and then gave him another two weeks in the punishment block for his itchy-feet interlude.

By this time, police were convinced that McVicar was either in his old haunts in London or sunning himself on a foreign beach. Billy, meantime, settled down to complete his sentence. He threw himself with enthusiasm into everything he was given to do, fitness training in particular. He found the hard work paid off. 'I'd served another 12 months at Wetherby when the officer again sent for me, and I naturally thought I must be in trouble. But the opposite was the case. I was ordered to take a seat and told, "I'm pleased to see you kept your word. A number of boys have been put forward for consideration for an outward-bound course, and the PT instructor strongly supports you as a candidate. We send one boy each year and he doesn't think you would let Wetherby down. No one else has so far. Would you like to take part?" I had to ask what an outward-bound course was. He explained that it involved taking part in character building through mountain climbing, yachting, canoeing and potholing. The course was being held at Brathay Hall, near Ambleside in the Lake District. When I was again asked, "Are you interested?" I said right away and without any hesitation, "Aye, definitely."'

Two months later, Billy was kitted out with an army-surplus uniform: boots, kitbag, four pairs of denims, shirts and pullovers. He looked like a soldier. He was given a train ticket and detailed directions for getting to Ambleside station, where instructors would meet him. He was also handed £100 and told that that had to last a month and that a further £100 would be deposited at Brathay Hall for him. On the journey west, he was apprehensive, unsure what to expect. At the station, two minibuses collected a group of students and drove them to their destination, a magnificent mansion overlooking Lake Windermere. It was a beautiful spot. Rob Roy would have loved the forest, rivers and lakes, and Billy was gobsmacked by his new surroundings.

When everyone had arrived, they gathered in the assembly hall to meet one another, and as they chatted among themselves Billy was surprised to see a number of girls among the candidates. Before setting off, he had been promised that no one, apart from the instructors, would know he was from borstal and that it would be left up to Billy to decide whether he wanted to tell anyone else. After a preamble from the instructors, everyone was asked to step forward and introduce themselves. First were the instructors and then the young people, who had mostly been sent by private companies such as major insurance firms or as part of apprenticeships.

When it came to Billy's turn, he found his mouth was dry and at first the words would not come. His public utterances had previously been restricted to speaking the word 'guilty' in court appearances, and now he felt the eyes of the women especially on him. He desperately wanted to make a good impression. Clearing his throat, he told the astonished assembly, 'My name is Billy Ferris. I'm from Wetherby borstal. I'm a young offender.' Had it been the right move? He could see everybody looking at one another, and even the instructors appeared surprised; previous borstal candidates had evidently given fictitious backgrounds. Now he had broken that mould. And there was more to come from him:

'I'm only telling you this in case any of you have money stolen – don't blame me.' Everyone relaxed and laughed at that. The ice had been broken, although he would never know whether the others thought it was a joke. Someone told him, 'We thought you were in the army,' and at that Billy felt he had been accepted.

It was announced that this was the first mixed course and that if successful it would become a permanent feature. At that, everyone cheered. Everybody seemed happy and excited, and the sense of adventure was infectious. Billy felt at ease; borstal was forgotten and his anxieties had been for nothing. Later, he learned he had been given the army uniform to enable him to say that he was an army cadet.

The next month went by in a delightful daze. He canoed, yachted, potholed, climbed Helvellyn, Scafell and others among the Lake District's highest peaks. He would remember it as one of the happiest months of his life. He knew when the time came to return to Wetherby that he had done everything asked of him and more, and he felt very proud and privileged to have been given the chance to take part.

In the same office where a year earlier he had been punished for running off, riding a horse and bringing chaos to a highly sensitive hunt for a wanted man, he was now complimented on his success. And he was told, 'Your reports speak only of good behaviour. Because of this, you are going home in two days. You've earned your release.' He was ecstatic, and on the way back to his room he told himself, 'Not bad for a horse thief from Blackhill.'

6

ON THE BUSES

BACK AT HOME, BILLY WAS welcomed into his family as though nothing had happened. Jenny, Willie, Paul and his sisters had remained loyal throughout his spell in Manchester and at borstal and only seemed glad the prodigal son had returned. If Willie felt he had been let down, he gave no sign of it, showing forgiveness and never once mentioning his son's excursion into lawlessness. While this might be put down to the behaviour of a loving father, it was shortly to emerge that Willie himself had secrets he would have preferred to remain in the shadows. Doubtless he remembered the well-used words from the Gospel of John: 'He that is without sin among you, let him first cast a stone.' Whatever his faults, Willie was no hypocrite.

Willie had seen that, as the working classes gradually became if not richer then certainly able to spare a few more pounds to spend on themselves, there was a growing demand for excursions. He'd decided to go into business for himself, starting off in the late '60s by setting up Hogganfield Coaches, first buying a second-hand minibus, then expanding to a 46-seater. It was a move that had the support of Jenny, as she remembers. 'At first, there was a lot of demand from football fans who wanted to be taken to matches and from weddings, for guests to be bussed to the venue. It also meant he was regularly up and away early in the morning to get men to their workplaces.' But as time passed, bookings and income had begun to drop off.

Following his release, Billy obtained work as a labourer with a company specialising in erecting huge chimneys for power stations. It was a good job, one he enjoyed, and the wages reflected the risks of working at great heights. He found himself travelling all over England, Scotland and Wales, but returning at every opportunity to Blackhill. He met a pretty young woman named Anne, fell in love and when he proposed, her acceptance excited them both. They were married on 24 January 1970. By then, Anne had discovered she was pregnant. With a baby on the way, due to arrive in late summer, the year promised much. At first, the young couple stayed with Anne's mum in Kirkintilloch, seven miles from Blackhill; they then managed to rent a home of their own nearby.

In August, Billy became proud dad to William, named after his father and grandfather. He had long known what it was like to have responsibility for someone younger and who looked to him for protection and guidance. Billy had been as a second father to Paul. Now, he threw himself into parenthood with a joy only a father can know. But though he did not realise it, dark clouds were already on the horizon, brought on by an incident that would lead to problems for the Ferris family, and Paul especially. It was something seemingly trivial, but the fallout lasts to this day.

In July, with Anne heavily pregnant, Billy announced that he intended to take her and his parents for a meal to celebrate his 20th birthday. Anne told him she preferred to stay at home, while at the same time encouraging him to enjoy the evening out with Jenny and Willie.

The celebration turned into a lingering nightmare, as Jenny remembers. 'On the way to meet us, William called into a shop, where he spotted a girl trying to lift the purse from an older woman's handbag while she was distracted. He shouted and as the girl ran off he chased after her, but her friends were waiting outside. They were the Welsh brothers, who lived in Blackhill. William ended up being jailed that night and I felt desperately sorry for him. He had simply tried to stop a crime, but somebody rang the police and claimed he had been fighting. He was arrested and because they had no station at Blackhill, they put him in an old police box to await the arrival of a van to take him away to be interviewed. That box was like something out of *Doctor Who*. It had been bashed to bits over the years, constantly being vandalised, and the door was almost hanging off. William was accused of kicking it and although he wasn't responsible, he got the blame. It was his first run-in with the Welsh family. He had no idea that they would go on to take it out on Paul at school.

Having seen Billy in trouble, it might have been expected that the Welsh brothers would let the matter end there. In fact, that incident was only the beginning of years of bullying and reprisal. Paul was aged seven at the time. Like Billy at his age, Paul had loved helping his grandfather in his vegetable garden, and continued tending the plot after Thomas's death. Like every schoolboy in Blackhill, he had heard about the Welsh family and was familiar with the name of their rival Arthur Thompson.

Thompson's rise to power and infamy had begun in the early 1960s. He would come to be known by the media as 'the Godfather', a tag he disliked and which was never mentioned in his presence. Tough and ambitious, he ran a pub and gambling club in Glasgow before moving into demolition and owning a timber yard. From time to time, he disappeared to London, where, it was rumoured, he carried out dirty work for the Krays. The twins had considerable respect for the gruff, barrel-chested Scot, and indeed, for most Glaswegians. In Glasgow, they would tell friends, there was as much violence in a fortnight as the main London gangs saw in a lifetime.

There was mutual dislike between the Thompson and Welsh families, each believing the other to be encroaching on their business activities and territories. The feud grew out of hand and began claiming lives. In mid-1966, Thompson was driving his Jaguar in Royston Road when he began overtaking a van in which sat Patrick Welsh and a pal, James Goldie. During the manoeuvre, the van was squeezed off the road and overturned, killing the occupants. An off-duty detective witnessed the incident. Thompson was accused of culpable homicide. Three months later, while he waited to face trial, he climbed into his motor outside the family home in Provanmill Road to give his mother-in-law, Margaret Johnstone, aged 61, a lift. Seconds later, the vehicle exploded in a fireball, killing her and seriously injuring Thompson.

On a dramatic day in November that same year, at the High Court in Glasgow, Thompson was cleared of the van killings before moving from the dock to the witness box to give evidence against three Welsh brothers, Martin, George and Henry, who were accused of murdering Margaret. Thompson looked around him and said,

'I cannot see any enemies in court.' It was commonly believed that he had merely stuck to the underworld code of not grassing even on the bitterest enemy. But observers of the underworld scene wondered whether he wanted the brothers at large so he could exact his own retribution for the killing of Margaret. They walked free, and the bitterness did not end there. Just under two years later, Thompson's fiercely protective wife, Rita, went to jail for stabbing a female member of the Welsh family in the chest. On the night of his 20th birthday, Billy unwittingly extended the feud to include his family.

Paul knew who the Welsh brothers were. There were six of them; Martin was regarded as the natural leader because of his strength. Unlike his brother, Paul had gone to St Philomena's primary, the same school as a number of the Welshes, and he would learn painfully that they were not going to forget the incident with Billy.

Meantime, the joy of holding his son meant the days seemed to pass quickly for Billy. But his happiness was soon to be marred. Driving to work on the outskirts of Kirkintilloch early one morning, he was stopped by the police. Checks at this time of day to see whether men heading to work had motor insurance, had paid road tax and were not driving stolen motors were commonplace. In Billy's case, officers had carried out a routine check of his number plate and discovered from that his name and the fact that he had a criminal record. Now they wanted to see his documentation. He had to admit that he had never bothered to undergo a formal driving test and get a licence. The inevitable outcome was a driving ban, as a result of which he lost his job. His life went into a downward spiral. With a wife and baby to support, money troubles soon piled up.

A solution was offered by a friend, who suggested robbing a shop in Glasgow of the contents of its safe. An insider had suggested a Sunday night hit, to take advantage of sizeable weekend takings, even assuring the pair that the safe key was usually left in the lock. They were dubious about the latter piece of information and so decided to go well prepared to break open the safe. Shops and sub-post offices throughout central Scotland were, at the time, being blitzed by a series of gangs, notably the Barlanark Team led by Thomas 'The Licensee' McGraw, and it was reasonable for Billy and his accomplice to assume that the blame for their own raid would be laid at the door of others.

The robbery was almost too easy. The pair forced the back door of the shop and were astonished to find the safe key still in the lock, as they had been told it would be. Inside was £1,138, a sizeable sum in 1971, when good-quality semi-detached houses were selling for less than £4,000. The theft did not attract more than a passing mention in a local newspaper. There were no clues as to the identity of the miscreants, and as the weeks passed Billy became increasingly convinced he had escaped undetected. Then came a knock on his door and police were waiting with handcuffs. His accomplice had carried out another robbery only to be caught in the act and, in an attempt to lessen his prison sentence, had told his captors about the earlier raid and named his partner in crime. When he came before the High Court in 1971, Billy was jailed for three years.

In prison, he could only listen helplessly as visitors told him of increasing problems for Paul and Willie. One story that reached him a few months after his jailing made him especially angry. His brother was just nine when, in 1972, he took on the bigger Martin Welsh in a playground fight and handed out a beating. That was an outcome for which his defeated foe and his brothers wanted revenge, and Paul knew that when he went back to his lessons the following day he would face the wrath of the other brothers. Sure enough, they were waiting. He would later tell friends, 'I really enjoyed school until I became a victim of the Welsh brothers. I was kicked all over the school yard by the brothers and then made to fight Martin Welsh again. I was truly frightened because I had another two years of primary school to go.'

The brothers would find that Paul, though slightly built, was no pushover. But he knew what they wanted – the sight and sound of him in tears – and he was determined not to give them that pleasure. He knew too that Billy would never have submitted, and that spurred him to even greater resistance, bringing even further pain. Paul quickly discovered that running away from an attack was no escape and merely created a delay before the punishment was administered. He realised too that the real intent of his tormentors was to humiliate him in front of his friends by forcing him to cry, so he vowed not to let tears show. As the beatings continued, Paul, bright and often demonstrating an astuteness beyond his years, nurtured a determination that when the time came for retaliation it would be sudden and without mercy.

For Jenny, there was nothing at that time to hint at the path her older son's life would take. 'I never saw William being violent when he was young. I saw Paul doing things that William never did at school, but then there were years between them. William and Paul were two different people; they were brothers, but like chalk and cheese.'

While he languished in his cell, unable to help the brother he loved, Billy was about to endure more misery. Willie's once thriving coach business had run into severe problems. As time went on and prices went up, customers he had previously given time to pay were making excuses as to why they couldn't come up with the money. This all started putting pressure on him.

There was worse to come. One of Willie's previous employers found himself on the receiving end of a random check of his books by social-security investigators. This led to his cash-in-hand system being unearthed, and checks were then extended to some of the recipients. A number had used false identities, but Willie had been too honest. His name and address were there in black and white and, inevitably, Hogganfield Coaches now came under the same scrutiny. Willie was charged with defrauding the Inland Revenue and jailed. Ironically, imprisonment would open up the prospect of a new career to him.

7

A ROOM WITH A VIEW

WILLIE SPENT PART OF HIS sentence in Perth jail, where he was visited by Paul and then Billy, who was released early in 1973. The latter experienced a very personal humiliation. 'Visiting my dad, seeing him in the same situation in which I had wasted years of my life, knowing the turmoil my ma was going through, left me for the only time in my life with a sense of shame that I hadn't been a better son, father, husband and brother. Now I knew how a father would feel at seeing his own son in prison.' He decided on a totally fresh start, believing there was no future for him in Scotland. He reckoned, with some justification, that if he stayed at home where the police knew of him and his record, that they would forever be at his shoulder. The outcome was that, with Anne and young William, he set up home in the Corby area of Northamptonshire, where he had relatives.

But, once again, a shortage of money soon became a problem. He thought he had learned a lesson from his first excursion into major crime: that if he needed assistance, he should choose only an accomplice who could be trusted completely and who would keep his mouth shut even if that meant receiving a longer sentence if caught. While doing his three years, Billy had been determined not to go back to prison. But that resolution was now being sorely tested by the demands of providing for his family. While in jail, he had found it relatively easy to convince himself he could say no to risking his freedom; the reality in the outside world of a screaming child and demanding wife was another matter.

It was soon obvious that moving to England had not been a good idea. In Scotland, he had at least had the support of his parents and sisters close at hand, along with friends whom he could trust and who would give him sound advice. Such guidance was missing when he was approached to take part in a robbery on a post office in Nottingham. He forgot his promise to say no, and the outcome was that before the year was out he was back in prison on remand, charged with another robbery. Billy was remanded to Bedford prison, principally to keep him apart from his partner in the raid, who had decided to turn Queen's evidence in exchange for a lighter sentence. While he waited for his trial, and the inevitable long jail sentence, his father was wondering whether fate had presented him with a solution to his own money worries.

The grim Victorian buildings that make up Barlinnie – known to many who have sampled its accommodation as 'the Big House' – dominate the skyline as seen by motorists heading into Glasgow from the east. Opposite the giant jail that is temporary home to more than 1,100 unfortunates, on the other side of the M8 motorway, is Blackhill. The prison is barely three-quarters of a mile from Hogganfield Street, where Jenny, Paul and the family lived. Willie had been moved to the Bar-L to prepare him for freedom. While he could not see his home through the bars of the little windows of his cell block, there was a view that attracted his interest and that of two others.

What they saw was a branch of the Bank of Scotland in Smithycroft Road, just a few yards from the prison. Over the years, countless inmates must have seen it too and it was odds-on that among them would have been bank robbers, men who would have spent many hours and days monitoring likely targets. Amazingly, the fact that a fortune lay on their doorstep appeared to have escaped their scrutiny. But it had not gone unnoticed by Willie, James Judge and John Davidson. The trio spent hours staring at the doors of the bank, watching customers and security vans come and go, timing arrivals and departures, noting times when the bank appeared busy and when it seemed to be quiet. Then they waited for freedom.

All three were due to be released around the same time in mid-1974. Willie would be the first to go free, and he had had much to think about, not least the fact that his eldest son was again serving a lengthy prison sentence, having been jailed for three and a half years for robbery, while his accomplice had been given a reduced sentence of three years. Society considered Willie had paid for his tax problems with valuable liberty. But he was about to exact recompense. On his way home on the day of his release, he took a slight detour along Smithycroft Road, past the front door of the Bank of Scotland. Willie faced hard times. Getting money from customers for coach trips had been difficult previously and now it would be almost impossible. But he had already worked out another use to which a coach could be put, and this time payment would be not only immediate but substantial, enough to secure the future of his business. In July, Davidson followed him through the gates of Barlinnie. Willie was waiting to greet him and to show him the bank set-up before taking him home to Hogganfield Street for a meal.

On 10 September 1974, casual onlookers would probably have thought nothing of the sight of a school bus packed with children drawing up at the bank in Smithycroft Road. Inside, six staff were busy when a teller looked up to see two male customers enter. A second glance caused her to ask a colleague, 'What's this coming in?' What she saw was a man with what appeared to be the face of a monkey. She would later tell police in a statement, 'When I saw the mask I was terrified. It was ape-like and grotesque, like something children wear at Hallowe'en.' Suddenly, a shotgun and revolver were being pointed, shocked customers and staff were ordered to kneel on the floor and then the robbers were fleeing with a massive haul of cash in sterling and foreign currency. They made their getaway in Willie's bus. By the time the alarm sounded, the raiders were long gone. After dropping off the youngsters nearby, the trio ended up at his home, where the haul was split three ways. The total take was made up of £9,631 cash plus the equivalent of £57,832 in foreign currency.

Paul Ferris was then looking forward to his 11th birthday. 'Dad had owned four or five different buses and used to transport supporters of Rangers and Celtic, take parties to Blackpool during Glasgow Fair fortnight in July, when just about everybody in Scotland seemed to head there, and generally be very busy. But then he went to prison for tax evasion and lost almost everything. In prison, he was in touch with two people who had been eyeing up the bank just a stone's throw from Barlinnie. While he had been away, it meant that us kids ended up at our gran's getting toast and beans for lunch, and we'd go back home from school when lessons were over for the day and mum would make us toast and beans. After a while, I associated toast and beans with my dad and his absence, which was very apparent. We were all over the moon when he came back home.

'My youngest sister Maureen and I played Monopoly quite a lot. One day, when our parents were out, I'd been looking around the house, going into places that as kids we weren't supposed to go, when I found this bag filled with money. It turned out to have been his stash from the bank robbery, but we didn't know that. We thought it was great, because we ended up playing Monopoly for real money. That's when the police turned up and saw money lying around the board. We couldn't understand why they took our game away. They went upstairs, where they found more money, while mum went off her head because my dad had owed her for provisions for that week.'

Paul could be said to be a double loser over the bank raid. As well as having his beloved Monopoly confiscated, he lost his ape mask after Jenny admitted to detectives it had belonged to her son. When he appeared at the High Court in Glasgow in November, two weeks after Paul's birthday, Willie, then aged forty-seven, was jailed for five years. He admitted being the getaway driver for the robbers, but the prosecution accepted that he had not gone into the bank or known that guns of any kind (they had in fact been replicas) were to be used. The judge, Lord Wheatley, told him, 'You have pleaded guilty to an offence which has become all too common and which has to be stamped out.' Two months later, it was the turn of Davidson and Judge to face his judgment and they were each jailed for ten years.

Both Billy and his dad were now in prison. 'I had already visited Billy in jail. Now I saw my dad inside as well,' says Paul. 'I knew where Barlinnie was, because as kids we used to hide in the bushes beside it and sing songs about the Black Maria. When it became common knowledge in the street that my dad had been arrested for the robbery, the other kids were asking me, "Was that your dad?" and I pretended it wasn't, telling them, "No, it was actually my brother." I was kind of familiar with the set-up at Barlinnie, but going up there to see him was like visiting the fictional Slade prison you saw in the television series *Porridge*. Obviously, it's had a facelift since then, but it was a dreadful place.'

Willie would never again be the same man after that second spell in prison. But while his health deteriorated, what he would never lose was a passionate pride in his sons. It was an emotion for which he would pay a painful price.

Billy began his latest sentence in Nottingham jail, where the authorities soon discovered he spelled trouble. Immediately after arriving, he had been sent to work in the prison's shoe factory. Most custodial establishments have workshops where inmates make a variety of items, from furniture to road signs and clothing for other prisons. In some cases, the working environment leaves much to be desired. It is, at times, not far removed from the cinema image of men dressed in grimy uniforms patterned with coloured arrows hunched over benches hand-stitching mailbags together.

The shoe factory was not a place where inmates volunteered to go to work. It reeked of the strong commercial adhesive Evo-Stik, and no matter how hard men tried through showering and scrubbing at the end of their daily stint to rid their bodies of the aroma, it continued to linger. An inmate did not need to be asked if he worked in the shoe factory; evidence of it could be detected from yards away. Billy determined from the outset he would not stay.

Because so many flammable substances were in use, smoking was meant to be strictly prohibited, but there were officers willing, for the sake of good relations, to turn a blind eye to a man who sneaked off into some corner for a quiet puff of a cigarette. On Billy's second day, everyone was evacuated from the shoe factory when it erupted in flames. He and three others were suspected of knowing how the fire had started and were locked in solitary confinement to await questioning by police, who had been called in to investigate. After 28 days, they were released into general circulation and he wrote home to tell his family, 'Obviously, the police realised that if a prisoner is going to risk having a quick drag in a non-smoking zone, accidents will happen. Cobblers no more – everybody got the boot!'

Later on, he was given work in the kitchen alongside a Londoner whom we shall call Roy. Roy was a master baker by trade, and he was a specialist in the manufacture of illicit alcoholic drink, known as 'hooch' or 'brew'. It was largely made from materials, especially yeast, purloined from the prison kitchen. The lessons Billy learned from the cockney would help him, and others, to spend many memorable nights and forgettable mornings in prisons throughout Britain. Billy named his own favourite brew 'Stairheid Dynamite' and told himself, 'This is the sort of stuff cowboys sold to red Indians. It's no wonder they stalked white men for more. I should have been Geronimo's brewmaster.'

Roy and Billy were soon joined in the kitchen by another Scot called Rab. Previously, nothing had been done about the taking of small amounts of yeast, but when Roy began allowing the Scots to have their share, a prison officer announced that in future he would dole it out. The response was that disinfectant was emptied into prison tea, salt into custard and soap into soup. All the food had to be dumped and the ten inmates working in the kitchen were lined up in front of an official who told them, 'If the guilty step forward, the rest can stay.' Kitchen jobs were prized, but nobody owned up and the entire canteen squad were sacked and marched back to their cells.

Billy later made no secret of having been behind a warning that anyone volunteering for kitchen work would be slashed. The threat was heeded, with the result that hungry inmates became restless. Fearing trouble, staff reinstated the kitchen team, but things only returned to normal when Roy was restored as sole distributor of the yeast.

'I didn't want any of you making hooch and going blind,' the officer said, but he was promptly told by one of his charges, in a fast-talking Glasgow accent, 'No, you didn't want us getting blind drunk, that's the real reason.'

The prisoners celebrated, believing they had won a victory that put Rab, Roy and Billy, 'the Booze Brothers', back in business. But the officer was determined he would have the last laugh and the result was that the convivial atmosphere the three enjoyed was about to be marred by the arrival in the kitchen of George David Duburiatte.

Duburiatte was nearing the end of a ten-year sentence imposed in 1965 for trying to rob the world-famous Shepperton film studios of £15,000. By a bizarre coincidence, he and an accomplice had chosen for the robbery a day when a replica of Newgate prison had been built in the studio as part of a movie backdrop. They stole for their getaway vehicle a car belonging to the First Sea Lord, Sir David Luce, but left empty-handed after a cashier at the studios pressed an alarm button. Police soon caught the crooks.

It was not the first time that Duburiatte had come to their notice. Five years earlier, while serving a sentence in Pentonville prison for possessing explosives and offensive weapons, he had complained of a swollen foot and was taken to hospital. In the waiting room, a stranger offered him a sweet from a packet. Suddenly, the patient made a miraculous recovery, throwing aside his crutches, vaulting over a windowsill and sprinting to a waiting car. Two men were jailed for helping him to escape. It was said the offering of the sweet was a signal that all was in place for him to flee.

The Scots had never heard of their new colleague and noted that Duburiatte was frequently absent. When asked where he had been, he told them it had been necessary for him to attend court hearings concerning family matters. Before long, they would discover the real reason for his disappearances.

The officer regularly in charge of the kitchen handed Duburiatte the prized job of adding the yeast to the bread and bun mix. At just under 6 ft tall and heavily built, the new man had an intimidating appearance, and clearly the thinking behind his appointment as yeast man was that the others would not dare steal from him.

Duburiatte took his role seriously, making it plain that yeast would no longer be slyly passed to anyone, thus threatening an end to the booming trade in hooch. That was bad enough, but the others suspected him of telling tales to staff about them and fellow inmates – an unforgivable crime in any jail and one liable to be met with severe beatings and even worse. In the Glasgow of Billy and Rab, grassing was unheard of, and the former determined to put a stop to it. He asked another Scot who worked with a party making concrete slabs to 'buff me up a bit of the steel rod you use to reinforce concrete' and the following evening was slipped a six-inch-long length of rod sharpened to a point at one end. It was not unlike a thick, sharp knitting needle and looked frightening.

Billy worked out his plan of action. In the mornings, kitchen workers had their cell doors opened sooner than other inmates' to allow them to prepare breakfast, and he decided to wait for his victim to enter the toilet area to take a shower, at which point he would attack. Duburiatte, wearing only a towel, was taken totally by surprise and slipped to the floor, where he appeared to have difficulty breathing.

As his attacker stood over him holding the weapon, he was able to plead only, 'Don't, don't, don't.'

He was told, 'If you fucking knock us back for yeast again, I will put this through you.'

'I'll give you anything, just don't stab me,' Duburiatte told Billy, before being rescued by Rab, who had rushed in expecting to see blood pouring from him.

'I've wound myself up all night for this,' Billy told Rab. 'I expected him to at least put up a show, not to bottle it.' Standing over his opponent, he spat on him and whispered, 'I better not have to come and see you again.'

Half an hour later, the two Scots were at work in the kitchen, but there was no sign of Duburiatte. 'That cowardly mouth has stuck us in,' Billy warned Rab. And he was right. At that moment, four officers arrived and carted first him and then his friend to the punishment block.

In the mid-morning, he was taken before a senior prison official, who told him, 'You are to be kept in solitary pending police enquiries into an assault on Duburiatte, who was slashed earlier this morning.'

Billy was astonished. 'He's a liar,' he protested. 'He must have done this to himself.' He knew Duburiatte had been left without a scratch.

As the other inmates were having their lunch, Billy was taken to be interviewed by the police. He was formally advised, 'We have reason to believe you can help us with our enquiries. A prisoner named George Duburiatte was slashed on the face. He said you did it while another inmate kept watch.'

Billy responded by telling them, 'I have nothing to say other than that Duburiatte is a liar and did this himself. I want a lawyer present before I answer any more questions.'

He was ordered to hand over his clothing, told to complete a form asking for the appointment of a lawyer and left to rot in solitary confinement for a further three weeks. At the end of that time, the same prison official who had originally accused him of the attack told him and Rab, 'No further action is being taken by the police or by myself. Consider yourselves very fortunate. You will be returned to your hall and back to work, and don't let me see either of you in front of me again.'

The Scots were not satisfied and demanded a full explanation. Later in the day, at an informal meeting with the same official, they were given one. 'For operational reasons, I cannot say too much, but what I can say will, I hope, be sufficient. It seems that Duburiatte had alternative motives for blaming you both for injuries that were very slight and possibly self-inflicted. He is being transferred and is at present in police custody.' There was more to follow, and the two listeners were not totally surprised by what they were told. 'Duburiatte is giving evidence against a number of London underworld figures and no doubt we will be reading about it in the tabloids. I accept, unreservedly, that you are both innocent of any assault on him.'

The reason for Duburiatte's absences was now clear. Instead of appearing in court to discuss his family, he had been meeting with police to give details of his crimes and the names of his accomplices. In the years that followed, it emerged that he had shopped almost 100 fellow criminals and, in exchange, was given a new identity by the police. In media interviews following his release, he told of keeping a double-barrelled shotgun by his bed and a crossbow nearby, of how major criminals had offered to pay huge sums to have him executed – and of the day two mad Jocks in Nottingham prison had tried to collect a £10,000 bounty by attacking him. His version was different from theirs. Duburiatte claimed that despite being slashed on the face, he had chased his attackers.

Billy remembers, 'It was the first time I'd heard of a supergrass. The morning that I pulled the weapon on him must have been his worst nightmare, because he obviously thought he had been exposed. That explained the look of utter terror on his face and why he was moved straight away into police custody. How strange that it all started over a bit of yeast.'

8

LOVE AND HURT

BILLY'S TIME IN JAIL WAS drawing to a close, and he began to be allowed short breaks to rejoin his wife and son.

In Scotland, matters were reaching a near crisis. With Paul's father and elder brother both behind bars, his schoolboy enemies doubtless believed he was now even more vulnerable. What they forgot was that he had always fought his own battles, never running home to tell tales of beatings and bullyings. Consequently, he continued to give as good as he got. A move to St Roch's secondary school had not shaken off the brothers, who, like him, were also due to transfer.

But there came a day when he flirted with death in an incident that shocked and horrified even those in Blackhill who were hardened to violence. Naturally, there were some who laid the blame at the door of the Welsh brothers, but Paul was a follower of the code that taught it was a sin to grass, even on enemies, and so he stayed silent, leaving even members of his family in ignorance of what happened.

In Glasgow at that time, stories were circulating of gangsters and moneylenders literally crucifying rivals or customers who found themselves unable to pay up in time. The escalating level of violence in the city was reflected in an attack on 13-year-old Paul. One day in 1976, word spread in Blackhill that he had been tied to a tree in the local graveyard and left dangling dangerously. Horrified adults cut him down, and when asked what had happened he said only that there had been an accident and refused to say who else had been involved. His friends pondered the story of a game that had come close to ending in tragedy, said little, asked no questions and wondered how long it would be before retribution came.

Meanwhile, Billy graduated from brief excursions home lasting a few hours, to days and then a weekend. The idea was to allow the prisoner and his family to get reaccustomed to having each other about. Men awaited these visits with eagerness, and Billy was no exception. He had a wife he loved and a son on whom he doted. But his world was about to be shattered.

Although he had begun to suspect that his feelings for Anne were no longer returned, he wondered if that was simply down to his wife's uncertainty as to how long her husband could stay free. In fact, the reality of the situation was devastating. During one short break, Billy's uncle Tommy, who had often visited him in jail, broke the news that Anne had been dating another man and was pregnant by him.

In the Maple Leaf pub in Corby in August 1976, an argument developed when another customer made comments to Billy about his wife. The other man, clothing worker Alan Thompson, aged 22, was stabbed and, despite efforts to save him, died. Billy was charged with murder.

Billy has never spoken about the emotions that tore him apart and caused him to act in the way he did that night, not even to his closest family. That decision to keep his thoughts locked away was one for which he would pay dearly over time. Just what did go through his mind?

'When I was told about Anne during one of my leaves, it felt like being given news of a bereavement. It was as though I'd been given a severe blow to the kidneys. I remember gasping for air and thinking, "This is how it must be just before you die, wanting one more, one final lungful of breath." In what seemed to be the distance, I could hear my uncle Tommy's voice telling me gently, "Billy, son, she's been fooling about and is pregnant. I didn't want to tell you in the prison visiting room. But now you're on home leave, it would be wrong for you not to know. I'm sorry it had to be me who told you." A devil inside me was screaming, "This is a sick joke." Had Uncle Tommy told me she was dead, I doubt the shock and the sense of loss would have been any greater.

'Thoughts immediately leapt into my head of a conversation I'd had on a visit with Anne when I'd told her, "You're putting on weight up top. Are you pregnant?" It was just the first thing that came into my head when I'd seen her, because I remembered that was how she looked when she was carrying our son William. As soon as the words were out, Anne was tearing into me screaming, "How dare you? How dare you?" I was taken aback by the violence of her response and felt guilty for having made what sounded such an insensitive remark. It was something said on the spur of the moment. I had no reason to think that what I was suggesting was true. Her reaction humbled me. Her words still sting as I remember them ringing in my ears. I have never felt like that before or since. Yet – call it intuition, perhaps – it turned out I was correct. The woman who was the love of my life had transferred her guilt to me. Over the years since, this must all have come back to haunt her.

'Yet when I was talking to my uncle, despite what he said, my only thought was, "Surely my Anne could never do that?" Looking back, I realise what a naive cunt I must have seemed.

'I remember walking around, kicking at a shop window and smashing it without realising what I was doing. On the train taking me from prison on my home leave, I had had but one thought, which was that soon I'd be seeing Anne and William again. Home, that wonderful word. I was going home to a wife and child who loved me and would give me all I could ask for and more. Sitting there, watching the miles speed by, I had thought, "I'm one of the lucky ones. So many guys are betrayed once the gates bang shut on them. Not me." Well, reality was waiting just around the corner. I had walked into a nightmare, into a horror story. And in this one, it wasn't the others who were being betrayed, it was me.

'Had my wife told me that what Uncle Tommy had said was untrue, I would have accepted her word without question. I wanted to believe it wasn't true. Why? Because I was so utterly and completely in love with her.

'I have never, ever shared these thoughts and feelings with anyone. Nobody. Instead, I maintained years of silence. Sharing a hurt is a no-go in jail. Getting mail can be a nightmare, because often the letters you receive are not from the person you most wanted to hear from. It's like when you're waiting for a call, and when the phone rings it's just a wrong number. So you discipline yourself not to look for mail and tell your family, "Don't write to me because I can't be bothered to write back." The reality of all this is that it's a cop-out to save you from disappointment. All the barriers you build to protect yourself only alienate you from everyone. You find yourself at your lowest point. Memories become a raw nerve; it's sink-or-swim time. Not giving a fuck seems to get you space; there's no aimless, senseless conversation to endure – a look or a jibe is enough of a signal that you want to be left alone. If cunts can't see how it is, fuck them. Their time will come to feel it.

'That is the only way out. Blank out thoughts of family and home so that as time goes by maybe the memories will dry up to be replaced by mere wishful thinking, thoughts not of how things are but of how they might have been. Of course, we can never know what might have been, what we have lost.

'Anne was put in a very difficult position by me because of the way of life I dragged her into. No doubt her hurt was greater than mine and I was all the bigger a disappointment – because she had married a loser. I was selfish and didn't care about consequences or the effect I was having on Anne.

'They say that the first cut is the deepest, but even 35 years later, the more a wound is probed the more inflamed it becomes. I read that in a book of Roman literature years ago and related to it instantly. The fact is there is no fooling yourself any longer; life has to go on. But nothing can prevent you remembering both the good and the very, very sad times.'

9

THE BOMBER

WHILE BILLY AWAITED HIS PUNISHMENT for murdering Alan Thompson in Leicester prison, mainland Britain was suffering regular and horrific outrages as the Troubles that were dragging Northern Ireland into despair spread like a cancer. Nowhere seemed safe, with London and the Midlands regularly targeted. In the capital, the Provisional IRA had waged a maniacal campaign during 1974 and 1975. More than 40 bombs had exploded, leaving 35 people dead and hundreds maimed and injured. In 1975, the organisation had claimed responsibility for the shooting dead of Ross McWhirter, co-founder of *The Guinness Book of Records*, who had offered a £50,000 reward for information about IRA activities leading to a conviction. Billy had frequently read of bombings and murders blamed on or claimed by Irish republican factions. During the years to follow, he would come face to face with many of the men who were responsible for these terrible acts.

One such was Raymond McLaughlin, who, the Scot discovered, was lucky to be alive. One night in November 1974, he had been acting as a lookout while his friend James McDade carried a bomb through the streets of Coventry. The expedition, on behalf of their IRA masters, was fraught with danger. Neither was familiar with their target, a newly built telephone exchange at Greyfriars, or even the streets around it. Both men lived in Birmingham, where McDade, then twenty-eight, had set up home with his wife and two young children, having left behind his mother in Belfast.

Then there was the added worry that police were on high alert. Just a few hours earlier, an IRA bomb had gone off at an RAF club in Northampton, causing massive damage, and there were rumours that another IRA unit was in the Birmingham area. Before the night was out, it would bomb the Solihull Conservative Club.

And just how stable was the bomb McDade carried? He and his minder were about to discover the answer to that. Shortly before half past eight, it exploded minutes early, literally blowing McDade into smithereens, bits of his body ending up in an alleyway 100 yards from where he had been standing. Remarkably, he was the only victim, but had McLaughlin been nearer, he too would have perished.

An enraged crowd spotted McLaughlin and gave chase. He was caught and kicked to the ground, but rescued by police who drove him off for his own safety. He was 23 and when he appeared before Birmingham Crown Court in March 1975 he was convicted of possessing a firearm and causing an explosion of a nature likely to endanger life. Jailed for 12 years, he was sent to Hull in the East Riding of Yorkshire, where he became caught up in a riot. He was transferred to the punishment block of Leicester jail.

The punishment cells were next to those holding remand prisoners, among them Billy, who found himself directly under the kitchen of the special unit, where long-term, major criminals were caged. By a strange twist of fate, John McVicar was one of these. McVicar and another inmate could sometimes be seen playing tennis in a small court marked out on a square of concrete surrounded by a 12-ft-high fence topped with razor wire. Players would carry out two posts with a net slung between them, being careful to return their equipment at the end of each game to a store.

Men on punishment, such as McLaughlin, were not so privileged. They were allowed, one at a time and for just half an hour each day, into a tiny exercise area in a small passageway between the tennis court and the windows of the remand-section cells. Spotting the Irishman one day, Billy had enquired how he was, to be told, 'Grand, just grand.'

'I liked Ray McLaughlin,' Billy remembers, 'as frankly I did many of those convicted of attacking the Old Bailey and Scotland Yard, but I did not like those who attacked soft targets like pubs. I saw the murder of Ross McWhirter as being in the same category as that of Lord Mountbatten – an assassination.'

Billy made friends with another inmate in the punishment cells, a man we are calling Jim Graham, and he found himself the cellmate of a man we are calling Don Andrews, with whom he had served time during his post-office-robbery sentence. Don too was awaiting his fate and, like Billy, allowed certain freedoms not available to others who had already been convicted and sentenced, including liberal use of the canteen shop, which sold among other items sweets and tobacco. They could spend as much as they wished. Through his cell window, Billy gave tobacco to McLaughlin, but because the Irishman did not smoke, he handed it on to Jim Graham, settling instead for sweets. As the friendship developed, Billy passed on juice and biscuits from the shop, and then a small quantity of hash.

Not a single prison in Britain can claim to be free of drugs. They are smuggled in with ease. The carriers may be unscrupulous officers, willing to risk their jobs and their own liberty for a few extra pounds or officers who have given in to intimidation. In fairness, however, these are rare. The inventiveness of inmates knows few bounds. Drugs have been smuggled into prisons even with the highest security ratings, sometimes simply by being thrown over a wall to a waiting inmate. While heroin and cocaine cause intense trouble inside prisons now, in the mid-1970s hash was the problem. This illicit intoxicant provided users who had only years of grim confinement ahead with a means of passing at least short periods in a feeling of relative well-being. For men and women, facing decades of incarceration, hashish was a welcome relief.

In the special unit above Billy, John McVicar was also restricted in what he could purchase from the canteen. The answer was for Billy to bang on the ceiling of his cell, the signal for a string to be lowered from the upper window so Don could attach a bag filled with tobacco and goodies that would then be hauled up. It was a pleasant enough arrangement in a situation where few had hope.

One day, the riot bell clanged and, after locking up every inmate, officers scampered to the special unit, where sounds of shouting and arguing were heard. These died down briefly before resuming until peace was restored and cell doors were unlocked by officers unwilling to talk about what had gone on. The answer to that was soon given by a special-unit prisoner, who told Billy that

two IRA offenders had been brought into the special unit and as a result all hell had broken out. It was inevitable that throughout the prison system there would be men and women who felt bitter towards those involved in terrorism.

There were few inmates who did not have families, wives and children walking streets now unsafe because of the activities of fanatics willing to bomb indiscriminately. In November 1975, a bomb thrown through the window of a Mayfair restaurant had caused a fatality. A month later, shots were fired through the windows of the same establishment. Police, realising the IRA frequently went back to former targets, were waiting. Many officers involved in that operation were still bitter over the cowardly shooting dead earlier that year by Liam Quinn of Constable Stephen Tibble, aged just 22. They did not know, however, that Quinn had been a member of the unit that went on to attack the restaurant. In the wake of the shooting, he had left London, eventually reaching Dublin, but four others had remained: Hugh Doherty, Martin O'Connell, Eddie Butler and Harry Duggan. With police hot on their heels, they fled into a block of flats in Balcombe Street, next to Marylebone railway station, where they took hostage two occupants of a flat, John and Sheila Matthews. Realising there was no way out, the gang initially demanded an aircraft to fly them to Ireland, and then, after six days, gave up and appeared in court to be convicted of murders and told they would die in jail.

Feeling also ran high in the Midlands. On 21 November 1974, bombs left in the Mulberry Bush and Tavern in the Town pubs killed 21 people, most of them young, and horribly injuring 162 others. Police arrested six Irishmen, Patrick Hill, Hugh Callaghan, John Walker, Richard McIlkenny, Gerard Hunter and William Power. Despite their protestations of innocence, in August 1975 they were all found guilty of 21 counts of murder and jailed for life. Four months later, fourteen prison officers were tried for assaulting them but were cleared by a jury. Other IRA supporters were suspected to have been the real bombers but no one came forward. The Birmingham Six remained in jail until 1991, when the Court of Appeal quashed their convictions.

Gossip had spread throughout Leicester prison that the two newcomers were part of the Balcombe Street gang. In the special unit, all that mattered was that they represented the IRA; a relative of one of the men already held there had been injured in one of the London bombings. This man made it plain to prison officers, 'If they come in here they will not be allowed to mix with anybody else, they will not be allowed to use the snooker table or watch television. They will not be allowed to use the unit kitchen but will have to go and get their meals from the canteen used by everybody else, and if that puts them in the firing line, that is their problem.' This man had a fearsome reputation as a prisoner not to be messed with, and during the time Billy was on remand in Leicester he heard numerous stories of IRA inmates being given a bad time by other prisoners.

This was the late summer of 1976, when on the outside of the prison walls the sun beat down day after day. Temperatures within rose too, as did tempers. Don Andrews was found guilty and moved to another part of the jail to await his sentence. He passed word to Billy that a newcomer due to arrive in the remand area had once cheated him. No sooner had this scoundrel dropped his meagre belongings in his cell than the Scot gave him a savage beating. Billy told other cons, 'I wanted to slash him, but Don said a good hiding would be enough.'

Battered and bleeding, the startled victim was carried off to the prison hospital while his attacker was given fourteen days' solitary and told he would not be allowed to watch television or mingle with other inmates for a further two weeks when his period in seclusion ended. In the punishment block, he found himself alongside McLaughlin and Graham, two men whom he would come across many times in the future in different jails.

Billy's time on remand ended at Northampton Crown Court on 31 May 1977, when he was sent to prison for life for the murder of Alan Thompson. By then, it had emerged that, in an extraordinary twist of fate, the victim was doomed to die anyway. He suffered from a highly infectious form of the hepatitis B virus characterised by the presence of the so-called Australia antigen. A medical expert reported that the infection was so severe that it would have been terminal. The judge, however, had no discretion over the sentence; life is mandatory for anyone convicted of murder. He did have a choice over how long he recommended to the Home Secretary that the accused man should stay locked up before he was allowed to seek parole. This period is known as the tariff, and the judge set it at 12 years. Parole is rarely granted to lifers on their first application, but friends of Billy believed he would be freed at the latest around 1990.

As he gazed through the tiny windows of the van taking him to prison through the streets of Northampton, he had no inkling of the ordeal that lay ahead. Instead, his immediate thoughts were of his son William, now approaching his seventh birthday. What, he wondered, was best for the child? 'I told myself I deserved to be jailed for the murder of Alan Thompson. This was a time of heartbreak on many fronts in my life, but there was no way back. I was in a boiling pot of hate, and more hurt about my marriage being over than worried as to what lay ahead in my life sentence. On reflection, I was drowning in self-pity.'

10

THE HATE FACTORY

HARDLY HAD THE WORDS OF the judge pronouncing life died away than Billy was on his way to Wormwood Scrubs in the heart of London. It was a grim place, originally built from corrugated iron using convict labour in the 1870s. In 1981, following a riot there, the prison's governor described the Scrubs as a 'penal dustbin'. Yet when Billy arrived in 1977, he was almost impressed. He was one of 1,300 men and found himself in D Hall, where long-term prisoners were held.

'Scrubs was a jail with a dreadful reputation as a hellhole. But I could have been entering Hell itself for all it mattered to me. I was angry, out of control, a time bomb ready to implode. I knew family visits and letters were always there for me, although I am ashamed to say I hated getting mail. But still they wrote. I was lucky in that if you could equate family love to wealth, then I was a billionaire. In jail, you never get really close to anybody. You have friends, good friends who stand by your side, but my attitude was that until someone had been tried and tested in a confrontation, I could never be sure just how loyal he would be. All I could do was hope he would live up to my expectations.

'The first thing to hit me was not the usual smell of boiled cabbage and urine but a pleasant aroma of food being cooked. I could make out fried onions and curries. This was different from any other establishment I had ever been in. I found that cons were allowed to cook their own food and buy their own groceries via the canteen from their prison wages. To say I was pleasantly surprised was an understatement.

'Four of us arrived at the same time, and I was given a cell on the second landing. On my way up the stairs, I noticed a prisoner with a black eyepatch, giving him the appearance of a pirate, and thought, "What a prick." As I walked past him, I eyeballed his good eye and felt it following me all the way along the landing. I felt like dropping my kit on the floor and poking that fucking eye out, because I had very, very bad vibes about this cunt.

'The pirate then moved his attention from me and started watching where the other three new fish went. Later on, I had a run-in with this rat and knew I had been right to have bad impulses about him. He was flashy, swaggered around as if he ruled the landing and you could dry wet sheets on his shoulders. Somebody told me his real name, but I'll call him Bill York. I dumped my gear on the bed, took a look around the cell, which was clean but nothing special, and walked outside and almost slap into an old friend who'd been transferred from Leicester, Jim Graham. It was good to see a familiar face and, after asking how I was and sympathising with me over my conviction and sentence, he introduced me to some of the others. Everybody made me feel welcome.'

Billy was soon shaking hands with half a dozen men whose exploits had produced dazzling headlines in the tabloids including Billy Gentry, Ian (also known as John) Barrie from Edinburgh, John Goodall, Jimmy O'Loughlin, who would become a long-time friend, and two others whom we are calling Norman Brown and Harry Parker.

He would soon discover that Gentry was an old accomplice of John McVicar, and the two shared many laughs about the night the borstal boy had briefly become the most wanted man in Britain. In 1966, Londoner Gentry, then aged 33, and McVicar were arrested in the capital after shots were fired at police during a car chase through the streets of Deptford and Bermondsey. The getaway car crashed into a lorry, and as the occupants ran off two police constables drove off in pursuit of Gentry, who was armed with a revolver. He pointed the gun through the window of the car and told one of the policemen, 'Get out or else it's your lot,' not realising that the chambers were empty. After being arrested, Gentry told a senior policeman, 'That driver of yours is really good. We thought we had a good one but we could not lose him. Tell your man he can have five grand to drive for us next time.'

The cockney was sent down for 17 years and in 1969 found himself in E Wing at Durham, from where McVicar had escaped the previous year. By then, the wing was holding Moors murderer Ian Brady, London gang boss Charlie Richardson and Paul Seabourne, who had been involved in the dramatic escape from jail of Great Train Robber Ronnie Biggs. At Durham, Gentry and other high-profile inmates including Richardson and Seabourne went on hunger strike in protest at restrictions placed by the authorities on visiting arrangements. Ironically, while their protest continued, it was reported in the press that Brady had taken on the role of cook to a number of sex offenders kept apart for their own safety. After his stint in Durham, and with freedom in sight, Gentry had been moved to the Scrubs to be nearer his family.

Barrie was a trusted member of the Kray twins' gang who had been in prison since March 1969, when he was convicted of a sensational murder. Aged 31 at the time, he was jailed for life for his part in the killing of George Cornell, who ran with a rival London outfit, the infamous Richardson 'Torture Gang'. Ronnie Kray was tipped off that Cornell was in the Blind Beggar pub in Whitechapel. It was Kray territory and, according to the strict code of underworld courtesy, he should not have been there without permission. Together with Barrie, Ronnie strode into the Blind Beggar where, just seconds earlier, Cornell had told his pal Albert Woods, 'Let's have one for the road.' Barrie shot into the ceiling, causing drinkers to dive for cover, at which Ronnie whipped out a Mauser pistol and from just ten feet away blasted his victim in the head.

John Goodall, from Finchley, had been captured at a hotel in the Costa Brava resort of Lloret de Mar. He was extradited to London and in 1974 jailed for 12 years after admitting to having taken part in an armed bank robbery. As the months passed, Billy learned that Brown, Parker and O'Loughlin were serving long sentences for their roles in robberies. All these men became Billy's close friends.

Billy remembers, 'A few things happened during my time in

D Hall that opened my eyes and made me see what the Scrubs was really like. I felt I was living in a factory that churned out hate. I called it "the Hate Factory". So many men I came across were filled with hate – hate for what they saw as the injustice of long sentences, hate for the staff who kept them under lock and key and often hate for one another. An attitude of every man for himself pervaded the place. Where the various elements from the London gangs were concerned, it was dog eat dog. I would learn just how this hate could twist a man's thinking. Had I not met Jim and Ray, I know I would not have had such an easy introduction to the place, but my friendship with them resulted in my having a much easier time than most received.'

Billy Gentry was the hall bookie, willing to take bets on racing or boxing, and together with Barrie he ran the hall, with Goodall as their third in command. The Glaswegian respected all three. 'They were gentlemen and good company, always told cracking stories, never moaned and did their time in style. These men certainly fitted the popular gangster image. Billy was a really good guy who had been stuck in by a female supergrass.'

Norman Brown and Harry Parker, with the help of Jim Graham, ran a thriving prison football-coupon system, to which most inmates contributed, and occasionally they would share a hash joint and a laugh with the Scot.

Jim introduced Billy to others, including a number convicted of terrorist offences. Cornelius McFadden, a man we are calling Peter Wilson, Patrick 'Paddy' Hackett and another whom we are calling John McIntosh would become allies. They trusted Billy because word had spread of the kindness and friendship he had shown not only to Jim but also to Ray McLaughlin.

In March 1975, at the age of just 21, Cornelius Michael McFadden of Acton, London, had been sent to prison for 20 years. Along with seven other Irishmen, he was found guilty of plotting IRA bombings in London and the Home Counties. Explosives had been planted a year earlier at Madame Tussauds, the Boat Show at Earls Court and outside the home of a senior army officer; several firebombs had been planted at a shopping centre in Uxbridge. Sentencing the terrorists, the judge, Mr Justice Melford Stevenson, had said that some defence counsel had acted as 'mere loudspeakers of a maladjusted set' and that it was 'a sad day for the Bar of England'. His remarks were countered by the Bar Council, which hit back in a statement declaring: 'It will be a sad day for the Bar when any barrister is deterred from doing his duty by any fear of official displeasure or hope for personal advantage.'

It was Paddy Hackett, though, who attracted Billy's admiration. 'Of all the people to make an impression on me, it was an IRA man. What I liked about him was not that he was IRA but his attitude to disability.'

Hackett, a butcher from Clapham Common, was a member of a Provisional IRA unit who had been jailed for 20 years in June 1977. In the dock alongside him that day at the Old Bailey stood Adrian Vincent Donnelly, and both were convicted by a jury of taking part in a six-week terror campaign in which there were sixteen bombing incidents.

Hackett told Billy how he and Donnelly had been ordered by their terrorist commanders to take a bomb and detonate it outside Wandsworth jail in London. It was the start of a remarkable sequence of bad luck. Somebody stole the car in which they planned to carry the device and, rather than abandon the operation, they decided to travel by Underground. However, outside the Tube station at Kensington on 1 March 1976, the bomb exploded prematurely, inflicting terrible injuries on Hackett. A Flying Squad detective, who discovered him lying in a pool of his own blood in the road, saw that one of his hands had been blown off at the wrist and that he had extensive injuries to his stomach and legs. Doctors saved his life but had to amputate a leg. While he was recovering, he told detectives he had become lost and that he belonged to the 'Sixth South Tyrone'. He said he had been working on a bomb when he blew himself up.

'Paddy said the police were squeezing his wounds to get him to talk and to give his name. He told them he was "Patrick Hennessy from Galway". It was only after his photograph appeared in newspapers that someone came forward and he was identified to the police. After months of treatment, he ended up in D Hall with us. He was given an artificial arm and leg that didn't fit and was forever arguing with the hospital screws over this. One day, he took off his artificial leg and used it to smash up the office. It took this, and some disruptions by other IRA offenders, for anything to be done on his behalf. Paddy never played on his disability. His IRA comrades were continually offering to make his bed and clean his cell, but he always turned them down. He was his own man and constantly cheerful, a truly amazing human being. I could never see him as a terrorist, just a very brave man.'

Thanks to his friend Jim Graham, Billy was allocated a job in the prison laundry, where he found himself working alongside Gentry, Goodall, Barrie and an unfamiliar face, Vic Dark. Londoner Dark was just 20 and at the start of what would be a terrifying criminal career. During an armed robbery, police arrived on the scene sooner than anticipated and in the panic his fellow robber called out Vic's name. Realising a security guard had heard, Dark shot the man, but the bullet passed clean through him and hit the accomplice. In the nightmare of alarm bells and sirens, he picked up his friend and, with gun in hand, took a policeman hostage, forcing him to drive off. Eventually, he ran off into a boggy potato field and buried himself in the mud while police and tracker dogs searched in vain. He was later jailed for 12 years.

Billy enjoyed laundry work because it was far from exhausting and the inmates often took breaks to play cards and even get stoned, the attitude of the guards being to turn a blind eye so long as the work was done.

But behind the bonhomie, the Hate Factory spewed greed and discontent. Convicted of involvement in robbing the Bank of America in Mayfair in 1976 (of which more later), O'Loughlin was believed, as a result of the multimillion-pound haul, to be wealthy, and to men whose schemes and hopes of earning fortunes had largely been shattered, the thought that another had succeeded where they had failed bred envy. Further, because the crime had been staged in London, some gangs from the city believed they were entitled to a share, a commission for work carried out in their territory. Jimmy and his fellow gang members disagreed. The final straw for some was that he employed an unofficial minder, one-eyed Bill York. Billy, as we have seen, had taken a dislike to York.

Jimmy knew Billy disliked York but told him, 'He's OK, Billy. I know he comes across as being flashy, but that's just his way.

Take it from me, he'll grow on you. He's no rose – more a jaggy nettle. Give him time.'

But Billy's reply was, 'Your trouble, Jimmy, is that you see the good in everybody, including him.'

The simmering jealousy towards Jimmy grew until one day he was mysteriously no longer at the Scrubs, and officers let word slip that he had been suddenly moved to Parkhurst because of security concerns. But those like Billy who knew and liked Jimmy suspected that the reason was simply that he was the victim of false whispers that he was in danger, rumours put about as punishment for not complying with demands for a share of his loot. Billy says, 'Here was a man being punished by other inmates simply because they hated the idea that he might have had money and they did not. It was typical of the Hate Factory. The prison system bred hate.'

Meanwhile, as the demand for drugs increased, so did the likelihood of trouble. The issue threatened to come to a head when the Londoners, who had a monopoly on drug trading, discovered that IRA terrorists had moved into the market. This was hugely risky, not just because it meant their being in direct opposition to the cockneys but also because their commanders over the water forbade them even to use hash. If caught, they faced punishment from their own allies.

During this time, McFadden and McIntosh were visited by a friend from Ireland. Two pinboards made in one of the workshops had been left for the guest to collect as he was leaving. But during a routine search, guards had torn open the boards and discovered £300 in cash hidden inside. Rumour had it that the authorities had been tipped off about where to find the contraband by Bill York.

The assumption among most inmates was that the money was payment for hash that was to be smuggled into the jail, and that the discovery spelled big trouble for McFadden and McIntosh from a number of quarters. However, the Irish contingent knew differently, and news of the discovery was greeted with dismay and anxiety. Because of it, the cells of McFadden and McIntosh were locked up, and in that of the former was an item the terrorists badly needed.

Peter Wilson sought Billy out and asked for a favour. Would

he agree to swap his name card with that of McFadden so that it looked as if Cornelius's cell was his and then ask a prison officer to open it up? 'If it works, bring us his stereo speakers, Billy,' he was told. 'We're scared they might be taken away if Con's cell is searched.'

'When Peter asked me, I didn't hesitate,' says Billy. 'I'd have done the same for anybody else. Trouble followed me anyway, and I welcomed it.'

The deception worked. Immediately he had handed over the speakers, Billy replaced the name cards. He suspected some plot was afoot and thought, wrongly, that the equipment contained money or hash. But when the speakers were opened up, he watched in amazement as a spanner, nuts, bolts and wheel spacers were hauled out. 'What the fuck's that?' he asked and was told by Wilson, 'It's a bleeding jack for forcing window bars, is what it is.' It looked as if someone had paid handsomely for the tools to be smuggled inside.

Later that night, during association, the period when inmates can mingle to play games, chat or watch television, six IRA offenders forced bars on a toilet window on the second floor and tied bedding together to lower themselves to the ground. They knew an escape was out of the question, as they could not climb the 15-ft-high perimeter fence. But they were hell-bent on making mischief and creating a panic. All six ran around causing a major security alert but were caught and locked up back in their cells within minutes.

While the incident caused hilarity among the other inmates, the full repercussions created intense bad feeling. The following day, every cell was searched and items such as extra clothing removed on the grounds they could have been used on the outside in an escape. All inmates were locked up for the day.

Gossip was rife that a full escape by the Irish contingent had actually been planned, with getaway cars supposed to be waiting outside the prison walls. Newspapers screamed that a major IRA breakout had been foiled. Stories persisted that nurses at nearby Hammersmith Hospital were to have been taken hostage and used to bargain for the release of more terrorist convicts. The six escapees were transferred elsewhere in the prison system.

Billy expected York to be beaten up for having endangered

the escape plan, but nothing was done, and Billy lost much of the respect he had held for the IRA, who not only ignored their own rules on drugs but also allowed informers to escape without punishment.

11

STRAIGHTENER

ONE DAY, WHEN BILLY HAD been in the Scrubs for a few months, he was told by Norman and Jim, 'We have opposition to our football coupon. A guy known as Brummy and two of his mug pals are taking bets, and we're not allowing this. We're going to ask them for a straightener on the third landing, where the screws can't see it going on.'

A 'straightener' was slang for a fist fight, a 'square go', and Billy announced that he would even the odds by joining in. 'We share everything else, so why not the hassle too?' he said. Violence, often brutal and sometimes fatal, is an accepted part of prison life. It is inevitable that when men are cooped up together for long spells petty jealousies develop into fighting and bloodshed.

What happened next, according to Billy, was typical of the banal brutality of prison life. 'Brummy worked in the laundry with me. I'd never liked or trusted him, and I think it was only a matter of time before things between us boiled over. Because the next day was a Friday, when work normally stopped earlier, the straightener was arranged for four in the afternoon. Jim told Brummy to tell his two pals to be on the third landing at dinner time. All that afternoon in the laundry, I would catch Brummy watching me. Then Jim was taken to the dentist for a filling.

'A few of the boys knew what was going to go down. John Barrie, Billy Gentry and John Goodall had all said, "Billy, don't get involved. You'll all get fucked out [transferred]. There'll be no winners." But by this time I was committed.

'Just when Jim left, I caught Brummy smirking at me. "You

won't be smirking when we get into the hall," I said, and he came back with, "Why wait? Let's do it now."

'John, Billy and John G jumped in between us, and that fucked him off. He was a big bastard and fancied his chances, and somebody said, "Billy, just leave it. Brummy'll pull your fucking head off." But no cunt was going to pull my head off, I was sure of that.

'Unexpectedly, for some reason I didn't know about, we finished at three that day instead of four, which could have put me in a tight spot. The opposition certainly thought I was in trouble, especially when I got back to the hall to find Jim still at the dentist, while Norman had an hour to go before finishing an education class. I decided I would wait on them to join me. I was in my cell having a pipe of hash when Vic Dark came in and said he wanted to sit with me until the others returned. Vic was a good guy, but I'd changed my mind and I told him I was going to see Brummy right then.

'I went to see the jail barber and asked for a shot of his scissors. When he handed them over, I just walked away with them towards Brummy's cell, where I snapped the scissors in two, pushed his door open and peered inside only to find it empty. Just then, I heard his horrible voice calling, "Jock, over here," and turned around to find him standing at the door of his mate's cell.

'I had the scissors up my sleeve, headed towards him, and as I entered the cell, Brummy punched me on the side of the head. It would probably have stunned anybody else, but we grappled with each other and I managed to stab him through the cheek with one blow and in the shoulder with another. Suddenly, he wasn't so brave and was trying to get outside. I stabbed him another three or four times before he managed to escape. He was in a real panic as I went out after him. He ran, dripping blood, into the shower area, as he had nowhere else to go. A lot of people had been watching and waiting, probably expecting me to get a right beating, and they were all surprised at Brummy bolting away from me. I was covered in blood as well, and Vic, John, Billy and a few others pulled me away to clean me up. I told them, "It's OK, guys, it's no ma blood."

'There was a lump on the side of my head, but otherwise I was fine. Somebody found me a change of clothes, and one or two people went off to see what condition Brummy was in. They came back to say he would have to go to hospital and all I could think of to say was, "Good." By this time, Norman and Jim had arrived and told me what a stupid cunt I was and that I should have waited as arranged. I told them, "Well, what's done can't be undone. I'm not finished. While I'm in this mood I'm just going to do York now for what he did to McFadden and McIntosh."

'The boys tried to talk me out of it, but I knew my time with them at the Scrubs was up and that I might as well be hung for a sheep as a lamb. I'd smoked another pipe of hash, too, and that had given me a lift. "York, here I come," I was telling myself, and I headed straight for his cell. My adrenalin was really pumping by now.

'He was in there, clearly not expecting me, and as I went through the door he could only say, "What? What?" as I tried to stab him in his good eye. His hand came up fast and the scissors went straight through his hand as he pushed me back and slammed the door in my face. I shouted through the door to him that everyone knew it was him who had set up John and Con. "It's only a matter of time before you're in intensive care," I was screaming.

'By this time, my friends had caught up with me. One of the lads disappeared with the scissors and got rid of them. A stretcher was brought in for Brummy, and as he was being placed on it and carried along the landing, I started mimicking the sound of an ambulance siren: "Nee-naw, nee-naw, nee-naw." All the others joined in and then we all just laughed. I knew I'd fucked up, that my time in D Hall was over, but I'd had a good run while it lasted. Now I was waiting to be taken to the punishment block, with Brummy in hospital and York not far behind him. Later, both of them pleaded to be put on protection.

'I smoked a hash pipe while waiting and thought it had been an eventful day in the Hate Factory, a place of double standards and divided loyalties. To be honest, though, while I would miss my friends, I was glad to be getting out of it in one piece. When my cell door was opened, the screws were there, mob-handed, and I walked out and headed downstairs. They had been warned by other inmates not to rough up the Jock or there would be a riot. I had the London mob to thank for that.

'In the punishment cell, I was stripped of all clothing and checked for injuries, but all they found was the huge lump the size of a boiled egg on the side of my head. It wouldn't have surprised me if they'd found a lion stamp on it. But I reckoned it was a cheap price to pay for the satisfaction of what I had done to two characters who deserved to be punished as far as I was concerned.

'The following day, CID officers came to my cell, told me, "Two prisoners have been injured," and began detailing what the doctors were saying about Brummy and York, and what they had heard in the hall. I was involved, they said. It was the usual crap, and I just told them, "I have nothing to say." One of the coppers asked, "Can you tell me how these men got their injuries?" I told him, "It was obviously a double suicide attempt," and burst out laughing, then told them to fuck off and go and catch some child molesters, saying, "This is a jail, not a fucking kindergarten." One of them was staring at me open-mouthed. When I made to walk towards them, they manhandled me back inside, the door was banged shut and I heard keys in the lock. One of the coppers was shouting through the door, "We will be seeing you again, Ferris," and I called back, "Well, make sure you bring some hash with you, arsehole." He clearly had no sense of humour. There was nothing more from him, just the sound of footsteps disappearing.

'Later that week, when I was allowed to go to chapel, Norman and Harry said York had already been transferred. They brought me up to date with the gossip, gave me books, magazines, sweets and juice, and did this regularly until I was eventually moved. I knew when I left I'd miss them, because they were both good guys. York had had to be moved for his own safety. So many different factions had reason to loathe him. A stronger man might have tried to bluff it out, but he had no stomach for a challenge and was too terrified to fight. Brummy ended up back in the prison hospital after a couple of days, but then made a full recovery. He was told he'd better do the right thing and keep his mouth shut, although I don't think he actually needed telling, as he wasn't a grass. But it was good to know I had guys out there trying to help me out. I got away with no further action being taken. After all, nobody was complaining or saying they had seen anything. In any case, what could they do? Take away my teddy bear?

'I was kept in solitary for several months before everything was resolved. Being dubbed up in the digger was easy. It gave me a chance to read more, think more and plan more in case any opportunity should arise that could be used to my advantage. Verbal abuse by the screws went with the territory, but my philosophy was "Give no quarter and expect none in return." That was the way it was in those days.

'During that time, I met a guy in his 50s with long grey hair down to his shoulders and a long grey beard to his chest. I was in one of two exercise pens, fifteen feet square, enclosed by a fifteen-foot-high fence. When he saw me going into the next pen, he turned and asked, "How the devil are you?" It was good to talk to someone, and he told me his name was Jack Tierney, adding, "My friends call me Bulletproof." I couldn't help bursting into laughter, and Jack went on to tell me he got the name after he was shot five times in the face and head by an IRA activist using a .22 pistol. This was amazing and many might not have believed him, but he showed me his scars and said a bullet was still lodged in his brain. Later on, I found out that this caused him to rant and rave from time to time, and the screws were terrified of him, because Bulletproof couldn't be ordered about easily.

'He was the funniest guy I had ever met, a real character. Our paths were to cross again years later. We would swap lies, with me swearing on the governor's life my story was true and him saying, "Away ye go, ya wild thing, Billy." He was from Waterford but after being released from hospital following the shooting, he'd decided to move to Camberwell in London. He was one of the strongest guys I've ever met, a real wild man. I liked his patter because it was so original. He was doing a lifer for murder.' A London newsagent had been killed during a robbery at his shop in 1975. Tierney and co-accused David Smart claimed that they had been led by Frank Johnson, who consistently denied involvement and who spent 26 years in jail before his murder conviction was overturned after it emerged that the victim had made a deathbed statement saying Johnson had not been there.

Billy had been told by the authorities at Wormwood Scrubs to expect a transfer to Parkhurst on the Isle of Wight, which had an interesting history. It had at one time been used as a prison for boys awaiting deportation to Australia, and at the time of Billy's planned move there, had a reputation as the toughest jail in Britain, holding, at various times, the Richardsons, the Krays and Ian Brady. He psyched himself up for the move but at the last minute he was told that an industrial dispute involving prison officers, which had been going on for months, had still not been resolved, with the result that they were refusing to take in any further inmates. It meant he remained in limbo, stuck in solitary for far longer than was the norm, and after a time he made it known he was fed up with his situation.

Punishment cells were cleaned by sex offenders, sometimes called 'nonces' or 'beasts'. One of their tasks was to put food on trays given to inmates by prison officers, and once an inmate had completed his meal the tray was washed by the same sex offenders, in a double cell opposite to that holding Billy. One day, hearing the hated sex attackers singing, he began banging on his door screaming, 'Shut the fuck up, ya beasts. What the fuck have you got to be happy about?' Bulletproof joined in the shouting, resulting in a prison officer ticking off the beasts and ordering them to be quiet. 'Some of your audience are complaining,' he said, causing the choir to roar with laughter and infuriating Billy. Minutes later, his cell was opened up for a routine exercise period and he bolted out, taking the prison officer by surprise. Jumping over a long table on which the food trays were kept, he grabbed a tray and began beating the nearest of two sex offenders who were still busy washing up. It was over in a matter of seconds, but not before the alarm bell had been sounded and officers appeared as if from nowhere.

He was thrown about like a rag doll and given such a beating that it was some time before he could remember what had happened. But he believed the pain was worth it: never again did he or Bulletproof hear singing. His outburst appears to have been the straw that broke the camel's back. Days later, he was ordered to collect his property, handcuffed and shackled inside a prison van and transferred north to Wakefield.

Finally, he had escaped from the Hate Factory, still bruised and battered as a result of the beating in the punishment block. But what he found when he arrived in Yorkshire brought a red mist to his eyes. Because it seemed to him that in Wakefield nonces outnumbered decent guys. He had arrived, he felt, in the original house of horrors, had swapped the Hate Factory for a haven for beasts.

12

TRIAL AND PUNISHMENT

ALTHOUGH THE HATE FACTORY HAD held hard, often violent men, Billy had understood them and felt confident of holding his own among them. But Wakefield, he discovered, was at the foot of the decency league, holding many perverts and beasts. A blind eye was turned to their sexual activities among one another. The reasoning was that if they were happy, they were less likely to cause problems. Anyone interfering with this arrangement could find himself in trouble.

Billy arrived at Wakefield still angry and smarting over the beating at Wormwood Scrubs for his attack on the sex-pest singers. His philosophy was simple: 'Sex offenders were fair game. Stab or slash, scald or cosh, it didn't matter how they were punished. They were the dregs.'

On arrival, Billy was taken to a hall blocked off by a grille gate and which stank of human faeces and urine. It was drab and dirty, and he was immediately aware of inmates who appeared sly and shifty, trying to avoid eye contact. He wondered if these impressions were the result of an imagination coloured by his having spent too long in solitary or by his lengthy and often bizarre conversations with Bulletproof. His cell was on the third landing, reached by a narrow steel spiral stairway, wide enough for only one person at a time and a potential deathtrap for a man encountering an enemy armed with a weapon. Inside, he found the usual bed, cupboard, slop pot and zero home comforts. It was a dump, but then such was his mood of bitterness that a five-star hotel would have got the same reaction from him.

Hardly had he dumped his belongings than he turned to see a

tall, thin man staring at him and asking in a welcome Scots accent where he had come from. Billy told him 'Scrubs' and the stranger introduced himself. He was a Scot from Nottingham and said a number of other Scots were scattered throughout the jail. The two discovered they had mutual friends, and the ice was broken. Soon afterwards, when Billy was heading to the canteen for his tea, he was summoned by his fellow Scot to meet two other men, who stood with outstretched hands. One said his name was Billy Armstrong and told Billy that he was a friend of Raymond McLaughlin, also in Wakefield, and had some stuff from him for him. The other was Vince Donnelly, who had been convicted alongside Patrick Hackett.

Billy Armstrong was aged twenty-nine when he was convicted in 1973 along with seven others, notably the Price sisters, of exploding two IRA bombs in London in March that year. The devices at the Old Bailey and Scotland Yard caused one death and left two hundred others injured, despite detailed telephoned warnings. The jury at Winchester Crown Court returned a not guilty verdict on IRA activist Roisin McNearney, aged 18, who was thought to have helped the police identify the other accused. The accused began humming Handel's Dead March and one threw a coin at McNearney saying, 'Take your blood money with you.' She broke down in tears and left the dock. She was later given a new identity. Like the others, Armstrong, from Belfast, was jailed for life and would spend the years that followed arguing that his sentence was unjust and unfair. He and the man from Glasgow became friends.

Donnelly had escaped injury in the 1976 Kensington blast, but was not deterred by the appalling wounds suffered by Hackett. Two weeks later, while he was carrying another bomb on the Underground, it too went off prematurely, on a Metropolitan Line train. Donnelly leapt out and shot the train driver, Joseph Stephens, at point-blank range, killing him. As police closed in, he turned the gun on himself and was overpowered when a policeman battered him with his truncheon. While Donnelly lay gravely ill in Queen Mary's Hospital in West Ham, police issued his photograph and appealed for anyone who recognised him to come forward. Officers were anxious to discover where he had been living in case more explosives were stored there. And, sure enough, when a tip-off led anti-terrorist officers to a bedsit in Brixton, they found bomb-making equipment. Donnelly was given 30 years.

Over the years, there were some who felt the Scot was too close to the bombers, but the same accusation could certainly not be levelled at him with regard to his dealings with the sex offenders. He vowed to revenge his treatment at the Scrubs by making plain to all child molesters what his attitude towards them was. He would show no mercy.

In his hall, a double cell had been fitted out so that inmates could cook their own meals using food bought from the canteen. It was a facility available to beasts, and Billy told another con, 'I'm not having any of these scum cooking near me. If they come close, I'll scald one of them without hesitation.' One day, Armstrong had been cooking a fry-up for a few pals, including Billy. Armstrong was carrying plates along the third landing with Billy, who had a frying pan in one hand and a tea jug in the other, when he spotted a diminutive, stocky figure and told Billy, 'That's Boris the Beast.' As the little man climbed down the narrow staircase, suddenly Billy was after him, beating him about the head with the frying pan all the way to the bottom and roaring with laughter. Boris the Beast fled to the safety of the basement floor, while Billy and Armstrong continued on to the kitchen cell, warning some sex offenders who were there to get out. They instantly complained and within minutes Billy had been huckled off to the punishment cells.

Officially, the punishment area was known as the Control Unit; among unfortunates sampling its accommodation, it was 'the Black Hole'. Throughout the prison system, there were men – criminals, maybe, but with a streak of decency – who held in abhorrence those with unnatural desires, and they often preferred the misery of the punishment blocks or solitary confinement to mingling with monsters who slaked their sexual desires on children or beasts who raped women.

The following day, Billy appeared before a senior official, on report for assault, bullying and being rude to prison officers. 'What about all the kids and women they raped and terrified?' he asked, but his protest fell on deaf ears, and a day later he was ordered into solitary for 14 days. 'I hope your wife gets raped by some dirty beast,' stormed Billy as he was led off. His cell in solitary consisted only of a bed on the floor and a slop pot. He was not given bedding until 8.30 p.m. and was allowed a single hour to exercise each day.

Two weeks later, he was back on his landing, continuing to torment any sex offenders he spotted on the ground floor by pouring boiling water over the railing then leaping back to avoid detection, or by throwing batteries, hoping to hear a squeal of pain.

Billy's circle of friends expanded to include a man we are calling Joe White, who had successfully appealed the severity of a life sentence and had it replaced by one of ten years. Smoking hash with a group of pals to celebrate the outcome, Joe began telling a story of how before the appeal hearing he had confided to Billy that he was feeling depressed. 'I said to Billy, "If I don't get a result, I'll top myself," but Billy didn't believe me and said, "Aye, right," so I pulled a box from under my bed and out of it hauled a 6-ft length of rope.' By now, the room was in silence as the other cons hung on his every word. 'Billy asked me if I was really serious and I told him I was, at which he shook my hand and said, "OK, pal, tell me when you're going to do it and I'll pull your legs in case you have second thoughts."'

One of the listeners, astonished at what he was hearing, interposed, 'Fuck's sake, Billy,' but Joe continued, 'I was a bit shocked by Billy's attitude, because I was feeling really down and just needed an ear, somebody to listen to me and say, "Don't be daft," but the bastard was serious.'

Everyone began laughing. 'Well, at least I put the idea out of your head, ya daft bastard,' said Billy.

'Too fucking right, you did,' Joe told him.

At the time Billy came to Wakefield, in order to create paranoia among prison staff, IRA men from his hall were calling meetings with comrades from elsewhere in the jail. Mainstream prisoners offered to increase the tension by beginning a disturbance, but the offer was declined. It could all too easily get out of hand.

Billy knew how determined and disciplined members of the organisation could be. At Wakefield, they were still talking about the ordeal of Frank Stagg, who had died there in 1976, aged 33, while on hunger strike. He had been arrested in 1973 along with six others alleged to make up an IRA unit planning a bombing campaign in Coventry. Stagg was given ten years and at Parkhurst prison began a hunger strike when his demands to be repatriated to a jail in Ireland were rejected. He gave up but at Long Lartin prison in Worcestershire he began another strike, lasting 34 days, over humiliating strip-searches on him and his family during visits. The two protests took their toll and he developed an acute kidney complaint that worsened when, in December 1975, having been transferred to Wakefield, he again began refusing food over the repatriation issue. Stagg died in February the following year after 62 days on hunger strike.

Following his death, Raymond McLaughlin, who had taken over as IRA commanding officer at Wakefield, had warned prison officials of possible reprisals. It was a move that did not go down well with the IRA hierarchy, because they were endeavouring to build a smoother relationship with the prison service in the hope it would support repatriation to Ireland for IRA prisoners.

The terrorists' numbers at Wakefield had increased with the arrivals of Sean Kinsella and Paul Norney in 1976. Kinsella had been sentenced to life imprisonment in 1974 for the brutal murder of Senator Billy Fox at his home in County Cavan. Two months after his conviction, he escaped from Portlaoise prison, joined an IRA unit in England and was arrested in Liverpool when police stormed a flat and discovered gelignite, guns and a list of Cabinet ministers' addresses. He was jailed for 20 years. At Wakefield, he was rumoured to be on the verge of taking over as senior man, commanders in Ulster having told McLaughlin that his threats to prison management were out of order.

Paul Norney was just 17 when he went to jail in 1975. He was arrested after a struggle in which a policeman was shot and wounded, and was convicted of five attempted murder charges, conspiracy to commit explosions, conspiracy to murder and possessing a firearm. He was jailed for life. Billy liked him. 'He didn't give a fuck, and that's why I took to him. He might have been the youngest of the IRA prisoners, but many in their ranks were cowards compared with him. He was a game boy.' He also took a shine to Kinsella, even though the latter blamed Norney for his capture because the shooting of the policeman had ultimately led to his arrest. He felt that while many of the IRA convicts were mere dreamers, used as cannon fodder by their bosses, Kinsella was the real deal, a man wholly committed to his cause.

One day, Armstrong had confided to Billy, 'Ray is in serious trouble and Sean has been told to take over command and do his best to defuse the tension with the screws. Ray's been given a thorough dressing-down. His problem is that he let his heart rule his head.' In the end, there were no reprisals over Stagg's death, although the same would not be said of that of another hunger striker, Bobby Sands, five years later in 1981.

Now another IRA prisoner was in trouble with his own. Armstrong told Billy that Joe Duffy was to face a punishment court and asked if he would allow them the use of his cell. Billy liked and trusted Armstrong, so he agreed and even kept watch outside the door as Kinsella, Armstrong, Donnelly and then Duffy entered. The last man in was the last to emerge, his face unmarked but chalk white, ten minutes later. Barely able to walk, he staggered along the landing to the stairs and down to his cell on the landing below.

Later in the day, Armstrong told Billy, 'Duffy is out.'

'Out of where?'

'The IRA.'

'What for?'

'He's been badmouthing Father Fell.'

Father Patrick Fell was an English-born Roman Catholic priest who had been arrested in 1973, when he was assistant priest at All Souls Church in Earlsdon, Coventry. It was alleged by the prosecution during his trial at Birmingham Crown Court that he and Frank Stagg were joint commanders of the same unit, but the priest never admitted to being a member of the IRA. He was jailed for twelve years and was at one stage held in Albany prison on the Isle of Wight where, after taking part in a sit-down protest, he became one of six republican prisoners charged with offences that included mutiny. He was freed in 1982 and became a parish priest in Donegal. Father Fell was well respected, and when Duffy entered Billy's cell, he must have known he was in for a hard time for gossiping disrespectfully about the priest.

Kinsella in particular was enraged, and as Duffy stood quaking before him he was told that the IRA leadership regretted ever allowing him to join the organisation. Armstrong and Donnelly were ordered to beat him up, being careful not to draw attention by marking his face.

Billy was later told, 'They kicked fuck out of Duffy. Then Sean told him he was out of the IRA, his family would no longer get help with expenses for visits, he was not to return to Ireland and he must never again mention the name of Father Fell.'

Billy tried speaking up for Duffy. He remembers, 'Joe was involved in the riots in Hull with the other IRA boys. Everybody there spoke highly of him and, like all the others, he never whinged when he was being beaten and banged up.'

But the response was a simple, 'Orders are orders. He's finished.' From that day, the other republican inmates ignored Duffy.

Billy had no qualms about letting them use his cell for the punishment beating. 'I willingly let them have it, because I just couldn't have cared less if they murdered any cunt in it. But here was clear evidence of the double standards of the IRA: one law for some, another for the rest. Here was a guy who'd done nothing but speak out of turn basically getting a kicking and being booted out of their organisation.'

Billy could not understand their logic. A man doing a long sentence for the same cause had been ostracised for just a few idle words of chatter. But then, as the weeks drifted on, he found prison life was never straightforward.

He discovered that men he thought he knew and understood, men who inspired others, who showed courage outside prison walls, could develop a determination to protect themselves even at the expense of friends once the gates and barbed wire enclosed them. Strong men who would never dream of betraying a pal became cowed and institutionalised through years of being deprived of the simple right of choice. Often the result was that when the opportunity arrived to make a decision, the path they took was one foreign to their nature. Then they committed that worst of offences: they became informers.

One day, a good friend to Billy whom we are calling Billy Simpson announced that he had decided to start a fire and escape under cover of the chaos that would inevitably follow. Some of the Irish prisoners went along with the plot. One of their number was James Joseph 'Jimmy' Ashe, a member of a group known as the Birmingham Nine, which also included Joe Duffy, Patrick Guilfoyle, Martin Coughlan, Gerard Young, Michael Murray, Anthony Madigan, Gerald Small and Stephen Blake, and had conducted the biggest wave of bombings in the West Midlands since the Second World War, setting off 20 devices between August 1973 and August 1974. Jimmy Ashe had admitted conspiring to cause explosions and left the dock shouting 'Up the People's Army' after being sentenced to 12 years. In Wakefield, in the run-up to the escape attempt, he picked an argument with a prison officer and was marched to the Control Unit. Almost immediately, Billy and Simpson were dragged from their work and within an hour found themselves in a van heading for Strangeways, while a search uncovered home-made metal weapons in the cell of an IRA inmate. Staff also swooped on their workmate, Franklin Davies, who was serving 18 years for his role in the Spaghetti House siege.

Four others were shanghaied to various jails throughout the country, leaving Billy to reflect, 'Somebody grassed us.'

Clearly, word that Billy and Simpson were friends of the republicans had preceded them to Strangeways, where they were looked on as IRA sympathisers. They were beaten, and a visiting priest who asked Billy how he was only to be told, 'I'm battered black and blue,' responded with, 'Oh, your friend is the same. Just try and keep calm. It goes on a lot in here.'

'Get to fuck out of this cell, ya fucking hypocrite. You're condoning this,' screamed Billy.

Later, he asked Simpson, 'Why did you send the priest over?'

'I thought you'd get a laugh. I had a right good one listening to you shouting at him.'

The two remained at Strangeways for twenty-eight days. It was Billy's first taste of what was known within the prison system as the 'cooler circuit': inmates regarded as troublesome would be constantly moved around, spending a month here and a month there. The idea being to unsettle, to 'cool down', anyone who was refusing to behave.

Back at Wakefield, Billy learned others had been victims of the cooler circuit with Frank Davies sent on a short stint to Durham, Raymond to Walton and Armstrong to Armley in Leeds. Donnelly had been sent to the Control Unit. Kinsella was moved to Gartree, near Market Harborough in Leicestershire, but unlike the others he did not return to Wakefield. 'They all got to keep their radios and never got any beatings,' Billy remembers. 'But at least we had a good laugh telling the others about the devil's advocate priest.'

13

BRAINS

IN WAKEFIELD, BILLY ENCOUNTERED ONE of the most terrifying men in the prison system. Robert John 'Bob' Maudsley was nicknamed 'Hannibal the Cannibal'. He killed a man, was jailed, slaughtered three more in prison and was believed to have eaten the brains of one of his victims. One of twelve children from Liverpool, Maudsley was brought up in a Nazareth House orphanage run by nuns. As a teenager in London, he worked as a rent boy to fund a drug habit. In 1974, aged 21, he garrotted a man who had picked him up for sex and shown him photographs of children he had abused. From then on, Maudsley displayed a hatred of abusers that bordered on an obsession. Sentenced to natural life in prison, he was transferred to Broadmoor Hospital for the Criminally Insane. In 1977, he and another inmate, violent psychopath David Cheeseman, locked themselves in a cell with a convicted paedophile for nine hours and tortured him to death. Horrified guards who crashed down the door discovered that the victim's skull had been cracked open and a spoon was wedged in the brain, part of which was missing. Maudsley was suspected of having dined on it. He was convicted of manslaughter and moved to Wakefield.

The presence of the man from Broadmoor dominated discussion. Billy Armstrong pointed him out, and after the story of the terror in the torture cell was related, Billy nicknamed Maudsley 'Brains', which relieved the tension and even drew laughs. Billy remembers Maudsley well. 'You couldn't forget him. He was a weirdo and needed watching. A couple of months after we returned, he approached a guy we knew and asked if he could get him a weapon. At the time, we'd been having a very pleasant smoke of hash in one of the recreation rooms and one or two of us were pretty stoned. But I can tell you, hearing that sobered us up pretty smartly. We remembered what had happened when he'd got hold of a spoon at Broadmoor. We wanted to know more. Someone said, "Get him in here," and about five minutes later Brains came in.

'Usually, nobody entered when our crowd was in that room, especially beasts, who knew they would get a beating if they dared show their faces without permission. We regarded it as our space. Brains had no reservations, though. He wandered in and I asked why he wanted a weapon. "I want to go back to Broadmoor. I don't like it here," he said. I asked how having a weapon would get him a return back there. "Oh, that's easy. I'll just stab a screw to death," he said, as if he was telling us the score in one of the World Cup games. We all looked at each other and for a few seconds there was silence. Then somebody with a sense of humour asked Brains, "Just one screw?" It was hard to take such a casual threat seriously. But the reply made us all sit up: "Maybe more. Can you help me out?"

'We told him we'd have a think about that and get back to him and he seemed quite happy with the answer, turned around and walked out. I asked, "What the fuck was all that about? Is he for real?" and someone said, "If we arm him, he might do one of us. Then again, it could be worth the risk." We all laughed and agreed, but I knew each of us was thinking to himself, "Better keep a permanent eye on this cunt, I don't want to be next."

'Two weeks later, Brains was giving off really bad vibes, acting very strangely, giving odd looks, and I said to the other lads, "I think we're going to have to nip him, put him in intensive care. At least then he's off the hall and out of our way." Joe said he thought we were getting paranoid just because we knew Maudsley was hunting for a weapon, but I didn't see it that way and told him, "Aye, right. A loony like Brains and we shouldn't be getting the jitters?" Then I said to the others, "Don't give Joe another joint, he's stoned," and that brought laughs all round.

'Either paranoia was running wild, or the hash was fucking brilliant, but the situation was about to be taken out of our hands. It was a morning in July 1978. Some of us were cleaning our cells when one of our crowd came and told us that Brains had just gone into his cell with a beast and it sounded like they were fighting. There was a scramble to Brains' door and, sure as fuck, you could hear a struggle, furniture being pushed about and so on. Then nothing, not a sound, and we all backed away. Brains came walking out of the cell and quietly closed the door. When he saw us, he began heading to where we were standing on the landing. Armstrong snapped his snooker cue, grabbed one half and held it behind his back. When he reached us Brains said, as calmly as anything, "I'm going back to Broadmoor, but first I'm going to do in a few beasts." His face was as white as a sheet and his expression was one of, "Fuck, what have I done now?" Then, as we looked at one another, he just turned and walked away as nice as you like.

'I said, "It's nearly dinner. If he's going to kill a few more nonces, I hope he does them before the bell goes, or we'll miss dinner. It could be a case of for whom the bell tolls," and we all fell about laughing. A few of us had thought about going over to his cell to take a look through the peephole, but somebody said, "No fucking chance. Let's not get drawn into this one." Then the dinner bell went off and we all went for our grub. I think we were all sure there was a dead beast in Brains' cell and that he was on the prowl for more victims. We were well to the front of the dinner line and couldn't wait to get back to see what else went down. After dinner, there was no sign of Brains, who, unknown to us, had done an old guy whose cell was next door to that of a robber pal of ours called Mickey. We were all crammed into Mickey's cell with our dinner trays at the time. Later on, when we eventually found out what had happened, he pointed out, "Just as well we all went down to dinner together."

'We all ate our grub in Mick's cell, not knowing if Brains was going to do others, and when we finished eating we stood out on the landing looking for him. And there he was, carrying a pillowslip with something inside. He quietly closed his cell door just as the screws were shouting, "Lock-up," which was until two in the afternoon. The screw on the landing spotted Brains on the spiral staircase and shouted, "Maudsley, where are you going?" and back came the reply, "Broadmoor." That made us howl with laughter, and the screw shouted, "Get up here, Maudsley." But Brains ignored him and went off towards the office with his pillowslip slung over his shoulder. I asked one of the others, "Reckon it's a head in the pillowcase?" We were all stoned and all these shenanigans seemed so surreal.

'We all split up and were heading for our own cells when a wee screw we called "the Concrete Gnome" screamed out, "Hostage situation! Lock down!" We all yelled, "Yee-ha!" because that meant Brains now had a hostage. The Concrete Gnome was panicking, so we made ourselves scarce, dodging to stay out of our cells. After all, why make things easy for screws? After about 20 minutes, we were locked up, with shouts of "Hope Brains murders him". With us locked up and out of the way, the screws were going mental and we could hear shouts of "Medic, medic".

'Later, we learned they had found one dead under Brains' bed, and a second in another cell butchered but still alive, although he only lasted a couple of hours. We were opened back up a few hours later, as if nothing had happened. In that place, the loss of a life didn't mean a thing. Two cells were taped off, police came into the hall and we went to the football field, where we picked up enough gossip to learn the full depth of the horror.

'Brains was the talk of the steamie. When we had last seen him, he was walking towards the principal officer's office carrying his pillowcase. The PO was behind the desk, facing the door, giving a rookie trainee screw a pep talk about his chosen career. Brains walked in, put a home-made knife on the desk and said, "You'll be two short at the next roll call, and if I don't get back to Broadmoor, it'll be screws the next time." At that, the PO leapt from his chair and ran out of the office yelling, "Hostage situation! Lock down!" According to the Concrete Gnome, the rookie was too shocked and terrified to move. I said, "Well, at least he used his brains," and we all had a laugh.

'The Concrete Gnome told us all the grisly details of the guy who he found still alive. He said there was blood everywhere, all over the walls. After the police left we had a nosey through the peephole and, sure enough, it was in a right mess. The screw went on to tell us he had found a pulse on the guy's neck as other screws stood back to await a medic. There was blood all over the guy's head. Someone had said, "Take that earpiece out of his ear," but when the screw took the thing out he found it was actually the inside of the victim's ear. The screw told us, "I don't remember fainting." We were all in stitches at that, but apparently it was all true. After that, the Concrete Gnome was always trying to be a nice guy to us. I bet he wished he had never told us, as we used to wind him up about it, telling him, "Now you're entertainments officer, producing ears out of ears." We had many a laugh about it. Maybe that sounds callous, but there was no sympathy for the dead, especially if they were beasts. Our only regret was that it was a pity Brains hadn't killed more sex offenders, or even some of the screws who went around bullying inmates. As for the beasts, they were petrified, knowing they had had a close shave with Brains.'

Maudsley's first victim that dreadful day was sex offender Salney Darwood, who had agreed to go to the killer's cell. Inside he was garrotted and stabbed with the home-made dagger and his body stuffed beneath the bed. After meeting Billy and the others, and closing his cell door, Maudsley had gone off with the knife to kill again, cornering and stabbing to death inmate Bill Roberts, then hacking open his skull. Five years later, the authorities decided that Maudsley was so dangerous he should be locked up in a special cell built in the Wakefield basement. He was allowed out once a day for exercise, always watched by at least five guards.

'Maudsley has become the bogeyman of the English prison system,' says Billy. 'Jail bosses know they aren't in danger from him, and nor is any other prisoner except the weak. He was a victim finder, and I know because I saw him often and regularly talked with him. He could have endeared himself to the bulk of the prison population, become a Charlie Bronson figure, by doing screws. But he picked on little people. He's a six-footer, yet one of his victims was under five feet and another an old guy who wasn't a beast. He got a weapon under false pretences by saying he intended using it to stab screws. Had he done that, there could have been a massive shake-up of the prison system and dramatic changes could have been introduced, because people would have wanted to know the reason why screws were attacked.'

Maudsley was not the only mass killer Billy would encounter. One day he went to the prison hospital for a check-up with an optician and took the opportunity to meet Billy Simpson, who had broken his ankle, and pass on hash. Simpson pointed to the door of a nearby hospital cell and said, 'You'll never guess who's in there.'

'It's not fucking Brains, is it?' wondered Billy, who looked inside as food was being passed in. But the occupant was Archibald Hall, known as 'the Monster Butler'. Born in Glasgow in June 1924, Archie claimed to have discovered the joys of sex while still a youngster when he was seduced by an older woman who was a neighbour. Eventually, he moved to London, where he found he was attracted to both sexes and became involved with wealthy society men, including celebrities such as Lord Boothby and the playwright Sir Terence Rattigan. He took elocution lessons and began calling himself Roy Fontaine, started working as a butler and came to know the inside of prisons due to a habit of pilfering jewels from wealthy employers or guests whose homes he burgled.

Hall landed in a political storm in the early 1970s when he got his hands on lost documents holding details of then prime minister Edward Heath's cabinet meetings. He was jailed for theft, and on his release in 1975 headed back to Scotland, where he took a job as butler to Lady Margaret Hudson in Dumfriesshire. Then one of his old cellmates, David Wright, arrived and began working as a gamekeeper. Wright stole some of her ladyship's jewels and told Hall he would expose his criminal past if he reported the theft. The outcome was that Hall murdered Wright, buried him and returned to London.

He was appointed butler to wealthy Walter Scott-Elliot, aged 82, a former Labour MP and junior minister, and his wife Dorothy, 60. Another old acquaintance, Michael Kitto, turned up, and Dorothy was murdered when she walked in as the pair plotted to rob her and her husband.

Her body was thrown into the boot of a car and the killers, who had been joined by Hall's prostitute mistress Mary Coggle, drugged Scott-Elliot and headed north with him to Scotland. There, he was killed and the bodies buried in Inverness-shire and Perthshire. Mary was next to die, because she refused to get rid of Dorothy's expensive fur coat. Her remains were dumped in a barn in Dumfriesshire, where a shepherd discovered them on Christmas Day 1977.

In Cumbria, the murderers met up with Hall's half-brother Donald, a paedophile recently out of jail. Now he too was killed and his body dumped in the car boot. It was decided to bury him in Scotland also. But bad weather forced the pair to book in to a hotel at North Berwick in East Lothian, where their behaviour raised the suspicions of the owner. He thought they might make off without paying and called the police, who made the grim discovery of the body in the boot. Kitto was immediately grabbed, and although Hall escaped through a toilet window, he was soon caught. Both were jailed for life, and police confided to Kitto that he had been lucky to be captured because he was next on Hall's death list.

Billy describes Hall as skinny and balding, small and inoffensive, almost like a ventriloquist's dummy. The one-time suave servant told him in a firm but squeaky Scots accent, 'I'm on hunger strike and I'll be donating my body to science.'

Billy called to him, 'There ain't much of you there, Archie.' Just as the pair were about to start up a conversation, he was summoned to his appointment with the optician and when it was over he found himself prevented from further access to the mass murderer by a metal door.

Two weeks later, Simpson, now sufficiently recovered to be back in general circulation and join Billy in the exercise yard, was called over by a prison officer, and when he returned he was laughing. 'The screw said Archie wants me to send him over some porn mags,' he said, causing Billy to burst into laughter at the thought that after three months without eating, Hall's sole thought was for pornography. Later, it transpired that staff had secretly been slipping Archie slabs of chocolate in return for stories that they passed to contacts in the media. Simpson didn't have the heart to let Archie down and arranged for a supply of suitable material to be delivered to him in hospital.

Archie was well liked, but the same could not be said of another inmate, Peter Colson, a used-car dealer from London who had taken part, with Jimmy O'Loughlin, in the raid on the Bank of America in Mayfair. At the time, their £8 million haul was believed to be one of the biggest ever taken. The seven-strong gang had failed in one attempt to drill through the lock of the bank vault. But then an insider, who would turn police informant, hid in the roof space and learned the combination simply by watching as officials opened it up. By the time they were caught, the man believed to have masterminded the scheme had fled to North Africa, leaving Colson and the others to be handed jail sentences totalling nearly 100 years.

O'Loughlin copped 17 years. Colson's share was 21 years, and he was also ordered by the courts to hand over £500,000. Some inmates tagged him 'Danny DeVito' because of his lack of height. The bank robber had tried bullying a sex offender, who blacked his eye, and had to be rescued from a savage beating by Frank Conteh, whose brother John was WBC Light Heavyweight champion from 1974 to 1978. Frank was liked and respected. In 1975, he had been jailed for five and a half years for taking part in a £6,000 wages robbery near Warrington. He was sent to Hull prison, where he became caught up in the same riot that had resulted in Raymond McLaughlin being sent to the Leicester punishment block. Frank lost 380 days' remission and spent six months in solitary in Dartmoor jail. He was one of a group of inmates who gave evidence against a number of Hull prison officers who were later charged with assaulting prisoners.

Billy looked on Colson with contempt and whenever the chance arose would sing the popular country-and-western song 'Coward of the County' at him. 'He was a legend – in his own prison cell, with the heart of a snake. He bought his friends and was the only guy I know who paid to do time.' In the exercise yard, other cons made fun of Colson. 'You're as false as a padded bra,' he was told. 'You can't let a beast get away with giving you a bashing. Do you want a blade to stab him or are you going to pay one of us to do it?' Angered by the wind-up, Colson retorted, 'I'll sort it myself.' He was a regular in the prison gym and spent a lot of time on the punchbag. Billy Simpson would taunt him, 'You think you're boxing midgets, Danny. You're OK fighting the bag because you know it can't hit you back. You can't fight sleep and you couldn't box an egg.'

One day, in an attempt to deflect attention from taunts that he was afraid to fight his sex-offender tormentor, Colson told a prison officer, in front of other inmates, 'I could escape out of here any time.' Asked, 'And how would you do that?' he replied, 'Steal the keys belonging to the screw who runs the gym. He puts them in a locker when he's working out with the guys. That would get me out of the gym and a rope would get me over the wall.' There was stunned silence. Another inmate had been planning that precise method of escape, and now his plans were in ruins. Immediately the comment was made the arrangements for holding the keys were altered. Colson's indiscretion and refusal to challenge the inmate who had punched him in the eye caused anger. 'It's fucking embarrassing,' said Frank Conteh. Billy agreed, and it wouldn't be long before he came into conflict with Colson.

14

THE IRA

BILLY ENJOYED THE COMPANY OF most of the IRA prisoners, in particular that of Billy Armstrong. They both liked playing practical jokes, although their humour was not always appreciated by others. Armstrong, for instance, came up with the idea of forcing off cell doors and hiding them in another con's cell, then watching prison officers trying to find them. Then Billy Ferris succeeded in convincing Raymond and other IRA inmates that a pal from Wakefield had just been released and was going to turn up on the next Saturday afternoon. At three o'clock, he would throw a rope over the wall and have a car waiting at the foot of the prison wall for their getaway. The Irishmen swallowed the bait and six of them spent the afternoon waiting in vain for the appearance of the rope.

On another occasion, Armstrong asked Billy to act as lookout while he tested out a key he had made for a cell door. 'All clear,' said the Glaswegian, and the Irishman told him, 'Look, it fits.'

Billy replied, 'Aye, it fits, but it disnae open the fucking lock. What are you smoking? How about giving me some? It must be really good stuff.'

Armstrong was offended by his friend's scepticism. It was the first sign of a chink in their relationship, but that chink would open to a yawning crack.

In early 1979, Armstrong was told of the death of his father, but he was refused permission to travel to Ireland for the funeral. To increase the hurt, his IRA colleagues were prevented from sending flowers. It was a prohibition that Billy felt should not go unanswered, but to his disappointment, nothing was done.

'I was naturally disgusted when the jail stopped the flowers, but even more disgusted at Billy Armstrong doing nothing. He would rant, "I'll kill one of those bastards for that." Billy Simpson and I would look at one another and say, "He can't say all this and do nothing." But that's what happened. He showed himself up to be as bogus as he was loyal to his cause, someone with feet of clay. In our eyes, he mugged himself and all his comrades by making idle threats that he didn't have the heart or will to follow through. He was a poor, weak cunt, and Simpson and me blamed our having spent time with him in the segregation unit for the growth of our friendship with him.'

The Scottish inmates said they would organise a floral tribute to Armstrong's father and wanted an accompanying note to read 'From your friends and comrades'. Prison officials refused permission but relented when Billy threatened a peaceful sit-down protest if the flowers were not sent. At six o'clock the next morning, he was dragged from his cell and sent to Winston Green jail in Birmingham, where he spent the next 28 days, accused of being a subversive. His friendship with Armstrong would never be the same. He had been punished because he had stuck up for the bomber, but Armstrong himself, for all his talk of vengeance, had done nothing in retaliation against the authorities.

On his return from Winston Green, where other prisoners had been generous, Billy confided to Raymond McLaughlin, 'I'd have done something about it if it had been my da. I've stood my ground with Billy Armstrong during a lot of things, and I would have expected more from him.'

He nodded in agreement as he listened to the reply: 'Armstrong's a dreamer. Don't take him seriously. He's been telling some of us that the IRA got them all the jail for publicity and then left them to rot, that they were all ordered to get on the same plane after bombing the Old Bailey and Scotland Yard and were then all arrested. It's not true. He's just bitter over his da. I've had to be firm with him and remind him to watch his tongue and stop talking out of turn.'

Billy remains disappointed over the response to his backing for Armstrong and many of the IRA faction. 'Billy Armstrong? I was a fool. I bought the whole IRA package. When you're friends with someone, you make allowances, then after a while they can become an embarrassment. Then it's not a friendship any more but a liability, a hump on your back. I'd had no doubt Billy Armstrong was the real deal. In hindsight, like others I met, he was a legend in his own cell. He became a figure of ridicule among his own crowd and amongst other prisoners.

'When his da died, I was gutted for his loss. He would say, "On my da's life, if I don't get repatriated for the funeral, I'll kill one of the bastards, then the rest of us will do one at a time until we get home." It was all bollocks, but I believed it at the time because he was saying things like, "We IRA guys have nothing to lose, especially when we're serving six, eight or twelve life sentences. It's the equivalent of a death sentence. I'll set off a chain of attacks." But when the KO from the governor came, not even a rollabout.

'Out of friendship, I was set to throw myself in with them, because I just didn't give a fuck about the consequences. I couldn't see myself ever getting out, so murder and mayhem went with the territory. In jail, you don't have the chance to think twice. You act on impulse. Either you are involved or you are not. Choice doesn't come into it; circumstances dictate the situation.'

Weeks later, Billy was tipped off that the IRA contingent was planning unrest. 'Something is going to go down,' he was told, but he was instructed not to say anything to Armstrong. He assumed this was a sympathetic move, because the Irishman was still grieving over his father, and that there was nothing sinister about it. 'Don't go to education class tomorrow with your pal Simpson,' was the word.

When Billy passed on the news, Simpson asked for his advice and was told, 'It disnae matter what's going down, it's going to look fucking suspicious for us if we suddenly go absent on the day it happens.'

Next day, when nothing had happened by the lunch hour, it was assumed the trouble had been called off, but then alarm bells began ringing and an inmate said the education block was on fire. Smoke began to permeate the halls and everyone was locked up for the afternoon. Through his cell window, Billy saw six fire engines and then heard bangs. These turned out to be incendiary devices exploded by army experts brought in to defuse them. Suddenly, the door to his cell was thrust open and he was in a van heading north to Durham, told he was suspected once again of subversive activity.

He bemoans the feeble effort at creating trouble. 'Had Armstrong and the others done what Maudsley did and killed, they would have been repatriated. In fact, had the IRA contingent done anything as a reprisal for the death of Frank Stagg, they would have been treated much better in jail. If they'd done a screw over the beatings they suffered, then things would have been made a lot easier for them. Screws would have known what to expect if they went over the top. But they did nothing. Had the same circumstances existed in the H Blocks of the Maze, the maximum-security block of Portlaoise in County Laois or any jail over there, then screws would have been shot or blown up. They had people in prison doing long sentences whose families – their wives, mothers, children – were forced to undergo humiliating strip-searches each time they visited. What did they do about that? Nothing.

'The movie *In the Name of the Father* showed London gangsters being threatened by the IRA. What bollocks. The truth is the English mob put the IRA people behind their doors because of outrage over the Birmingham pub bombings. The only reason the Irish contingent were eventually accepted was because of the 1976 Hull riots, where Ray McLaughlin and Joe Duffy and others of their cause stood their ground with mainstream prisoners in the fight against the screws. IRA prisoners in mainland Britain endured all sorts of shit that would not have been tolerated in Ireland. Any genuine supporter of these people would have been disgusted at the absence of response. Bobby Sands, God rest him, died a man for his beliefs, as did Frank Stagg. Yet Frank is forgotten, another sad example of IRA double standards.'

Billy guessed he would be back at Wakefield after a further 28-day spell on the cooler circuit. He found the constant upheaval pointless and, more importantly, an unfair burden on his family. 'My being sentenced to the cooler circuit made no difference to their determination to continue seeing me. No matter which jail I was in, they visited it. As for being punished for assaults on sex offenders, that went with the actions. Punishment followed assaults. I knew that. No big deal. Had it bothered me, I would not have continued doing it. I saw it as a way of getting away from the beasts. I never knew where I would end up or what to expect on arrival at the next destination. But once you had done the rounds, been in the digger a few times, it became no problem. I knew I could cope. I was most conscious of being the new boy on the first cooler circuit. After that, it was a piece of cake. Anybody who says otherwise is just a sympathy seeker.'

In fact, Billy would not be returned to Wakefield; he was out of the beasts' haven for ever. As soon as he arrived at Durham, he wondered if John McVicar's escape of a decade ago had been to simply rid himself of the filth and smell that pervaded the century-and-a-half-old building. Billy found it difficult to understand the north-east of England accents of the officers but felt more kindly disposed towards them when he was given his radio.

The following day, he was walking around an exercise area when the inmate in the next pen, an older man, asked him in a strong cockney accent, 'All right, son? What you here for and where from?' Billy wondered who was asking. 'I'm Billy Ferris, from Wakefield. What's your name?' he replied and was told, 'I'm Frankie Fraser.'

Billy had met a man with legendary status in the underworld. Born in Lambeth in 1923, Frankie spent most of the 1950s as bodyguard to London criminal kingpin Billy Hill. Hill respected the Scottish criminal fraternity and once tried to hire Victor 'Scarface' Russo from Coatbridge to help out in a plot to discredit one of his rivals, Jack 'Spot' Comer. Being asked to work for Hill was a big plus on the CV of any would-be gangster. In the early 1960s, Frankie met up with Charlie and Eddie Richardson and with them set up Atlantic Machines, a fruit-machine venture, to act as a front for criminal activity. During the brothers' infamous 1967 torture trial, Frankie was accused of pulling out victims' teeth with a pair of pliers and jailed for ten years.

He was one of the ringleaders of a terrifying riot at Parkhurst in 1969 that resulted in him needing an extended stay in hospital for his injuries. It would be 1985 before he was finally released.

Billy would describe Frankie to his brother Paul as 'a gentleman who asked me if I needed tobacco or anything'.

'Frankie told some stories and said the screws were terrified of him. He said to me, "I heard you come in last night. Albert Baker is in the next cell to you. Are you Catholic or Protestant?"

'"Catholic," I said, and Frankie told me, "Albert don't like Catholics."'

In October 1972, James McCartan, aged 21, a Roman Catholic, had left a party in a notoriously hardline loyalist area of east Belfast. Trespassing over the sectarian divide was a fatal mistake. He was grabbed by a gang of men and taken to a UDA safe house. There he was beaten and repeatedly stabbed before being driven to the Mersey Street Bridge, where three bullets were fired into his head and his body left for police to discover. A year after the murder, Albert Baker, a former soldier who had deserted to the UDA from the Royal Irish Rangers, pleaded guilty to killing McCartan and to three other murders. He was jailed for life. In a series of letters to public figures written in his prison cell, he claimed that the UDA had a special relationship with the army, allowing the leaders of the terrorist organisation to operate freely so long as they followed the orders of the security services. He also alleged that the Royal Ulster Constabulary had provided weapons to the UDA for assassinations.

'Frank was forever winding Albert and me up,' remembers Billy. 'He was a funny, funny guy, and Albert was really good company too. Frank was well mannered, cheerful and a really nice guy to speak with. He commanded respect from screws and cons alike. He was a man among rats. I didn't know much then about his exploits. As time went on and the years passed, I often heard his name mentioned and people would tell me of what Frank had done. I would never have taken him for the pain machine that he was. But then, I learned that the vast majority of London villains and gangsters did not need to impress, because their reputations went before them. These guys weren't talkers, they were doers. But Frank – he was in a league of his own.

'And Albert? Like a lot of us, he didn't give a fuck. I could never decide whether he was a political puppet or an extremist. But at the end of the day, he was only dangerous with a gun in his hand. He would tell me of times he'd sat down in Hull, Gartree, the Scrubs or Albany and shared meals with IRA guys. Yet had they been a few yards away from each other on the outside, they would have been killing each another. Jail was a crazy place, with no consistency. When I was told, "Watch out, he's a Catholic-hater," it wasn't a threat, just a bit of fun. Albert would laugh and tell us how he and the IRA guys cooked for one another. The joke was that hating Catholics only applied when he wasn't hungry.'

After the customary 28 days, Billy was on the move once again, this time to Leeds for a month, then back to Winston Green, followed by Walton, Liverpool, Strangeways, the giant Wandsworth in London, back to Strangeways and then a return to Wandsworth, where he met another prisoner who had made headlines, Freddie Sewell.

In August 1971, Sewell was a member of a gang that raided a jeweller's shop in Blackpool. As they fled, a police car chased them and the London car dealer said later in a statement:

> Eventually we all panicked. There was some fighting and I ran into three policemen. Two of them stayed back, but one chased me around the corner. He dived at me and we went on the floor. The gun went off. He said, 'You have shot me.' I can never forget that.

The victim, Superintendent Gerry Richardson, aged 38, died in hospital. During his trial at Manchester Crown Court in March 1972, Sewell, a year older than his victim, said the shooting was an accident, but he was found guilty and jailed for 30 years. Sewell had been caught up in a disturbance at Gartree, where, he complained, he had been smashed over the head with a baton held by a prison officer trying to restore calm. Like Billy, he was on the cooler circuit.

Billy remembers Sewell vividly. 'Freddie was a tall, big-framed man. He was quietly spoken, well mannered and really interesting to talk to. He was not suited to prison life. He'd lost a lot of weight and had deep-set, dark-rimmed eyes that gave him the look of someone who was always tired. During an earlier prison stint, he had been smashed over the head with a hammer. Freddie talked incessantly of his mum and son. He would tell me, "Money ain't no good in here, Billy. I'd give every penny I have just to be with my dear old mum and my son again."

'One day, I asked him if he thought he would ever get out of prison, and I instantly regretted it. Freddie looked at me as if I'd winded him with a body punch, his eyes seemed to go blank and then he replied, "Maybe some day, provided I keep my health."

I felt ashamed at having asked the question, and it made me realise that you simply did not ask that particular question of somebody in his situation, for whom the possibility of freedom was such a long way off. I had a lot of admiration for the way Freddie handled himself.'

His 28-day stint in London over, Billy was taken north, back to Durham followed by further stints at Winston Green and then Walton, where he met Liverpool drug dealer John Haase. Haase was a minor-league criminal then, but was destined for fame, or more accurately, infamy. Billy liked him from the outset. 'He looked after me while I was at Walton. He was the real deal, flashy but well respected and able to back it up. There were plenty who badmouthed John, but only behind his back, and he never let anybody down. No one ever went to prison because of anything he said or did.'

From Liverpool, Billy was returned to Wandsworth. Fed up by this time with the continual moves, he asked a lawyer to intervene. The official response from the Home Office to a request to be told the reason for the moves was that prison intelligence officers at Wakefield had information that Billy was involved in arson and various subversive acts with IRA prisoners. It was said that there was firm evidence to back up these claims and it was proposed that he be moved to Dartmoor, the grim establishment in Devon originally built in 1809 and which had held French and American prisoners of war. The Home Office warned that any involvement in subversive activities would result in him being kept out of circulation for a long time.

15

BATMAN

In DARTMOOR, BILLY WAS AS far away from Glasgow as it was possible for a prisoner to be. He was now convinced that he had been the victim of a plot by prison informers to get him into serious trouble, but he was helpless to prevent this latest development. The van journey over the moors to Princetown was a nightmare. Eventually, through a mixture of mist, rain, hailstones and sunshine, a building appeared. The same sight, Billy remembered, had once greeted Éamon de Valera, who went on to become President of Ireland. Billy wondered if the Baskerville hound of Sherlock Holmes fame was somewhere about. Then he saw the dreaded Latin inscription above the entrance, 'Parcere subjectis'. It means 'Spare the vanquished', but to Billy it might as well have read 'Abandon hope all ye who enter here'. It was enough to make him ask himself, 'What the fuck have I got myself into?'

At reception, he was given a formal introductory talk and told, 'We will not put up with any trouble from you, Ferris. Keep your head down and get on with your sentence or you will be on the move again and in solitary.'

Billy said, 'That disnae bother me,' but was told, 'We have tamed harder than you, Ferris.'

Two other inmates handed him his uniform, a pair of grey trousers that were too long and too wide and a grey woolly jumper that was so big he felt it could have covered eight men. When he said, brusquely, 'Change these,' he was told, 'No way, Jock, you'll get them altered tomorrow in the workshop.'

He protested, 'I'm not walking about like a fucking clown from Billy Smart's circus,' and tried to grab the nearest prisoner, intending to thump him. Hardly had he moved when two guards from the reception desk seized him from behind and all three ended up rolling about on the floor.

More officers rushed to help, expecting a furious reaction from Billy. But he realised he had fallen into a trap, had been antagonised into lashing out, and he simply waited to be dragged off to the punishment cells as blows landed on his back and legs. He heard one officer boast, 'We tame lions here.'

He was frogmarched down a flight of steps and into a basement, where in the gloom the door of a punishment cell creaked open and he was pushed inside. It was freezing and stank of urine and damp; condensation ran down the dark-green painted walls and over the slate floor. A 2-ft-high block of wood, like a tree stump, was bracketed to the wall for him to sit on. His bed consisted of a foot-thick concrete slab. There was no sign of a mattress. He heard a shouted command to 'stand face to the wall' and made the mistake of responding with 'fuck off'. He waited for the next beating, intending to get in at least a couple of blows. But the cell door flew open and there stood a group of officers, two holding metal buckets, and suddenly he was shocked as ice-cold water was thrown over him. Then the door was slammed shut and he could hear his tormentors laughing as they walked off. He screamed, 'Fucking pricks,' but there was no one listening.

His clothing was drenched. There was no means to dry himself and no chance of a change into dry garments. Hours passed in which he tried walking up and down the cell to keep warm. His teeth chattered and never before had he felt so cold or miserable.

At half past six the next morning, the cell door was thrown open and one of the officers who had watched the previous evening as he was drenched asked, 'Still want to fight, Jock?'

'Naw,' the shivering Scot meant to reply, but he realised it sounded like the bleating of a sheep: 'Na, na, na, na.'

He knew there would come a time in the future when he would laugh at the ordeal, and he was cheered when the officer told him, 'Right, good lad. Go and take a shower. There are clean, dry clothes there. Put them on and we'll get you a hot cuppa and a breakfast.'

He went to a single shower and was disappointed to see what appeared to be filthy brown water emerging. Naked and freezing, he turned to watching officers and asked, 'What the fuck is going on?' to be told, 'Don't worry, the water's fine. It's bog water from the moors. Just don't drink it.' He stepped under the shower and to his delight, it was gloriously warm. Closing his eyes so he could not see the colour, he luxuriated in the warmth. Later, he learned that this was the colour of all the water in Dartmoor and that from time to time a work party had to pull dead sheep out of the bog.

This was his baptism at Dartmoor, his welcome to a jail that felt as if it had been forgotten by time. It had a reputation among inmates as the worst jail in the country with the toughest officers. He recalls, 'Like most of the other cons there, I had been moved to Dartmoor for allegedly causing trouble, and I wondered if the same applied to the officers.' Things at Dartmoor quickly began to look up, but nonetheless, for the remainder of his life Billy would regard Dartmoor as the dustbin of the prison system, the place where men whom no other prison wanted were sent.

His introduction to Dartmoor had been harsh, but when lunchtime arrived, Billy was pleasantly surprised. For the first time in many long months, he was allowed to collect his own food. While on punishment in other establishments, it had been delivered to him through his cell door. He also discovered that he had a choice of what to eat.

One of the inmates serving up the dishes asked him in a friendly Scottish voice, 'How are you doing, son?' The questioner was Tommy Flannigan, a co-accused of Freddie Sewell. Tommy had been acquitted of conspiring to use firearms but found guilty of taking part in the robbery. He told Billy, 'I'll get your door open after dinner and get your kit altered for you, so keep the heid.' Billy thanked him and went back to eating, but hearing a Scots voice for the first time in many months had cheered him considerably. The food was warm and tasted good, and he was confident he would soon regain the fitness he'd lost through spending so long in solitary.

Tommy, he discovered, was as good as his word, managing to open his door that afternoon for a chat and put him wise as to how Dartmoor was run. He introduced him to his friend John, a burglar from Bristol who could have doubled for the television comedian Benny Hill, and another man whom Billy describes as 'brilliant'. This was big John Cook from Newcastle upon Tyne, a pal of the Kray twins. Like Tommy Flannigan he was likeable and funny.

John had served ten years for shooting at a policeman during a car chase in the north-east of England. On his release, he was recruited by farmer Joseph Langton to murder his wife, Florence, so that Langton could set up home with a young mistress. Langton gave Cook £30 to 'think it over' and he went to a pub in Gateshead, where he and two younger friends laughed and told the crowded bar about the 'mad farmer'. But Langton was deadly serious, and in May 1970 Florence was murdered as she made tea at Stand-Against-All Farm in County Durham. The killers buried her body in a remote spot called Beggar's Wood. The grisly details emerged when Cook complained to the mistress that he and the other murderers had not been paid. Police became involved and at Newcastle Assizes that year Cook, Langton and two helpers were jailed. Billy soon made friends with the big man, who said he had been injured in the Korean War when shrapnel was blown into his intestines. Tommy Flannigan's version was less heroic: 'He cut his arse sitting on a can of bully beef.'

Tommy, Cook and John worked in the pantry and got Billy a job with them, handing out meals to inmates. One of their tasks was to take hot-water cans round the cells at weekends so that inmates could make tea. Billy discovered that John Cook's intestinal problems resulted in him having to take daily laxatives, which he said tasted like chocolate, and certainly they looked like chocolate granules. Billy's mischievous nature was soon at work. The Scot filled a two-litre jug with six spoonfuls of the laxative. He decided not to try the mixture, accepting Cook's description of the taste, but to make it even more palatable he added sugar and milk. He did not tell his pantry colleagues what he had done, but instead offered to do the water round by himself, thus allowing them to watch television. Accompanied by two prison officers, he took the hot water in an urn on a wheelbarrow around the hall, distributing water to about two hundred inmates but secretly giving ten the laxative mix. They seemed grateful for a change of drink to hot chocolate, unaware that there would be inevitable after-effects.

Billy was finding it hard to conceal his laughter. He rejoined the others, who looked up from watching television to enquire if there had been any problems. 'Not at the moment,' they were told. A while later came a wave of noise as inmates began pressing bells to be released in order to head for the nearest toilet. Pleas of 'Fuck's sake, open the door', could be heard across the hall.

Cook asked Billy, 'What the fuck have you done?' and was told, 'I gave a few of them some of your laxative granules. They thought they were getting a treat.' The recipients were running in and out of their cells, desperate to empty slop pots, and a rumour spread like wildfire that they were victims of food poisoning. A couple of days later, Cook told the unfortunates the cause of their heaving bowels. It was the last time Billy was invited to distribute anything, and a few of the victims wanted him strung up. They might have succeeded had it not been for the intervention of Cook, Flannigan and the Bristol burglar.

At Dartmoor, bats were regularly to be seen flying around outside the prison, and occasionally would get in through a window. Not long after Billy's tea round, a robber called Brian was washing food trays when a bat became entangled in his equipment and he caught it. 'Look what I've got,' he began shouting, and prisoners working in the kitchen and pantry gathered around to take a look. The tiny creature caused the hairs on the back of Billy's neck to rise and made his skin crawl. Brian had been one of the laxative victims. Now it was payback time. 'Remember you spiked me, Billy?' he asked, and without waiting for a reply carried on, 'I'm going to stick this down the neck of your shirt.' Billy ran off with the robber in hot pursuit and was saved only by the welcome appearance of the hall supervisor, who called out, 'Less noise or I'll sack the lot of you.' Brian was made to release the creature out the window.

Brian was a hypochondriac who constantly believed he had contracted some serious illness. A simple comment that he looked unwell was sufficient to send him in the direction of prison officers to complain he had fallen victim to influenza in the damp, dark conditions inside Dartmoor and needed copious amounts of paracetamol. Billy had read *Nightwing*, the novel by Martin Cruz Smith, and still had a copy of the book, about killer bats plaguing an Indian reservation in New Mexico, feeding on the blood of herds of cattle and sheep. Now he read a paragraph to Brian in which bubonic plague was mentioned and asked, 'Did you wash your hands after touching that bat?' His listener turned white, protesting, 'You can't catch that now. It's been eliminated,' only to be told by Cook, 'I'm not sure, but I think you need to get a tetanus jag.'

Brian tried putting on a brave face, saying, 'You're having me on,' and headed for his cell, but half an hour later he had gone sick. 'I have a sore throat,' he told a medic called to examine him. 'I want a penicillin injection. I've been bitten by a bat.' The nurse tried to explain that he was the victim of a wind-up, not a bite, but Brian was adamant his life was in danger. Eventually, he was taken to the prison surgery by the medic, who first jabbed him in the backside, simply to get peace, and then told him he would have to lock him up in his cell because he was getting too excited and needed to relax.

When the medic left, Billy shouted to Brian through his locked door, 'The real reason you're locked up is you might have rabies. It's to keep you away from us.' He heard a faint voice reply, 'You're fucking joking,' and called back, 'You'll know you have rabies if you get a sore throat and start foaming at the mouth.' This left the hypochondriac in such a state of fear that he began shouting for help and banging on his cell door until prison officers were forced to open it up. The medic was summoned and ordered Billy, 'Tell him you're joking. This has gone too far.'

'Aye, you're right, I'm joking. It's just a wind-up,' he said.

'Oh, thank fuck. I thought I had the plague,' said Brian. 'You're a little bastard.'

Billy settled in well at Dartmoor and before long was offered a job as a cleaner in the boiler house. It was easy work and the boilermen working with him were civilians who treated him with kindness, often sharing with him the food prepared for them by their wives. 'The prison had a scary reputation and even guys who had never been there would tell you there was a curse over the place. Often when I sat around talking with the guys in the boiler house, we would wonder how many French or American prisoners had died there, how many hearts had been broken inside over the years.'

One day, a new inmate was transferred from Hull. We will call him simply Jack. A Gypsy, he initially tried to conceal the reason why he was inside, which was for strangling a woman.

He was serving a life sentence. He was soon well liked. However, on one occasion when he was badmouthing some IRA offenders, including Father Patrick Fell, he was warned by John the burglar to watch his words. 'Billy has friends among the IRA people in a few prisons,' he said. 'Just be careful.'

In Hull, Jack had been threatened by convicted terrorists, who regarded him as a beast after discovering that his victim had been a woman. Jack claimed he had stabbed another man after taking a fit, but when the truth about his offence became known in Dartmoor, Billy and others wanted to stab him for what they saw as an abuse of their trust and friendship.

The Gypsy complained to senior staff about the threat and Billy was confronted. He denied any wrongdoing but was told, 'You are too unpredictable, Ferris. We know you have settled down well here, but we cannot take a chance of something happening, so you are being sent to Maidstone. Your reports are good, but it's time for you to move on.' Another brick was being cemented into the wall enclosing his life.

16

THE COW'S LEG

IT WAS JANUARY 1984 AND as Billy was driven through the gates of Maidstone prison in Kent, he had a sense of déjà vu. It was as though he had been taken on a round trip back to Dartmoor. Maidstone had the same grim appearance – hardly surprising, because it had been built in 1819, only ten years after Dartmoor. Inside, he found good training facilities, an easy-going regime and even an outside swimming pool. A pal in Dartmoor had said, 'It's like a health farm, Billy,' and he wasn't disappointed. He also discovered himself among many old friends and a smattering of enemies. Peter Colson was there, and Billy felt sure it was only a matter of time before he and Colson clashed. He geared himself up for a fight against him and others whom he had come to despise in the course of his journey through the prison system. This would be no Wars of the Roses, he mused, but a battle against weeds.

On arrival, he heard an accent he was sure was from Glasgow and found himself shaking hands with a man we are calling David Sanderson. He was awaiting trial, accused with another man of holding an assistant governor hostage at Parkhurst. He had sparked a nationwide alert after escaping from police custody in Canterbury the previous November. Three weeks later, David gave himself up to officers from the Serious Crime Squad after walking into a Glasgow lawyer's office. 'It was a very civilised surrender,' said police. Jimmy O'Loughlin was also in Maidstone, as were Bulletproof and Vic Dark.

Billy's arrival was expected, because John Cook had written to a long-time friend, a convicted UDA arms smuggler we are calling Jack Flower, guaranteeing the Scot could be trusted. Through Jack,

THE COW'S LEG I
he met a couple of robbers, one whom we will refer to as Bob

he met a couple of robbers, one whom we will refer to as Bob England, the other by his real name of Ted Wallace. Wallace had been jailed for manslaughter after a robbery in which a security van was rammed, causing the death of a guard on duty in the back of the vehicle. Tragedy struck during his detention when his son was murdered. Ted too had a long-standing dislike of Peter Colson.

Billy was also introduced to George Davis. At that time, few people, in or out of prison, had not heard of Davis. In April 1974, he was identified as one of five men who tried to snatch a payroll as it was being delivered to the London Electricity Board at Ilford in Essex. Police had been tipped off about the raid and were waiting. Davis was convicted, despite producing witnesses who said he was working as a taxi driver that day, and sent to prison for 20 years, later reduced on appeal to 17. His distraught friends, with supporters including Ronnie and Reggie Kray's mum Violet, started a campaign to free him. One publicity stunt, in August 1975, involved digging up the cricket pitch at Headingley, forcing the postponement of an Ashes Test match and earning one of Davis's friends, Peter Chappell, an 18-month prison sentence.

So strong was the evidence supporting Davis's alibi that two years into his sentence Home Secretary Roy Jenkins decided to exercise the Royal Prerogative of Mercy and release him, while at the same time pointing out this did not necessarily mean that he believed Davis was innocent. But a year and a half later, Davis was back in jail after he and a gang that included Mickey Ishmael, who had fought strenuously to win Davis's freedom, attempted another payroll snatch, targeting £58,000 that was being delivered to the Bank of Cyprus in Seven Sisters Road in Holloway. Once again, the Flying Squad was waiting and George was arrested. Now he was doing a 13-year stretch at Maidstone, where Billy joined him. Soon the pair were working together in the kitchen, where the latter was very quickly able to resume his hooch-making sideline.

Despite the 450 miles distance, Willie Ferris visited his son whenever he could, sometimes taking along Paul or one of his daughters. Paul remembers: 'When Billy was doing his life sentence we corresponded all the time. In the early stages, I wrote about what was happening at school. He once sent me a photograph of himself in which he had a big, bushy beard and was wearing dark glasses. That picture actually put me in mind of one of the IRA hunger strikers. Once, during a visit, he had told me, "I'm in here because of you. The minute you're a good boy, they'll let me out." It was Billy's way of trying to make me behave myself. I believed him, thinking I was to blame for him staying in prison, and he had that over me for years. I remember thinking even as a teenager when I got nicked for my first offence, "Oh no, my brother – he's never going to get out again."'

Sometimes Jenny went along. 'Mostly, we didn't have a car when we visited William and eventually I stopped visiting those places, because it was really bad. To get to Maidstone, for instance, we had to get a bus to Glasgow Central Station, a train to London, and then use the Underground to get to another railway station and finally catch yet another train. When we reached Maidstone, we discovered a supermarket where we could get washed and changed. At the prison, they knew we were tired and had travelled a long way. Sometimes they sent one of the other inmates to bring us tea and coffee with biscuits. Once, when a man brought plain biscuits, Billy packed him off and told him, "These are for my ma – get her chocolate biscuits." They let us meet him in a separate room. We were in there one day and I was admiring the decor, in particular a potted plant, and when I mentioned this to William, he said, "I'll get you the plant. And do you want one of the pictures hanging on the wall as well?" It was all a joke, of course.'

Billy remembers, 'I started going to the gym every day and got really fit. It was a party jail, where you trained hard then partied hard. There was always plenty of hooch and hash, and the London mob certainly knew how to enjoy themselves.'

Billy made friends with another cockney, whom we are calling Paul Bailey, at one time a highly rated amateur boxer. Paul told a funny story about a high-profile robbery. The crime had had half of Britain laughing over breakfast when reports had appeared in the newspapers. A very well-respected gangland figure and an associate had turned up one day in 1981 outside the fashionable London jewellery house of Kutchinsky's in New Bond Street in a gleaming red Rolls-Royce. The pair disappeared into the shop and moments later astonished shoppers saw the Roller driving off towards Piccadilly at high speed, crashing into parked cars. It was later found abandoned in Westminster, the thieves credited with having pocketed gems worth a mind-boggling £500,000. The Rolls-Royce, said to be worth £40,000, had been stolen from an underground car park in London, where it had been parked by its owner, impressionist Mike Yarwood, while he rehearsed for a television show. 'All I am worried about now is my no-claims bonus,' he cracked after being told the police were returning the car.

A few months after Billy arrived at Maidstone, David Sanderson barricaded himself into the prison hospital, taking two guards hostage. All inmates were ordered back to their halls, causing Colson to moan, 'Slag, fucking up our workout,' a complaint that brought a rebuke from Bailey, whose wife was from Glasgow and who therefore wanted to show loyalty to the Scottish prisoners. Billy recalls that when his dad next visited, he told Willie about David: 'He started chucking snooker balls at the medical officers, who were pressing alarm buttons. He has a history of taking hostages. It was never anything serious, but the staff did their best to dramatise the situation by making out people were in danger. David was just making up his own form of snooker, trying to hit screws with the balls. He carried on until he ran out of balls and realised he was snookered. He never got a break – just a move to another jail on the grounds he was a troublemaker.'

Meanwhile, Billy's hooch-making enterprise was thriving, and some of his fellow inmates were brought in to help with arrangements to allow the booze to gain extra strength by giving it time to ferment. Working in the kitchen gave Billy access to areas not normally available to other prisoners. One of his robber friends stole a screwdriver, which Billy used to loosen asbestos tiles above the ovens. In the empty space, he hid five one-gallon containers at a time. After a week, these would be removed, hidden in metal tea urns and delivered to customers in the various halls. The success of this venture gave birth to ambition and the skills learned over the years by the robbers were again put to use, as Billy remembers.

'We ended up breaking into the pantry and main fridge area. The door to the pantry was in two sections: the top half was locked, but once opened it gave access to the bolt holding the bottom door. Breaking into a fridge was kids' work for guys used to opening up safes, and once the top was free, you only needed to reach down with a slice of frozen fish to slip the bottom bolt. I was sceptical at first. "Aye, right, sure," I told them, but sure as fuck it worked, and we regularly broke into the fridge, stealing blocks of yeast, joints of beef, eggs, whatever we wanted. The screws were blaming other screws for stealing, as they never thought it could have been us. Eventually, they put on a new steel door and lock. Try as we might, we couldn't get hold of the key. Still, we'd had a good run.

'But then we found that we were back in business. We started helping to unload the butcher's van when it arrived with supplies for the prison. We'd carry two huge cows into the pantry freezer, where the butcher would cut them into sections. One day, I got hold of the butcher's saw and cut a leg off one of the cow carcasses. George Davis was in stitches and asked me where I was going to hide it. I stuck it in a kitchen laundry bag without the guards seeing a thing. I even asked one of the screws, "Want me to take the dirty kit to the laundry, boss?" The guy answered, "Sure, Billy," so I pushed the trolley towards the laundry and asked Bulletproof to pass it on to Jack Flower and ask him to hide it in his cell.

'By the time I got back to the kitchen, the screws were going nuts. They'd discovered the cow leg had disappeared. They lined up all 18 cons who worked in the kitchen, but half of us were stoned from drinking my hooch. Then they even searched everybody, patting us down looking for a cow's leg, and one officer, who was turning as red as beetroot and looked as though he was about to have a heart attack, was threatening to order everybody to strip and be body-searched. One of the staff stormed off into the pantry shouting, "Think this is funny?" and came out with this huge cow on his shoulders. He slung the frozen carcass, with three legs sticking into the air, down onto the table and walked up and down the line staring into each man's face, one at a time, and yelling, "Where is the other fucking leg?"

'I didn't help, because I told this guy, "It certainly didn't come past this way because I'd have noticed a cow that only had three legs," and at that the guy went nuts. Everybody was howling with laughter, and the angry screw was threatening to sack us all from our jobs in the kitchen. Then one of the other screws whispered something to him and he started sneering, came over to me and told me the missing leg had been found under the pillow in my cell, wrapped in kitchen whites.'

Billy soon discovered what had gone wrong. Never the brightest spark, Bulletproof had asked Jack to hide it in Billy's cell, not his own. The following day, when Billy appeared before the governor accused of stealing meat, he did not help his cause by replying to the charge with, 'Look, gov, somebody's pulling your leg.' He was warned, 'Ferris, this is serious,' but only aggravated matters by telling the official, 'OK, I'll put my legs up to it. Guilty as charged.' He was told he would lose fourteen days' pay, be restricted to his cell for two weeks and be sacked from his prized kitchen job.

His punishment served, his dad visited him. Jack Flower and the Londoners knew what an ordeal it was to travel from Glasgow and arranged to have someone not only meet Billy's father but also put him up for the night and drive him to the jail. Sometimes Billy would encourage Bulletproof, who had very few visitors and was worried about his wife's health, to sit in on these reunions. Willie Ferris had constructed a remarkable device for smuggling in booze. Under his jacket was a plastic bottle filled with vodka. A tube ran from it down his leg with a crocodile clip attached to prevent leakage. Father, son and Bulletproof would casually sit around the table in the visiting area and, from time to time, Willie would cross his legs, pull the end of the tube from his trousers, undo the clip, hold a cup beneath the tube and pour the two inmates drinks. 'Bulletproof and me always loved it when my dad came alone, because mum would have been terrified that we'd get caught. We never did get found out and even got drunk a few times. God bless my old da, a lifesaver he was. He loved helping us and getting one over on the screws.'

One day, Billy was strolling around the exercise field, chatting with George Davis and Paul Bailey, when a smiling Jimmy O'Loughlin approached. They had not seen him for more than a week and, at first, his expression seemed to be that of a man who had been overindulging in Billy's hooch. His speech too sounded garbled, almost incoherent.

'It's your Hampsteads that's different about you, isn't it, Jimmy?' asked Paul.

'What the fuck's Hampsteads?' wondered Billy.

'Hampstead Heath, teeth' was the reply.

Jimmy told the trio, 'Three grand these cost me. The prison let me get private treatment so long as I paid all the bills. What do you think?'

Paul said, 'To be honest, mate, you look like Shergar.'

Billy said, 'No, he's more like Mister Ed, the talking horse.'

Jimmy had clearly not expected such a response, and his disappointment turned to anger when Paul added, 'For three grand, I'll get somebody to kick fuck out the dentist.'

'Fuck you,' said Jimmy and stormed off. After this exchange, he rarely spoke to any of the three as friends again.

'Now we know where Shergar's teeth are,' said Paul. 'But it's odds on he paid over the odds for them. Only an Irishman with money to throw away would spend three grand on teeth that made you look like that.'

At Maidstone, Billy met several inmates whose names were familiar to readers of newspaper headlines. Bailey introduced him to Londoner Tony White, who had been remanded accused of involvement in a sensational robbery in November 1983. A six-man gang broke into the Brinks Mat warehouse at Heathrow Airport. They had been tipped off to expect to find £3 million in cash, but, to their delight and astonishment, discovered three tonnes of gold bullion, worth a staggering £26 million. Billy took an immediate liking to White. 'He was a gentleman, like most London gangsters, who never moaned, could do his porridge, unlike some others I knew, and was the real deal.' White would be cleared of the Brinks Mat allegations and sent home.

Bob White – no relation to Tony – had not been long at Maidstone, and in a few months would be moved on for his own safety and because of concerns over his health. In 1974, along with an accomplice, he had been found guilty of what the prosecution at his trial at the Old Bailey had described as a cold-blooded gangland execution of a suspected informer. The victim, Christopher Whitaker, aged 16, had been lured to St Mary's Cemetery, Neasden, because it was believed he had passed information about White and his accomplice to the police. When he was told he would spend at least 18 years in jail, White calmly said to the judge, 'I still say I never shot the boy. What you do with me is immaterial. I intend taking my own life anyway.' White was not liked, especially since rumour had it that he had informed police and prison officials investigating riots at Parkhurst jail that one of the troublemakers had been Frankie Fraser.

Other cockneys often talked to Billy about the underworld in the capital and some of the characters running it. One name that often cropped up was Arif. The Arif brothers were Ozer, Bekir, Mehmet, Dogan, Michael and Dennis. In 1979, police had investigated allegations that Dogan had strolled into a pub in London carrying a sawn-off shotgun that went off while pointed at a man's shoulder. Although the bar had been busy at the time, nobody could recall the incident. Four years later, Dogan was acquitted of taking part in a bogus arms deal aimed at cheating Iran's leader, Ayatollah Khomeini, out of £34 million.

It was at Maidstone that Billy first met a co-accused in that racket, Ben Alagha, who would come to play a treacherous role in his life. What was his first impression of him? 'Ben Alagha was a very religious man who seemed to be always on his prayer mat. Although he had an arrogant manner, I placed huge faith and trust in him.'

To his list of acquaintances, Billy also added Nizamodeen Hosein. In 1969, he and his older brother Arthur had been short of money and decided the solution was a kidnapping. They targeted the wife of the media mogul Rupert Murdoch, but they were mistakenly watching the wrong family and snatched Muriel McKay, the wife of a close business associate of Murdoch's, taking her to their farm on the border of Hertfordshire and Essex. After demanding a million pounds, they killed Mrs McKay. No body was found and police believed her remains had been fed to pigs. The brothers were jailed for life, but Naz was released after 15 years and went back to Trinidad, his birthplace. While in Gartree prison, Naz was beaten up by a band of inmates in an effort to force him to tell them where Mrs McKay's body was buried. Their intention was to collect a £10,000 reward for information that would result in her family being able to give her a proper burial. He stayed silent, but the same could not be said of Peter Colson.

When Billy had been in Maidstone for about a year, word came on the prison grapevine that Colson had been badmouthing Ted, Paul Bailey and Billy. For Billy, it was the final straw in a long-standing feud, and he told Paul, 'I'm going to do that rat.' He asked one of his friends who worked in the kitchen to sneak him out a machete, normally used for halving cabbages. He hid the weapon in a bag under his exercise clothes, then headed off to the gym, warning Paul and the others to return to the hall, where their presence would be noted by prison officers, so that they could prove later that they were not involved in what was about to happen. He made for the exercise yard and then headed towards the education block, where he knew Colson would be. He planned to attack as Colson emerged. He waited and waited. In fact, Colson was not there. He had been tipped off about Billy's plans and had taken refuge in the cell of Billy Murray.

Murray, a Londoner, had been jailed for life in July 1974 for taking part in a payroll robbery at Springburn, Glasgow, in which just under £10,000 was stolen at gunpoint from a British Rail depot. He and his fellow gang members left behind the dead body of brave security guard James Kennedy. The other robbers were caught and jailed for life, but it was many months before Murray was tracked down to Brighton. He claimed that he had known guns were to be used on the raid but had been promised the shotgun cartridges were to be 'riced up' so that if they were fired the victims would only be stung by rice. However, after fleeing, he read in a newspaper that Mr Kennedy, with whom he had been struggling when he heard a shot fired, had died. 'You can't give life back, can you?' he had said in court.

Now he was giving refuge to a fellow robber, and as Billy ran along the landing towards Murray's cell door, it was banged shut. A voice had already called out, 'Better be on your toes – Ferris is nuts, he's bladed up.'

Realising his hopes of attacking Colson had been foiled, Billy now knew he must get rid of the machete. He returned it to the kitchen, but it had already been missed and the kitchen door was locked because a full-scale search had started. He buried it in gardens close to the kitchen and went back to his hall.

He spotted Colson and Murray as they emerged for a meal and drew his hand across his throat. Soon after, George Davis approached and told Billy, 'Things have got out of order. I've been asked to calm things down – I hope you'll listen.' Others joined in, warning Billy, 'You and those pricks Colson and Murray are sure to be transferred.'

That evening, all three were called before a senior prison official

Billy as a toddler in 1951.

Visiting Santa Claus in 1953.

lly and his sister Catherine
Blochairn Park, Glasgow.

Billy hated having his photograph taken, as this shot of him with his sisters in 1956 demonstrates.

Billy in 1977, the year he was sentenced to life.

Billy and Paul with their dad Willie.

Official mugshots taken when Billy arrived at Dartmoor prison in 1983.

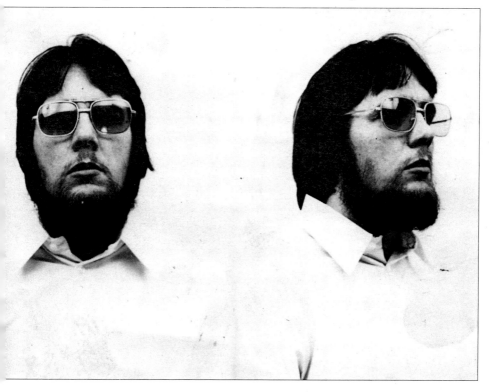

The family took this shot of Billy after travelling from Glasgow to visit him in Maidstone jail in 1984.

Billy with Arty the goat at Dungavel Castle in 1991.

Billy ended up in trouble after dressing as Dennis the Menace to liven up his nephew Paul Jr's birthday party in 1992.

On the run in Blackpool in 1993. Billy was visited by Jenny and Willie.

Lorraine Casey met and fell in love with Billy after meeting him in a Blackpool night spot.

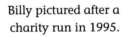

Billy pictured after a charity run in 1995.

Billy with his mum during a brief home leave in 1995.

Billy visiting Paul at Frankland prison in 1999.

Billy and Carol-Anne's wedding day in 2000.

Billy and Paul reunited on Paul's release in January 2002. (Photograph by Brian Anderson, *News of the World*.)

Billy relaxes with Carol-Anne at their home in Irvine shortly before he was arrested for a second murder.

Because he insists he is innocent of the murder for which he is currently serving life, Billy refuses to do prison work, instead building dolls' houses and furniture for charity.

and warned that unless the missing machete was returned, every cell in the jail would be searched, a move that would bring intense dislike towards anyone suspected of being the cause, as valued hidden and illicit items such as drugs and weapons would be uncovered and confiscated. Back on the hall, Paul offered to retrieve the machete. He asked Billy, 'You got a backup weapon?' and was told, 'Yes, I always keep a small lock-back for emergencies. I'll be OK.'

For the next two days, Colson and Murray went about as though they were Siamese twins, always watching warily for any sign of Billy or those they regarded as his closest friends. He enjoyed witnessing their discomfort and was aware that they knew he would not let his anger subside.

Then, suddenly and without warning, he was marched from the hall to the punishment cells and an hour later hauled up in front of a senior officer and told, 'We have received information that you and another prisoner have been planning to escape by smuggling a gun through the visiting area.'

Billy spat back, 'Fucking lies.'

'We are satisfied with our intelligence,' he was told, and he knew then that someone had informed on him. A move to another jail was inevitable, and an hour later he was on his way to Wandsworth, where he was classed as an escape risk.

During the journey, he wondered why the prison authorities had apparently so readily believed whatever it was they had been told. He could think of no firm evidence against him and even wondered if his growing a beard had aroused suspicion. Had intelligence officers surmised he was preparing a disguise, he pondered? The motive for the beard, as he recalls, was far from sinister. 'I grew it out of pure laziness. If anybody asked me what kind of beard I had, I'd tell them, "It's a cowboy beard." They'd usually have a puzzled expression and ask what that meant, and I'd explain, "It's got wide open spaces."'

Through the bars on the windows of the prison van he could see houses and people going about their everyday chores. But he had allowed no prospect of being among them to enter his mind. 'Freedom wasn't a thought I entertained in my situation. Thinking of freedom was a sign of weakness, something you cannot allow yourself in prison, and so I had to find ways of putting such thoughts to the back of my head. If I didn't, I knew I'd crack up at the enormity of the situation I was in. I knew I wasn't going anywhere for a long time. If I'd started letting the prospect of freedom enter my mind, I could have gone under, a blubbering wreck. I've seen that happen to too many good guys, and they ended up losing hope altogether.'

Ben Alagha was transferred at the same time, to Parkhurst, and he later wrote to Billy to say that he had been told that he was suspected of having paid Billy £30,000 to smuggle a gun into Maidstone to help him escape. He said that Billy's dad and brother were suspected of helping him.

Billy was furious that his family had been dragged into the supposed escape plot. Whatever plans Billy might have had, he would never have put at risk the liberty of his dad or Paul.

He suspected Colson and Murray had concocted the story, and remembers telling his dad during a visit, 'I can't see any mileage in it for anybody else. This smacks of a typical London stroke: get rid of the opposition by any means. I'm not the first these rats have set up and I surely won't be the last.'

At Wandsworth, he was told he would be placed in solitary confinement, 'pending a full and thorough investigation' by police and prison-service intelligence officers. No evidence was found to back up the allegations. In February 1975, after eight months of being classed as an escape risk for an attempt that never was, Billy was moved to Lewes jail in East Sussex.

17

DIRTY PROTEST

HE WONDERED IF THERE MIGHT be an omen in his move to Lewes. He and Éamon de Valera had both been inmates of Dartmoor and now he was following the great man to Lewes. De Valera had won friends and ultimately a presidency through his refusal to knuckle under. The Irishman was constantly suspected of trying to escape, a feat he achieved from Lincoln jail in 1919. He, like Billy, constantly defied authority. Billy had been at loggerheads with officialdom for as long as he could remember, and, while it did not accurately reflect the facts, his record now showed that he had been plotting an escape, the outcome being that he found himself locked behind those same grim Lewes walls that had housed de Valera.

Shortly after the move, Billy received bad news. His friend Ted Wallace had been moved to Leyhill open prison in Gloucestershire, but, with the end of his sentence in sight, he had suffered a massive heart attack and died. Billy grieved over Ted's death, but at least found some consolation in the fact that Lewes was pleasant and had a relaxed regime.

Among the inmates there were three of the Springburn depot robbers. He had made no secret of his dislike for Billy Murray, who had also been transferred to Lewes, but he quickly became friends with the others, John Murphy and Alan Brown.

Irish-born Murphy had caused a sensation as he was leaving the dock of the High Court in Glasgow in April 1974 having been found guilty of shooting and murdering 42-year-old Mr Kennedy. He gestured towards the judge, Lord Kissen, held a white handkerchief on his head in mockery of His Lordship's wig, turned to the public gallery and shouted 'mammer', described in the papers as 'the Jewish word for bastard', presumably a reference to the fact that Lord Kissen was Scotland's first Jewish high court judge. It was done so quickly that none of the 32 police officers in the courtroom had time to react. But most of the concern was over how Murphy had managed to whip out the handkerchief and get it on his head while surrounded by prison staff.

At the same trial, Brown and Jim Aitken, who was from Milton on the outskirts of Glasgow, were also convicted of murder, along with two others, while a sixth accused had earlier pleaded guilty. It was said by the prosecution that the depot had been watched for weeks before a decision was made to 'bring in a London team', which comprised Brown, Murphy, Murray, Sydney Draper and Stephen Doran. The convicted men were all jailed for life and given a total of 183 years for various offences including murder, attempted murder and robbery. Never before at any trial in Scotland had the penalties added up to such a huge total. Brown was told he would stay locked up for 25 years, Aitken and Murphy for 18. Draper also copped 25 years.

During the long evenings in Lewes, Billy especially enjoyed listening to the stories told about the London underworld by Terry Millman, who was serving a long sentence for robbery. Terry would prove to be a diamond of a friend.

Another con for whom Billy had and still has a high regard was Mark Leech, who would go on to become an accomplished playwright and editor of *The Prisons Handbook*, a valuable guide for those behind bars. 'If he had been around in the 1930s, Mark would have been called a cad. He had a vast knowledge of the law and of prison rules, but the only problem was that he never stopped talking on any subject you raised. Because he knew more about the regulations than the people running the jail, they tried to keep out of his way. Some of the cons were jealous, mainly because he was an educated guy, while they were not. When Mark sneaked into the chaplain's office, he pinched one of the bosses' standing-order books, while had most of the other inmates got in, they would have stolen the communion wine. Screws even went to the extreme of encouraging other prisoners to attack Mark. They thought that if they could prove they had intelligence he was in danger, they could put him in solitary on Rule 43 for his own protection, which would mean he would be unable to communicate with others and pass on advice.'

Just as he began to feel he had settled in well in Lewes, one day in September 1986 Billy was called before a governor who broke the bad news that his father had been taken into hospital. 'Fear clutched at my heart. I loved my da and his illness tore the soul and strength from me, killed me emotionally.' He was told he could have a temporary transfer north of the border to be near his family, but, within weeks, it turned out that the move would be made permanent.

As he gathered his belongings for the drive to Scotland, Terry Millman appeared at the door of his cell and handed over a two-ounce block of Nepalese Temple Ball hash, telling him, 'Have a big party with your mad Jock pals on me.' Had one been organised, the party would have been short, because immediately he arrived in Scotland Billy discovered he had walked slap bang into a hostage situation.

His first stop was Saughton, where he was supposed to remain for 48 hours before being moved west to Barlinnie. The day after he arrived, he was approached by a stocky man who asked, 'Are you Paul Ferris's brother?' When Billy told him, 'Aye, that's right,' he gave his name. Billy had heard of him, because Paul had briefly found himself in the same jail as the man. There had been a confrontation between the two and the other prisoner had backed down. Billy wondered what he wanted now and was astonished to hear, 'Me and a pal are going to take a screw hostage and could do with some help.'

'Not with my help, mate,' Billy said, adding, 'Good luck, but I'm not interested. Anyway, when are you going to do it?' He was perturbed to be told the attempt was to be made that night at recreation, because he was expecting a visit from Paul the next day and realised that the seizing of a hostage would result in the jail being put on lock down, with every inmate kept in his cell and visitors banned. 'I'm going to phone Paul to get him here on a visit tonight, so don't do it before then, OK?' he demanded, and was told, 'Aye, nae bother. Tell Paul I was asking for him.'

He telephoned his brother, who asked, 'What's the rush, Billy? I'm coming tomorrow,' but Billy replied, 'This is of major importance, Paul. You have got to get here tonight,' and Paul agreed. That evening, the brothers had just had time to embrace and sit down facing one another in the visiting room when alarm bells shrilled. 'What's up?' Paul asked. Billy told him about the guy he'd spoken to earlier and told him, 'That madman was going to take a screw hostage and I wanted you to have a word with him, but I guess he's done it anyway.'

'Fair play to the guy for waiting until I came,' said Paul.

The visit was abruptly ended. Policemen and soldiers had surrounded the jail. A full-scale riot was expected, and the prison officers were anxious. 'Just my luck,' mused Billy. 'As soon as I get here, there's trouble, and it's nothing to do with me.'

Late that night, he and nine others were herded onto a coach and driven to Craiginches prison in Aberdeen. He arrived hungry and on the downward spiral from the high of hash-taking into tiredness and dejection. Billy remembers, 'We were put into five cells and the next morning we got up for breakfast. In the dining hall, the existing inmates, the locals, were surprised to see ten new refugees. We grabbed the nearest tables, which didn't go down too well with the locals, who complained to the screws that we had taken their places. The screws told them, "Don't worry, they won't be here long."

'After porridge and a roll and sausage, one of the governors asked how we were. The others had elected me spokesman and I said, "We have no toilet gear, no tobacco, no phone cards and our families don't know where we are." He said he would try and get us kitted out and that we should try and settle in till the situation in Edinburgh was resolved, which he thought would be soon. I told him, "I was meant to move to Barlinnie today. I only came up from Sussex to be near my father," but he said no prisons were taking cons till the hostage situation in Edinburgh was sorted out and once that was done we could go back there. Privately, I'd realised that would be the situation, but I felt like a moan. I was determined to get my own back for being stuck in Aberdeen when I wanted to see my dad and was worried about him.

'Later on, we were taken to the canteen for our freebies, the items we had asked for because all our stuff was still in Edinburgh. While we waited for the canteen screw to open up, I told the other guys that it was no use sitting here and we would be better making ourselves unpopular, otherwise we'd be in Aberdeen for a long time. Somebody asked, "What should we do?"

'I told him, "Well, for starters, the phone." I told them to get some excrement and rub it into the earpiece and the mouthpiece. One of the lads said, "I'll do it," and off he went to the toilet. He came out with it in a piece of toilet paper, then rubbed it all over the handset. I gave him his reward, a bit of hash for a job well done.

'A big screw, he must have been over 6 ft tall and built like something out of the *Highlander* movie, took us to the canteen and gave us soap, toothpaste, shampoo, a half ounce of tobacco and a phone card each. He was about to say, "OK, now back to the cells," when the phone rang, and everybody shouted, "It's for you-hoo!" I got as far away as possible, along with one of my pals, John, and we winked at each other just as he picked up the phone. He got as far as answering, "Dining area-aaaaarrghh!" before he started spitting, throwing up, kicking tables about and shouting, "You fucking animals!" His face was the colour of a beetroot, and as he tried to rub the filth off his ear and face, he was only making it worse. Other screws came running in on hearing the racket he was causing. We were all standing there open-mouthed at his antics. The other screws had to restrain him as just what had happened to him started to sink in. Before he was dragged away, his parting words were, "After all I've done for you lot! Fucking animals!"

'I told the other lads, "He's only done his job for us," and that brought roars of laughter. When the other screws came back in, we said it was nothing to do with us and that he had lost the plot, cracked up. They put us in the cells, but we never kicked up a stink about that. It was one of my funniest moments in jail and worth the few joints I had to hand out to the guys who helped. After that, we were barred from the dining room and fed in our cells.

'After five days in Aberdeen, when we asked what was happening at Edinburgh and were told the hostage situation was still not resolved, I was beginning to wish the con who had taken the hostage would just murder the guy and get it over with. To make matters worse, one of the governors told us we would have to go to the work sheds because the screws were complaining that we were lying in our cells doing nothing. I thought to myself, "Work? No fucking danger."

'It was time for the ten of us to use new tactics, and when we were all together during exercise I said, "We've got to push them hard enough to get rid of us, so let's see what we can do." Everybody agreed, because we were all fed up.

'What I never expected was to see this big knitting machine, separated from the workshops by a long glass partition, with two doors at one end and one at the other. Our side of the work shed consisted of about 20 wooden benches, nearly 10 ft long, where prisoners sat making fishing nets, filling spools to feed the knitter. Just as we sat down, this fucking machine roared into life. It sounded like a train. I wondered how we could get in to sabotage this monster, because the noise was driving us potty. I went into the toilet and pulled two toilet bowls away from the wall, flooding the area. Then I sat down beside John and told him what I had done. We looked at one another, and I knew each of us was thinking, "Is there another toilet?" Sure enough, there was, so we gave it the same treatment as the first, then sat down laughing as water flooded out from both of them. Screws came running out to turn the water off and said, "No matter what you do, you are staying here and if you need the toilet you'll have to wait till you go back to the halls."

'I asked one, "Why look at us when you say that?" and he pointed to two lines of wet footprints that led straight to me and John. We just laughed as he walked away, but I was determined they would not win, that we would get our way. There were four workshop screws, who wore white coats over their uniforms. Two were supervising the cons in the knitting machine area, with the others watching us in the net section. It was as if we'd been thrown a challenge. They'd told us, "There is nothing you can do that will get you a move," and I thought, "We'll see."

'The guy who did the dirty work on the phone for me was my secret weapon. When it came to tea break, I told him to smear all the doors with filth and gave him a bit of hash as a reward. By the time the tea arrived, the handles on the doors were coated with muck. We didn't have long to wait to find out what would happen. The screws came out of their office, two heading to each side of the knitting machine doors while the remaining two went to the main door, where we were sitting. The local inmates had seen what we'd done, and there was no way they were going to watch in case they were blamed. They all looked at the floor, pretending to be busy, as we watched the screws heading towards the doors.

'The screws were trying to look tough, keeping eye contact with us as they inserted the keys into the locks. Then, as they pulled the handles to open the doors, they felt the filth on their hands. You could see the disgust on their faces. They were screaming, "Fucking animals! Glesga animal bastards!" One of the bosses shouted, "That's it, lock the lot of them up." I shouted, "Goldfinger," and that brought laughter from our crew, but John and me were taken to the punishment cells.

'A couple of days later, we were told we were going back to Edinburgh. All of us were assembled in the prison chapel, where we all had a good laugh at the turmoil we had caused, and as we marched through the halls we all began singing, "Here we go, here we go, here we go." All the way back to Edinburgh, we were singing, "Aberdeen no more."

'I was moved to Barlinnie later that week. It was my local jail and all my mates were there, so I was on my best behaviour. They even let me out a few times to see my dad in hospital. As usual, screws came along and we had a police escort, so things weren't absolutely perfect. I was handcuffed to the bed, and that left Paul raging, but I told him, "Paul, it doesn't matter. At least I'm seeing our da." The nursing sister noticed the handcuffs and ordered them to be taken off in case my dad took a turn for the worse and they needed to move him quickly. When the screws argued, she turned on them and asked, "Where on earth can he go with the number of prison officers and police around him?" There were four screws with me in the intensive-care unit, three storeys up, with police outside the door and sitting in a car beside the hospital entrance. She shamed them into taking the cuffs off. I think the screws would rather have had me causing a scene, so they could use that as an excuse to terminate my hospital visits and stop me seeing my da again. But I was too wide to be tricked into that. Da was too important to let down, and I wanted to see him as much as possible, so they could do all they could to humiliate me, but I wasn't falling for their stupid games.

'But they never gave up trying to upset us. When I was due to see him as he was about to be taken off the critical list, the police stopped other members of my family being there on the grounds that they had received a tip-off that I was going to escape with the help of Paul. That was a feeble and pretty childish excuse, solely calculated to cause hurt. Any escape attempt would have been suicidal, because the place was surrounded by police and I was assured that some of them were armed. I didn't let these antics spoil my visits or the time I had with Da, and because by then he was on the mend I didn't need to bite my tongue any more. For the first time since he had collapsed, I was feeling great and ready for anything, no matter what was ahead of me.'

But Billy was about to discover that he would need all his wits to survive in the deadly atmosphere of hate and gang rivalry that permeated every Scottish jail.

18

THE ROLLING JOINT

DURING HIS BRIEF STAY IN BARLINNIE, Billy met Arthur 'Arty' Thompson, son of the Glasgow Godfather for whom Paul worked as an enforcer, a collector of debts, a steward entrusted with protecting the secrets of his employer's empire. But while his father was discreet and devious, Arty, known by some as 'Fatboy' and by others as 'the Mars Bar Kid' because of his liking for the chocolate treats, was rash, even reckless. At times, his indiscretion bordered on stupidity, and he appeared hell-bent on a policy of making enemies – a highly dangerous strategy in the dog-eat-dog environment of prison.

In 1985, Arty had been jailed for 11 years for heroin dealing. A sidekick, John 'Jonah' McKenzie, went inside with him but received a shorter sentence, prompting the Thompsons to assume that this was a reward for turning traitor and helping the police. And, prior to the trial, old Arthur had wanted principal rival Tam McGraw to agree to be a defence witness. McGraw refused and was removed from the Thompsons' rapidly diminishing Christmas card list.

In prison, Arty foolishly continued drug dealing instead of taking fellow inmates' advice and keeping a low profile. Thompson Jr rashly began to issue threats against men whose help would have made life behind bars easier and safer, and in the course of doing so earned the additional nickname of 'Trumpet Arse'.

In Barlinnine B Hall, Billy soon discovered that Arty was arranging for hash to be smuggled in, with which he bought protection. One day Arty sidled up to Billy and pointed out another inmate. 'Ma da says for me to get him nipped,' he murmured. 'There's a few quid in it.'

'Who is he?' Billy asked, and the reply was 'Charlie Swan'. Few at that time had not heard of the handsome six-footer, who had been convicted in February 1986 of possession of a pistol, while already serving a 30-month stretch for assault. He had been having an affair with the pretty wife of a prominent golfer, which included raunchy sessions in the sport star's luxury home in Ayrshire. Swan told newspapers that while he and his girlfriend romped nearly naked on a bed at the Central Hotel in Glasgow, two men had burst in and taken photographs. A quarter of an hour later, the telephone rang in their room and a stranger warned that unless £10,000 cash was paid, the photographs would be shown to her husband. No money was ever handed over, and the whereabouts of the snapshots remained a mystery. The golfer and his wife eventually divorced.

In Barlinnie, Swan was terrified, having been told that there were people out to get him. He assumed the reason was that they were jealous at the thought that he had made a fortune by selling his story to newspapers. In fact, the threat came from an even more sinister source.

Arthur Thompson had a holiday house at Rothesay on Bute, and the island was also home to a number of families who were keen golfers and respected the husband. They knew he was too dignified to treat Swan with anything other than contempt, but when Arthur and Rita took a short break there, they made clear their revulsion over the way the sportsman had been deceived. Typically, the Godfather said nothing, but to those around him who knew him well, his silence spoke volumes.

A message was passed to Arty and the 'few quid' went on general offer. Billy knew why money had been mentioned. Arty couldn't have attacked anyone; his build was more akin to Billy Bunter than a tough. 'The only thing he can set about is his food,' Billy joked.

One of Arthur's closest friends was in prison, and it would have been natural to assume Arty would approach him and ask if he would sort Swan. But this man, an ally of the Godfather for many years, was actually wondering if Fatboy had grassed him up to police in an effort to save himself. Too timid to meet the situation head-on by having a heart to heart with his accuser, the Mars Bar Kid had gone bleating to his dad to help him out.

Now the Godfather was having to negotiate with his old friend not to take revenge on Arty. So, for the time being, there was no chance of this man doing Fatboy, or the old man for that matter, any favours. That meant Arty had to look elsewhere for a hit man willing to take up the contract on Charlie Swan.

Billy was not interested, but later in the day Swan found himself on the receiving end of what others laughed off as a 'hole in one', a stabbing with a screwdriver, and was carried out of B Hall on a stretcher. Billy was standing next to Arty as he trumpeted his delight at the sight of the ashen-faced victim being loaded into an ambulance. 'Did you get that, Charlie?' he chortled. It would emerge that Swan's attacker had told him that the screwdriver used in the stabbing had been contaminated with hepatitis, although subsequent tests showed no trace of the deadly virus.

'Arty was a joke, an embarrassment to his father,' says Billy. 'He was a dangerous, cowardly bastard, a fat, obese, smelly cunt. His father was a liberty taker. When I arrived, I hadn't seen Arty since he was a boy. He had a gang of cronies sitting in his cell and he asked, "Do you remember me, Billy?"

'I told him, "You used to masturbate dogs when you were a boy – no wonder dogs were forever rubbing up against your leg."

'That brought howls of laughter from everybody and the laughter became even louder when Arty blushed. Paul was in Barlinnie too at the time, accused of a shooting on a bridge over the M8 motorway near Easterhouse, Glasgow. Arty appealed to him, "Paul, tell them it's not true."

'But Paul was in tears, doubled up laughing, and told him, "But it's true, Arty. That's what you used to do."

'Arty stormed off with jeers ringing in his ears, shouts of "Woof, woof".

'Paul told me afterwards, "That was a bit low, bro."

'I said, "That's what Rover told Arty."

'A jury found the motorway shooting allegation not proven. Our da was forever warning Paul that old Arthur was a low-life who bought his friends just as his son did.' Billy sought permission for him and Paul to share a family visit but this was refused, a sore point with the brothers.

Jonah McKenzie, Arty's co-accused, was also in Barlinnie, able to see out of only one eye after an attack in a bar in Shettleston. He had been a friend of Tam McGraw, a welcome visitor to the McGraw home in Barlanark, but in 1984 he had viciously attacked the Licensee after throwing in his lot with Arty. After his release, McKenzie also turned against Paul Ferris, telling tales to police that Paul was behind the kneecapping of a minor underworld player named William Gillen, an allegation that would subsequently be dismissed by a jury. McKenzie died from a drug overdose not long after he was left totally blinded as the result of a vicious street stabbing. It was cruelly said that his brain swelled up because of the attack and that in order to relieve pressure on it doctors opened up his skull and inside discovered a photograph of Fatboy.

Now Billy was to leave Fatboy behind and head back to Saughton, but he would have considerable cause to think about the Thompsons in the years that followed.

In Edinburgh, details slowly emerged of just how serious the hostage taking and subsequent riot had been. Units of the SAS had been called in, the first time they had been used in a prison hostage situation, and, as a result, it was decided to set up a training programme for an elite specialist unit of prison officers that could be called in to deal with riot situations. Five inmates had seized prison officer Keith Stewart, aged twenty-five, and held him for four days. One of the ringleaders, armed robber Gordon Smith, was serving ten years and had a further seven years added for his role in the incident. Years later, he would claim that an officer who had received criminal injuries compensation as a result of being assaulted by him had sent him a postcard from Florida with a message hinting the incident had paid for the holiday.

Now, as the prison settled back into normality following the trouble, Billy and others discovered payback time for them had arrived already. He was told the property he had left in his cell had been destroyed during the riot. Prison staff claimed the damage was the work of other inmates, but he did not believe them, because it was rare for prisoners to damage one another's belongings. His view was strengthened when others discovered they too had suffered in the same way. As the men talked among themselves about what had happened, he told them, 'The cons pulled off a good one and this is the screws trying to pay us back and blame the rioters. It's fucking pathetic, and I won't forget what they've done. Maybe they think they've won the first round, but we'll have better days ahead. Material things are easily replaced.'

His mood was not helped when he learned that a young friend from Glasgow, also in Saughton, had been threatened by a gang who had warned that he would be slashed if he did not provide them with drugs and money. Billy and other inmates had a lot of respect for the victim of these threats. In an effort to convince a jury to acquit two pals, he had gone to court to give evidence on their behalf. They had carefully tutored him in what to say, but at the last moment they had changed their story without telling him, and as a result he had been jailed for perjury. Now he found himself at Saughton facing another ordeal.

'Point this gang out to me,' Billy told him and, heading along a landing, they spotted one of the ringleaders, followed by a crony named Gordon Modiak. As they came near, Billy booted the first man in the face and he fell back into Modiak, who scuttled off to the safety of his cell. The target of the Glaswegian's foot had been the bully's nose, which was broken and bleeding. He was grabbed by the hair and savagely told, 'Don't ever threaten one of my friends again or I'll put you in intensive care. Stick to robbing sex offenders. That goes for Modiak.' Prison officers had watched the attack but took no action for the time being.

Another to suffer Billy's wrath was a drug dealer from Aberdeen who was also suspected of being a police informer. He had badly let down a friend who was jailed as a consequence, but he strutted around prison as though he was lord of the manor. He was very proud of an impressive moustache, on which he lavished considerable care, and one day Billy and another inmate seized him, tied him to a chair, shaved off his pride and joy and lifted him, still bound, onto a table tennis table, where he became a figure of fun until rescued by staff.

In yet another confrontation, Billy was put on internal report – effectively laying him open to disciplinary action – for a bizarre attack on an inmate who had been jailed for assaulting women by knocking them to the ground, stealing their shoes and sniffing their feet. Spotting this oddball as he was walking along a landing, he seized the first item that came to hand, which happened to be a pair of boots outside a cell door, and used them to bash his target over the head, shouting, 'See if you enjoy sniffing these.' This and the attack on Modiak's friend were sufficient for the authorities to decide it was time for Billy to continue his shuttlecock journey around the prison system.

He found himself at Perth in February 1987. His initial impression was of dirt and the combined odours of boiled cabbage and urine. And his welcome to C Hall was not helped by the appearance in his cell late at night a couple of days later of a masked man dressed in dark-blue overalls who announced that the building was on fire. Two remand prisoners had set fire to their mattresses, forgetting they were locked inside their cell. Both ended up in hospital, but at least the other inmates, ordered outside to the exercise area, had the consolation of a fry-up during the night on the instructions of those running the prison, followed by a lie-in until noon.

The following afternoon, Billy was approached by a prisoner named Martin Ross, who handed him some hash. 'Billy, a parcel was thrown over the wall in a tennis ball and I was told it was for you. My own stuff came from one of your friends, and when I phone him I'll tell him you received it safely.' In addition to being a hypochondriac for whom the merest sniffle was a sign of the onset of pneumonia, Martin was one of the main heroin dealers in Glasgow, running a lucrative business that was the envy of Arty Thompson. Martin was tricked into driving a car to a rendezvous with a prostitute hired by the Godfather. As the couple set off, police, acting on an 'anonymous' tip-off, intercepted the motor. Heroin had been planted in the steering column of the car and the searchers, ignoring more obvious hiding places, went straight to it, with the result that Martin's journey ended not in a bedroom but a prison cell.

Billy began to enjoy life at Perth, where he made many friends, including Springburn payroll robber Jim Aitken, and he felt his impish sense of fun returning. It was impossible to ignore the conditions, particularly when it was necessary for contractors to make regular calls to spray chemicals on the hordes of cockroaches that seemed to scuttle out of every wall and corner. After these visits, cockroaches wriggled in agony, some in their death throes. One day, using the hash given to him by Martin and watched by a couple of friends, Billy rolled up four joints and placed a dying cockroach in each. Calling over two other inmates, he offered them the smokes, and before long two of their friends had joined the group. Soon seven prisoners were smoking joints in his cell.

'This is braw. Oh yeah,' one of them said to Billy, who was looking on convinced he could actually see the joint moving between the man's fingers. The unusually sweet smell made no difference to the enjoyment of the smokers, one of them asking the others, 'Ken, fit kinda gear is this, mon? It's fair braw stuff.'

Billy promised him, 'Aye, ye'll be crawling about in a minute.'

The last of the doctored joints was being finished off when a length of it fell onto the floor and began running around. 'Whit the fuck is that?' asked the owner, aghast at the sight of a glowing cigarette end speeding about in circles and rolling around.

'Don't worry, it's just a roach,' Billy told him.

'You're fucking heavy, mon,' shouted the smoker as he ran to the toilet.

'That's class hash,' Billy told his companions. 'A couple of drags are enough to make you crawl on the floor.'

He reflects, 'Pulling wind-ups like that kept me sane.'

Later in the year, Billy was transferred to Dungavel, an open prison near Strathaven that had originally been a hunting lodge for the Dukes of Hamilton. It became world famous in May 1941 when Rudolf Hess, Hitler's deputy as Führer, flew from Germany aiming to land a Messerschmitt 101 there in a bizarre bid to seek the help of the Duke of Hamilton to negotiate peace. Hess told secret service interrogators he had met the Duke five years earlier, during the 1936 Olympic Games in Berlin. After jumping from the plane in a parachute and landing at Eaglesham, near Glasgow, he was taken briefly to Dungavel, before being imprisoned in the Tower of London and later in Spandau jail, Berlin, where he saw out his days. Billy's first visit to Dungavel was as brief as Hess's.

On arrival, he had the customary introductory interview with a senior official, the idea being to acquaint him with the local rules and discuss his future. 'What can I do for you?' he was asked.

'Well, I want to see my dad. He's been very ill for months. That was the reason for my transfer from England.'

He was told, 'Ferris, you'll have to wait three months, and if an officer is willing to take you, your application for a visit may be approved.'

Billy protested, 'My father's medical file should be enough to get your support for my visiting him.'

But the reply gave him no more hope. 'These are the rules and if you don't like them, you can always go back to where you came from.'

Billy left the office, lifted a fire hydrant and proceeded to smash every window in sight. Within minutes, he was in handcuffs. He was sent back to Perth and from there to grim Inverness, infamous for the humiliating cages that had once held Jimmy Boyle.

There, he read of the sensational escape of Sydney Draper, one of Jim Aitken's co-accused, from Gartree maximum-security prison in Leicestershire in a helicopter. Draper was at large for 13 months before being recaptured, but that experience would not dissuade him from another attempt at illicit freedom.

Billy remained at Inverness for three months. Officially, he was on punishment, but he found the regime relaxed and the food good, and he built a rapport with the prison officers. In March 1988, he was told to pack because he was being transferred back to central Scotland. This time, his destination was the recently opened Shotts high-security prison in Lanarkshire.

19
PAYBACK

SHOTTS PRISON WAS INTENDED TO HOLD men classed as tough, violent and dangerous. Experts had decided that replacing brutality with humanity, encouraging a sense of having greater freedom while still locked up, might cool the ever-present burning threat of revolt. It was doubtless well meant, but the regime was regarded with suspicion by men used to harsh treatment intended to erode emotion and spirit. Some of the inmates had survived their share of bitter times, none more so than Tommy 'T.C.' Campbell. Four years earlier, in 1984, six members of the Doyle family had perished when someone set fire to their flat in Ruchazie, Glasgow, during an infamous period known as the Ice Cream Wars. Strathclyde Police had been under intense pressure to track down whoever was responsible, and justice and fair play buckled under the heat of public opinion. Campbell and Joe Steele, both from the east end of the city, were accused of being the arsonists responsible for the deaths of the Doyles. They vehemently protested their innocence but were found guilty of murder and jailed for life.

It would be almost twenty years before the word of the two men that some policemen had acted wrongly, planting incriminating evidence and presenting false testimony, was accepted and they were released, declared innocent victims of a miscarriage of justice.

During the intervening years in prison, they determined to keep their campaign for freedom before the public. Joe staged a series of dramatic escapes, during one of which he superglued himself to the gates of Buckingham Palace, while T.C. simply demanded his rights as a prisoner, which did not go down well with some of those guarding him. He suffered regular and vicious beatings, one of which, at Peterhead, left him close to death and resulted in the prison service having to fork out damages.

Others who were now Billy's neighbours included Dennis Currie. Currie had been jailed for life in 1985 for murdering pensioner Mary Martin. Shortly before Billy had arrived for his first stint at Perth in February 1987, Dennis and two other inmates had escaped by piling up chairs and tables to clamber from the prison laundry into the yard and using a home-made rope to haul themselves over the 30-ft barbed-wire-topped wall. Dennis managed to hide in an attic above a doctor's surgery in the town but grew hungry and thirsty while below him patients went through catalogues of aches and ailments with the doctor. He left telltale dusty fingermarks on the trapdoor to the attic and a coffee mug ring on a table in the surgery when he briefly emerged during closing hours. The excuse given by Dennis and the others for the prison breakout when they appeared before the High Court in Edinburgh later that year was that so many inmates were HIV positive, they were terrified of catching AIDS. It failed to help them escape an extra six years behind bars.

Of Shotts, Billy says, 'Almost every prisoner in my hall had been beaten, worked over or tortured, whatever you care to call it, by screws at one time or another. Now the screws wanted to talk to us, play pool and act as if nothing had happened. The cons had been brutalised, and now it was time to socialise with them. Most of us remembered the days when screws dressed up like Knights of the Round Table in brown overalls, body armour, elbow and knee pads, helmets and shields, and carried 4-ft-long batons when they went looking for a victim. This wasn't to protect themselves from their victims, it was a disguise so nobody could sue them afterwards. The screws at Shotts wore Mr Nice Guy uniforms and put on a Mr Nice Guy image, trying to kid us that along with their appearance their attitude had changed. Well, they weren't fooling me. Once a rat, always a rat. It took me only a few hours to find out that things were actually the same.

'I had been hoping to provoke an incident over the refusal to allow Paul and me shared visits. The prison service argued that I had to wait to be assessed as suitable to mix with other mainstream cons. I had never heard of this anywhere else and complained loudly, but nobody was biting and I told them, "None of you had better collapse or I'll give you the kiss of life with my boot." I tried recruiting as many cons as I could to come round to my way of thinking, that when it came to the crunch, the screws would just go back to despising us and treating us in the same old way. But I was shocked to hear, from people categorised as Scotland's toughest, comments such as, "Oh, Billy, we've had enough of being banged up. We don't want to get involved and spoil our chances of being moved on."

'I knew I was right, and the proof came one day when T.C. fell down in the exercise yard and broke both his wrists. He came back from hospital with plasters on both arms and told the screws that one of them would have to wipe his backside when he used the toilet. The new spirit of friendship vanished then, because there were no takers.

'I was disappointed at what I saw as the subservient attitude of many of my fellow prisoners. I expected more loyalty from Scotland's so-called toughest. Truth be told, they wanted rid of me so they could safely talk the usual rubbish to the screws, make themselves look good and the rest of us like troublemakers. They were an embarrassment, bogus, and no way was I going to join them and play goody-two-shoes to get a move to mainstream. Jail is jail, and it's not the conditions that make it good or bad but the other cons around you and how they handle themselves.'

The easier regime allowed less strict security during visits, something of which inmates took discreet advantage, and smuggling became marginally easier. It was a valuable benefit that most inmates were anxious to preserve. But then a prisoner turned up for his visit high on smuggled Valium and threatened his wife and another woman for not bringing him more drugs. The exchange was heard throughout the visiting room, and the terrified wife complained to the prison for allowing her husband to get himself into such a state, with the result that the old strict rules about visits were reinstated, leading to anger and disappointment.

Billy confided to another prisoner that he intended to punish the offender by slashing him across the face. This man, whom Billy had trusted, was so nervous about it that he made himself ill by taking too much Valium and, after being helped to the prison hospital, babbled out a story that Billy Ferris was about to commit murder. The outcome was that the intended victim and the informant were placed on protection for their own safety.

Billy spread a rumour that the two were having a gay relationship and, as word spread, local-radio DJ Tom Ferrie unwittingly played a request for them on one of his radio shows. The song was 'My Ding-a-Ling' by Chuck Berry. Another presenter thought he was congratulating a young man and woman on their engagement after being sent the names of the Valium takers and asked 'by all their pals at Shotts' if he would play Eddy Arnold singing 'Make the World Go Away'.

The aggro didn't end there. A riot at another prison was soon to give Arty Thompson an opportunity to stir up trouble for Billy, who wasn't about to let him get away with it. In September 1987, inmates at Peterhead, sickened by constant brutality and torture, had gone on the rampage, taking hostage prison officer Jackie Stuart. He was beaten, stripped, chained and dragged across the 90-ft-high rooftop of D Hall. A second officer, Bill Florence, was stabbed in the leg but quickly escaped. For decades, prisoners had told how Peterhead was a hell in which they were effectively used as punchbags by a minority of sadist officers (although no one suggested that Stuart or Florence was such an officer). The inmates had felt that nobody wanted to listen; with the nation's media camped outside striving to see their every move, it was a golden opportunity to draw attention to the nightmares that went on unseen behind the walls. Once again, an SAS unit was called in. Troops wearing body armour and carrying 9-mm pistols and sub-machine guns took a back-door route into the jail. Four soldiers climbed along a narrow parapet 70 ft above the ground and out of sight of the rioters; then, at 5 a.m., they exploded stun and CS gas grenades on the prisoners.

Now, four of the ringleaders – John 'Jake' Devine, Malcolm Leggat, Douglas Matthewson and Sammy 'The Bear' Ralston – were facing trial, accused of a variety of offences including rioting. The accused men were allowed to call as witnesses others who had been inmates of Peterhead. It meant that regulations restricting the use of telephones were eased so that prisoners who might have valuable evidence could be contacted and sounded out about what they might have seen or heard. For some, this was a chance to speak to cronies in other jails, and for Arty Thompson it presented an opportunity to lay a trap.

From Peterhead, the Mars Bar Kid contacted Shotts and spoke with lifer John Gallagher, who had been jailed for his role in a bungled but deadly attempt to rob likeable Glasgow butcher Thomas Woods of his takings. In 1978, Gallagher and two others, John Haig and David Cochrane, all wearing masks and armed with iron bars, had burst into their 64-year-old victim's shop in the Gallowgate and demanded money. The butcher and his wife desperately tried to fight them off, but seconds later Woods staggered into the street, covered in blood, and died. Inside, off-duty police constable Brian Coppins, a close friend of the couple who often helped them out and was passing when the raiders struck, had joined in the battle, managing to rip off Cochrane's mask. Coppins was badly injured but recovered. Gallagher left his palm print on the butcher's scales and was later arrested in Glasgow by armed police, while clever detective work led to the apprehension in Amsterdam of Cochrane. The killers' haul was less than a hundred pounds. All three were jailed for murder.

Arty was furious because he had heard that Billy had spread word that he and his dad were police informers and the Godfather's son was also venting his ire against Paul, badmouthing the younger Ferris for having stopped working for the Thompsons. Three Edinburgh men held in Shotts agreed, for a price, to beat Billy up, and Gallagher vouched for them. The trio discussed the plot amongst themselves, not realising that they had been overheard by a friend of Paul, who was quickly on the telephone to warn him what was in the offing. Paul arranged for a friend of T.C. Campbell to smuggle a lock-back knife to Billy, who had been told what to expect.

Armed with the knife, he went alone for his morning shower, hoping to lure the three men into following. When they failed to appear, he went looking for them. He slashed one in the neck, a second punched him in the face before his head was split open as it was smashed against a wall and the third took to his heels. The carnage was over in seconds. Before prison officers dragged the combatants apart, Billy slipped the knife into his shorts. All three casualties were taken to hospital, where Billy was treated for a depressed fracture of the cheekbone. No one made a formal complaint. After word reached the Edinburgh three that Paul Ferris had declared it was open season on them, they staged a demonstration to be moved. They had their way.

Much to his consternation, Arty found that he was joined at Peterhead in August 1988 by Billy, his intended target, in a transfer intended as punishment for the latter's knife attack in Shotts.

In Peterhead, Billy met Ronnie Neeson, whose brother John was a friend of Paul. In March 1983, Ronnie and drug dealer William 'Toe' Elliot had been jailed for life after being convicted of murdering pusher Robert Kane at a flat in Maryhill, Glasgow. Elliott became furious when he discovered that Kane was an addict, had been enjoying some of the heroin he supplied and, as a consequence, was unable to pay what he owed.

At the murder trial in March 1983, the prosecution said that, on the night of the murder, believing it would give them an alibi, Elliot and Neeson went to a disco in Tollcross. But they left and drove to Maryhill, where they donned masks and battered and stabbed Kane to death. They then returned to the disco. There was actually little evidence against either man until police arrested Elliot's younger brother John, who was described by witnesses in court as 'the poison dwarf', on unconnected charges. He volunteered the information that the two men had told him they were involved in Kane's killing.

In prison, Ronnie fought to prove his innocence. There were many who felt that Toe Elliot should have done the decent thing by accepting the murder was his responsibility alone and disputing his brother's claim that Neeson had been involved. That he did not left him a despised figure, described by Billy as 'the most hated man in Scottish prisons'. Ronnie, on the other hand, was well respected because he had endured frequent beatings, willing to suffer over his protestations of innocence. He and Billy played one-touch football each day in the exercise pen. It was hard, uncompromising and the highlight of the day.

One day, as he was being led to the pen, Billy banged on Ronnie's cell door and shouted, 'See you outside, Ron,' to which his friend replied, 'OK.' But it was a quarter of an hour before he appeared and when he did he was not looking his customary cheerful self. 'You OK, Ron?' he was asked, and he unenthusiastically mumbled a single word of reply: 'Aye.' Ronnie was losing five goals to two when he told his friend, 'Billy, I can't be bothered.' It was obvious something was wrong. 'I saw the doc before I came out. He looked me in the eyes and said, "You've got a cunt of a virus."'

'You sure, Ron?' asked Billy. 'Maybe you misheard.'

But Ronnie was adamant: 'I can still hear the doc telling me as he looked me in the eyes, "You've a cunt of a virus, Neeson." I felt numb and walked out.'

They returned to their cells and when teatime came around a medical officer gave Billy his normal medication for psoriasis, a family complaint.

'You on duty when Ronnie saw the doctor?' Billy asked.

'Yeah, I'm on my way to give him his medicine,' came the reply, followed by the production of a small brown bottle.

'What's that for?' Billy asked.

'Conjunctivitis. They're eye drops. He has to take them three times a day.'

Billy's laughter produced an odd look from the screw. A few minutes after he had gone, Billy heard banging on the wall separating him and Ronnie, who demanded, 'What's so funny?'

The reply came, 'You looked at the bottle he's left?'

'No, why?'

'It's not a cunt of a virus, it's conjunctivitis. You put the droplets from the bottle in your eyes three times a day.'

There was a brief silence followed by an outburst of laughter and then Ronnie called back, 'I was sure that was what the doc said. I had a joint before I saw him and it must have confused me.'

Billy's other neighbours on the landing in their Peterhead hall included Douglas Matthewson and Andrew Walker. Matthewson, one of the rioters, had told other inmates he was a biker who was serving life after stabbing another man dead in a fight. To them, this seemed just another murder until newspapers began covering the trial of the rioters and giving details about their backgrounds and convictions. It was not unknown for cons to hide the reason they were in prison. In Matthewson's case, his victim had been not a man but former beauty queen Audrey Williams, who was strangled by him in Montrose in 1982 after she rejected his advances. That offence meant he was classed as a beast, and now his secret was out it was only a matter of time before he was attacked or stabbed. He became reviled, and after being allowed a brief spell of freedom to attend the funeral of a relative, he was placed on protection for his own safety.

Andrew Walker had been sentenced to thirty years for an atrocity in 1985 in which he gunned down three army colleagues with a machine gun in snow-covered hills near Penicuik. Major David Cunningham, Sergeant Terence Hosker and Private John Thomson had been carrying a £19,000 payroll from a bank to their base at Glencorse Barracks, Edinburgh, when Walker, a fellow soldier, asked for a lift and executed them. He tried to make the crime look like the work of an IRA active service unit collecting funds, but was arrested when experts matched the murder bullets to a gun that had been in his possession. The cash has never been found. Walker was a witness at the rioters' trial.

Billy had managed to hold on to the lock-back he had used to stab the men hired by Arty to attack him, and now he reckoned payback time had arrived. He thought his best opportunity would be during a visit and hoped that one by his family might coincide with the Godfather coming to see his son. Because he could not get advance notice of when Arthur might call, he knew he would have to be always prepared. He had made up his mind to stab both Thompsons.

When visiting time came, he looked forward to meeting Paul and queued up for the customary search by a prison officer to ensure he had nothing concealed on him. The screws never touched his groin, and he had the tiny knife secreted down the front of his Y-fronts. But, to his consternation, he realised that a hand-held metal detector had been introduced. Ronnie was alert to the situation. He walked over to the officer carrying out the searches and began an argument, which quickly became heated. Billy joined in, complaining, 'Fuck's sake, our visitors have travelled for hours to get here and you start fucking about with a vibrator, robbing them and us of the time we're entitled to have together.' It was clear this was a situation that could easily erupt into trouble, and the officer, not wishing to be blamed for another riot, began cursorily waving the detector over the prisoners then waving them through to the visiting room.

Billy looked around and was gutted when he realised that neither Thompson was present. He said to Paul, 'Fatboy is here and I'm hoping the old man arrives for a visit. I still have the lock-back and I'll do him and anybody who shows up to see him.' Paul laughed and told his brother, 'Great. We'll both be rolling around if the old grass shows.' But neither of the targets did.

Later on, Billy explained to Ronnie about the plot Arty had orchestrated to attack him in Shotts. Neeson looked surprised and said, 'Gallagher? John Gallagher? He's here working in the hospital ward.' Billy told him, 'I hope he gets a visit at the same time as the Thompsons, then I can do all three.' He had still not given up hope of attacking Arty, and now decided on another ploy.

Inmates who were alleged to have taken part in the riots had been caged in the punishment block and were allowed 30-minute sessions to discuss evidence with other prisoners whom they might call as defence witnesses. These meetings were held in private in an office, out of the hearing of prison officers who sat on guard outside the door. Another of the defendants was to be Jake Devine, who had been serving a long sentence for a serious assault. Billy wanted him to act as a go-between, passing a message from him to Arty saying that Paul had been on a visit and had asked him to get important information to the younger Thompson urgently. 'I want to meet you to get a few things sorted out, so tell the screws you want a defence visit with me,' was the message.

Billy told Ronnie, 'If he goes for it, I'll do him there and then in the office. It's a square go, because he could just as easily do me.' But those in charge of prison security had other ideas. They had been tipped off that the Ferris–Thompson feud was threatening to spill over and disrupt the rioters' trial. Hardly had the message left Billy than he was summoned to the office of a governor and told, 'You will not be allowed anywhere near Thompson, not in the visiting room nor for defence meetings. In fact, you are to have no contact whatsoever with him. He does not want any trouble with you, so staff have been told to make sure you and he do not have visits on the same day. This will prevent you or your brother coming into contact with him or his father.'

Walking back to his cell, deep in thought, Billy reasoned that a ban on direct contact with Arty did not prevent others from reaching him. He arranged a defence visit with Jake Devine and asked him to approach another inmate, whom we will call Stan

Short, with a simple request for him to break Arty's nose and tell him, 'That's from Paul and Billy.' Billy had once saved Stan from being stabbed and knew one good turn deserved another.

When he heard Arty had been seen 'giving an impersonation of a fat panda bear', sporting two black eyes and a bruised face, he was content that the debt had been repaid in full. But it also meant that the war had escalated, and as time wore on an increasing number of combatants would be called on to take sides.

20

ARTY AND THE BIRDMAN

ARTY THOMPSON'S RESPONSE TO BEING beaten up was to hire a minder, Bill Varey, an Australian and one-time member of the Scots Guards who had also spent a stint in the notorious French Foreign Legion. That service alone was sufficient to give him an awesome reputation. Varey had been jailed for fourteen years in 1976 after being convicted of two armed robberies on banks in Edinburgh, a sentence later reduced on appeal to ten years. But in 1984, not long after being freed, he again found himself in prison, this time starting another 14-year stretch, for robbing the Lockerbie branch of the Clydesdale Bank while armed with a sawn-off shotgun. Sent to Peterhead, Varey twice made failed escape attempts, first threatening staff with a pair of shears and then using an imitation handgun to subdue a number of prison officers so they could be tied up. He became known as 'the Birdman of Peterhead' after developing an interest in caring for budgies.

His gentleness with the birds did not carry over into the work he had promised to carry out for Arty. On Thompson's orders, he thrashed Stan Short in retaliation for his attack on the Mars Bar Kid's nose. That upset a number of inmates who liked Stan, among them well-respected fitness fanatic Frank Ward, a sidekick of Paul Ferris's long-time friend James 'Jaimba' McLean and a man with a fearsome reputation for violence. Frank set about Varey, beating him so badly that he damaged his hands in the process. While the victim went off to hospital, Billy was joined in the punishment block by Short, sporting a badly bruised face, and Frank, his hands swathed in bandages.

Varey already had a bad reputation among other inmates. Donald Forbes accused him of being an informer, a most serious transgression in the eyes of any criminal. Forbes was infamous for having been sentenced to death in 1958 for murdering a night-watchman in Granton, Edinburgh. He was reprieved as the noose loomed. He was released from jail in 1970 but just seven weeks later was guilty of a fatal stabbing during a pub fight in Leith and was again given life. Ronnie Neeson told Billy, 'If Donald ever gets his hands on Varey, he will do him.'

Varey's enforced absence left Arty defenceless once again, so he took on a replacement bodyguard, Frank McPhie, who was serving a five-year sentence imposed in 1986 for an armed robbery, having completed a similar term following another robbery in 1978. McPhie would never be short of enemies. Oddly enough, having first employed a lover of birds, Arty had now turned to a prisoner with an intimate knowledge of dogs, an interest that he used to run a vile sideline as an organiser of dog fights.

Billy heard just how deceitful McPhie could be from one of his former associates, whom we are calling Chas. He told Billy, 'Frank's a good robber and a cunning bastard. A few years back, he, me and a third guy robbed a bank in central Scotland after pointing guns at the staff. We got away with a lot of money, parked up in woods and split up the haul. Frank reckoned the police would have set up roadblocks and it would be risky going back to our homes in Glasgow. If we were stopped and searched, we would be done for. He suggested we each bury our share out of sight of the others and retrieve it in our own time later on. That way nobody would know where the others had hidden their money.

'He had a spade in his van and gave us each a bag. We took it in turns to go into the woods and dig a hole, making sure to remember where it was. Just to make sure there was no way we would get into trouble if we were stopped, Frank buried the guns with his bag. Then we went back to Glasgow. We were actually checked over at a roadblock but the police waved us on when they found nothing in the van.

'I had known all along that Frank was going to rip the third guy off, because he told me what he planned to do. It left me doubled over with laughter and I went along with it. Frank had a bitch in season and before the job he'd smeared the three bags with her scent. The day after we pulled the job, he went back to the woods with the dog he used to cover his bitch and it had no problem sniffing out all three bags. The other guy went back every day for a week but couldn't find his bag. When he complained to me, I said I couldn't find mine either and we must have messed up remembering where they were buried or somebody else had found them. Frank used the same sting to con another guy a couple of years later.'

Several years afterwards, Billy was recounting this story to a friend, who almost choked as the tale reached its climax. 'The bastard! It was me who was ripped off!'

As the summer of 1989 approached in Peterhead, McPhie was on the Thompson payroll, and there were many who believed he had placed himself in danger by taking sides in the dispute between Billy and Arty.

Varey, meanwhile, was on his own. As far as his erstwhile employer was concerned, he owed the former legionnaire no further loyalty once he had been sent to hospital. No sooner had Varey been released back into the mainstream at Peterhead than he was set upon with pool cues by Jake Devine and Malky Leggat, resulting in Bill returning to hospital, Malky being transferred to Inverness and Jake finding himself again in the digger.

Nobody doubted the sincerity of Varey's interest in birdkeeping, or his genuine affection for budgies, but eyebrows were raised when, two weeks after once more returning from hospital, he sawed through the bars of his aviary and escaped. That sparked a massive manhunt and he was recaptured after two days on the run. He was caught as he stood at a bus stop, causing fellow inmates at Peterhead to joke that he had simply wanted to travel to the safety of some other prison where he would not be constantly on the receiving end of beatings. 'He's the first prisoner I've ever known who tried to transfer to another nick at his own expense and without prison transport,' said Billy. He was said to have told another prisoner, shortly before taking flight from the aviary, 'I just want to do my time in peace.'

Billy comments, 'He just couldn't handle the heat. Paranoia set in and he thought everybody was out to get him.' For some reason, Varey was moved to Inverness, the same jail now holding one of his tormentors. He would eventually be freed in 1998, after which he set up a decorating company in Glasgow, having turned to religion.

Meanwhile, others were on the move too. Arty headed to Shotts and there were many, including Billy, who wondered if peace might even break out in Peterhead, but Billy had little time to find out. In Glasgow, a truck had knocked Willie Ferris down. He was lying seriously injured in hospital. So grievous were his injuries that Paul telephoned Peterhead prison to ask that Billy be moved to Glasgow, a reasonable request that was quickly granted. So he found himself at Barlinnie in June 1989, warned that at the first hint of trouble he would be returned to Peterhead. But his thoughts were solely for his father and he had found the journey to the Big House a nightmare, desperate for news and unable to communicate with any member of his family.

Escorted by four prison officers and policemen, he was taken to Glasgow Royal Infirmary, where he found Willie ashen, in intensive care and encased in plaster, bandages and tubing. He wondered how the old man could survive. 'I was completely shattered when I saw the tubes and the oxygen mask covering my da, a feeling worsened by knowing I was helpless to do anything. Any son would surely be anxious seeing his dad in such a condition and my being in jail made it all the worse.' However, as the weeks passed, Willie slowly recovered, graduating from being bed-bound to shuffling about while hanging on to a Zimmer frame and finally being able to walk slowly with the aid of walking sticks.

To Billy it was an amazing and courage-giving transformation. His thoughts being concentrated on his dad, he had no time for mischief-making and confirmed to friends and family who commented on his seemingly healthier looks that he felt better than he had for many years. He was asked if he wished to join a working party making concrete slabs and agreed, provided he was allowed to use the breaks to run circuits around the football pitch. He was told that was fine as long as he didn't abuse the privilege, and he embarked on a gruelling daily routine of work and exercise.

Three months after arriving at Barlinnie, he was completing a training session when he spotted a party of visitors being escorted around the jail. One of the strangers approached and was introduced to him as Susan Baird, Lord Provost of Glasgow.

When she asked the purpose of his circuits, Billy told her, 'I'm hoping to organise a charity run involving some of the prisoners. If anyone will sponsor us, then we'll raise money for the children's hospital at Yorkhill.'

The Lord Provost told him, 'That's a wonderful idea. If it goes ahead, count me in as a sponsor.'

He had taken the prison officials by surprise. One told him, 'I haven't heard anything about this. Come and see me later. Nothing of this nature has ever been done in a Scottish jail.'

At a meeting later that day, Billy took a gamble and suggested he train twenty-five other cons for six weeks.

'Why are you doing this?' he was asked.

'The nurses and doctors who saved my da have been fantastic,' he said. 'I want to repay them in some way, and the family thought we should help the kids in Yorkhill.'

Willie McGurk, Barlinnie's much-respected PE supervisor, agreed to arrange training sessions, while Paul bought a trophy and medals for everyone taking part. The runners were joined by a number of celebrities, including athlete Tom McKean, who would be crowned European 800 metres champion the following year, Rikki Fulton, the legendary creator of the hilarious Reverend I.M. Jolly, and welterweight boxing star Gary Jacobs. Many years later, popular Gary from Glasgow discovered that in 1987, two years before the charity fun run, Paul Ferris had been approached by Arthur Thompson and asked to slash the boxer as a punishment for quitting Scotland to base himself in London. The request was refused.

Now Gary and the other volunteers, including men from prisons all over Scotland, had raised more than £3,000, including £2,000 from Paul and his friends, for the sick kids at Yorkhill. The event attracted considerable media interest – too much in the view of some.

Billy remembers telling his brother, 'I've never ever felt so proud of anything I've done, but some of the screws think I've been getting too much attention. The writing's on the wall. I reckon I'll be off on my travels soon. But I don't care, because our da's looking better again.'

He was right – his days at the Big House were numbered. But it would be a stranger who would unwittingly punch his ticket out.

21

THE WHACKING OF WHACKO

BRIAN DORAN HAD BEEN A QUIET, bespectacled schoolteacher who dreamed of excitement that no classroom could provide. A devout Roman Catholic with a knack for languages, he was fluent in Spanish and a chat with a friend one night convinced him this was a talent of which he ought to be making greater use. 'Why not get work with a travel company, Brian?' his friend suggested. 'There's no point in learning a foreign language and then using it to read a few books. You need to get out and about.' Doran's response was to become a rep for a travel agency. He went on to run Blue Sky Travel, a Glasgow-based firm that cashed in on the growing demand for package holidays.

His customers ranged from policemen to crooks, and extensive trips overseas to check out locations before recommending them to clients soon brought him to the notice of expats, and in particular the thriving community of on-the-run criminals holed up in Spain, where they were safe from extradition back to Britain. In Glasgow, Doran gained near-celebrity status. Money poured in, enabling him to buy a big house and expensive cars and to entertain royally, even running his own football team. His social life thrived, and it was through spending time with younger Glasgow partygoers that he was introduced to drugs. Doran's downfall would hinge on ever-increasing amounts of cocaine.

In the mid-to-late 1980s, Scottish drug barons were mainly interested in hashish, and Moroccan hashish in particular. Huge amounts were farmed in the Rif Mountains, shipped to the

Spanish mainland and from there taken by a number of routes to Scotland. The chief problem for the smugglers was that hash is bulky; a similar volume of cocaine could bring a return worth many times more. Because of the risks involved in smuggling it, cocaine was expensive.

A chance meeting in a Glasgow club between Doran and two Scots living in Holland, George Duncan and Thomas Sim, led to the start of a thriving racket that would change the course of Doran's life and that of many others. Duncan and Sim began smuggling cocaine to Doran – known as 'Whacko' because of his resemblance to Jimmy Edwards, the star of a television comedy of that name about school life – and others, including successful baker Andy Tait. The group was known as the Happy Dust Gang.

The police, alerted by increasing amounts of cocaine becoming available, began an investigation and were soon making arrests. Doran, panicked by the prospect of prison, decided to try to save his own neck, and at a secret meeting with two detectives in the Blue Sky Travel offices he offered to give the names of his accomplices in exchange for his own freedom. While police hedged on any deal, Doran went ahead and passed over names that led to Duncan and Sim and then Tait being jailed, the latter for four years. Whacko, meanwhile, did not hang around and wait to be collared. He went on the run to Spain but kept in contact by telephone with the officers who had investigated the Happy Dust Gang.

In Spain, he found his fluency in the language made him much in demand with anyone in need of a trusted interpreter. Among these was Glaswegian Walter 'Wattie' Douglas, known in drug-smuggling circles as 'the Milkman' because it was said of him that he 'always delivered'. Walter was well known among the multitude of wanted crooks living in southern Spain on the so-called Costa del Crime. However, like so many of these rich, often violent, criminals, his ability to speak or understand Spanish was almost non-existent. Now, in Doran, he discovered a first-rate communicator, and, with the promise of vast rewards, enlisted his help.

Soon, through his appearances at high-profile meetings, Whacko was being looked on by men controlling large sections of the European drugs market as a major player. During negotiations over huge deals, Douglas would sit by Doran's side, relying on his fellow Scot to interpret, saying little if anything, occasionally nodding agreement. Whacko took advantage of these negotiations to exaggerate the importance of his own role, describing himself as a co-director rather than a mere translator. On occasion the pair travelled to Amsterdam to conduct their discussions, a move that enabled Doran to study the Dutch city and arrange a possible bolthole in the event of his ever having to leave Spain in a hurry.

For Doran, the problem was that his role in the arrest of other members of the Happy Dust Gang had not gone unnoticed. He had been tarred with the reputation of being an informer, and it was only a matter of time before the same slur rubbed off on Douglas, the criminal fraternity reasoning that their closeness was an indication that Douglas approved of his partner's deceit. The outcome of this was that Doran became known as 'the Squealer Dealer' and Douglas 'the Tartan Pimpernel' because of his seeming ability to wriggle out of tough spots with the police. Detectives in Glasgow, however, never gave up hope of getting their man.

In 1987, Doran was one of 16 people, including 11 from Britain, arrested in Spain by police investigating hash smuggling. The evidence against him was weak and he was released on bail, but he knew that if he stayed in Spain he would have to take his chances should there be a trial, so he upped sticks and moved to Amsterdam, where his previous visits with Douglas had not gone unnoticed by the authorities.

The suspicion that Whacko was a grass meant that he had left behind talkative enemies on the Costa del Crime, and soon detectives in Glasgow were aware of his Amsterdam base. The outcome was that in February Doran was arrested following an undercover police operation in which an officer posing as a potential drug buyer had talked with the Scot, who could not resist boasting that he was an important player. After his arrest, he changed his story to claim that Douglas was the main man. But if he hoped his betrayal would get him out of being extradited to Scotland, he was out of luck. Hard though he fought to stay in Holland, he was flown back to Glasgow and banged up in Barlinnie. Back in Amsterdam, his claims had not fallen on deaf ears, and from then on the Milkman would be watched.

Meanwhile, word that Doran was in custody in Glasgow quickly leaked out to the Costa del Crime, and a telephone call was made to a well-known criminal family living in London whose enquiries showed that the brother of Paul Ferris was held in the same jail. During a visit from a friend, it was explained to Billy that he would be £20,000 better off if he would arrange for Doran to be stabbed as a warning to keep his mouth shut should he be approached by the Dutch police for more information. Billy explained that others were interested in Doran, principally the police, who were worried about the possibility of just such an incident, with the result that Whacko had been placed in the prison's segregation unit, the Wendy House.

'The only time Doran can be got to is when he is being escorted to visits or taken for court appearances,' he told his visitor. 'It would be very difficult, but I have plenty of friends who would willingly stab anybody for an earner, especially one as big as this.'

He wondered if an opportunity would arise. When it did, it was from an unexpected source. One day, while he was waiting to be taken to hospital to visit his father, a prison official asked, 'Billy, do you know Brian Doran who's in the segregation unit?'

'No, I've never met him,' was the honest reply.

'What it is, Billy, is that we have been told there's a contract on him.' He was not surprised to hear that word about the threat to Doran had spilled out. With such a sum at stake, it would have been impossible for rumour of it not to have spread. Prisons are notorious for gossip and the inmates' grapevine is as speedy and efficient as any modern communications system.

'That's rubbish, I would have heard about that,' was Billy's response. 'In fact, I think it's a liberty your keeping him down there in solitary simply because of jail gossip or malicious gossip from outside.'

'I'm glad you said that, Billy. You have a lot of influence in here. Could you guarantee he would not be injured if he was allowed to mix with everyone else? The guy's nerves are shattered. He isn't your normal run-of-the-mill prisoner and finds it hard to cope. By the way, are you enjoying the visits to your dad?'

Billy could barely conceal his delight at what he had heard. 'Of course I'll make sure he's fine,' he promised, at the same time thinking to himself, 'Like fuck I will.'

Visiting Willie always put him in good fettle and now he had even greater cause to have a spring in his step. He was ecstatic at the prospect of getting someone he saw as a rat off protection and into the firing line. He was confident he had more torpedoes (jail slang for assassins) on standby than the nuclear submarines at Faslane and could hardly wait for Doran to be moved to his hall so he could hire an attacker and then collect the bounty.

'That official will rue the day he took my word a grass wouldn't be stabbed,' he thought. 'Asking about my father! It isn't the first time a screw's thought he could use emotional blackmail to get me to keep the peace. They want me to do their job for them.' He believed the exchange contained a veiled threat that should anything untoward happen to Doran, further permission to see Willie might be refused. 'Fuck you. If you do that, I'll stab you,' he mused, trying to hide his displeasure and admitting to himself with a wry smile, 'I have more fucking faces than are on show at Madame Tussauds.'

Returning to his hall after the visit to his father, Billy saw a slightly built man with receding hair waiting to greet him. Doran extended a hand, which Billy shook, thinking, 'Ya fucking beauty! Twenty thousand quid just smiled at me.' He could see worry etched on the face of the stranger. During recreation that night, as cons sat about chatting, playing dominoes or pool, watching television or reading, Doran was stabbed. Billy was heading back to his cell when he felt a hand grab at his sleeve. He turned around, thinking he was about to be attacked, to find that Doran was at his elbow, pale and evidently in shock. All he could say was, 'I've been stabbed,' and as he turned around Billy saw what appeared to be a home-made weapon sticking out of his back. The injury did not seem at that stage to be unduly serious. Doran was standing upright and able to walk. Instinctively, Billy pulled the blade out. He saw it was about eight inches long. He handed it to Doran, who, by now on the verge of collapse, gasped, 'What will I do with this, anyway?'

Billy was now in an awkward situation. If Doran died, he would be the logical suspect, having blood from the weapon on his hand and clothing. Supporting the stabbing victim, he said, 'I'll take you to the end of the hall where you can get an officer to help. Don't let go of the blade. If anybody tries to have another go at you, at least you have something you can defend yourself with.' The words were meant to reassure Doran, but they appeared to have the opposite effect. He was obviously terrified.

Reaching the desk where the duty officer sat, he handed over the weapon and then collapsed. The officer panicked and pressed his alarm button. Billy told him, 'That's a bit over-dramatic, isn't it? The guy's here and nobody's shouting or making threats. Why not just get him some help?'

When other officers arrived, Billy was asked, 'What happened?'

'He can tell you better than me,' he replied, pointing at the stabbing victim as he was being placed on a stretcher to be taken to hospital.

Billy knew the police would want to interview him and was surprised that they didn't appear until the following morning. He told them honestly, 'I know nothing and I don't even know Doran. I never met him until he turns up with a knife in his back.'

'Why did you pull it out?' he was asked.

'In case somebody hung their jacket on it.'

It was clear that not everyone had seen Billy's actions as those of a Good Samaritan. 'Do you know that the worst thing you can do is pull a knife out of someone? He could have bled to death.'

'No, it wasn't the worst thing I could have done,' he told his interrogators. 'I could have shoved it in further. Look, there's nothing I can tell you. Why not ask Doran what this is all about?'

As he returned from the interview, an officer pulled Billy to one side and said accusingly, 'I find it hard to believe you don't know anything about this.'

The only response was, 'Well, you would say that, wouldn't you?'

Among the inmates, rumour was rife that the weapon had been coated with blood given by a prisoner who was HIV positive. Doctors at the Royal Infirmary told Doran he was lucky no vital organ had been pierced. The wound turned out to be not serious and tests confirmed that he had not been infected with the virus. He was soon back at Barlinnie. No one was ever charged with the attack, but Billy knew the suspicion that he was somehow involved would remain.

Doran's trial on the charges resulting from the activities of the Happy Dust Gang was fixed for October 1989 at the High Court in

Glasgow. On the eve of its beginning, a mystery woman arrived at the comfortable Utrecht home of George Duncan and offered him £110,000 if he did not give crucial evidence for the prosecution. Duncan did not show up at the High Court, where Doran denied charges of cocaine smuggling and failing to appear for his trial in April 1983. He was jailed for two years. Some were surprised by the fact that this was half the term given to the luckless Andy Tait. There was even more good news for Doran when he was told the sentence would be backdated to the time of his arrest in Holland, meaning that if he behaved himself he would be freed in June the following year.

Two months after Doran started his brief sentence, staff at Barlinnie told Billy that he was suspected of paying a prison officer to smuggle in drink and drugs for him. Demands to be shown proof and given the officer's name were ignored, and he was moved back to Peterhead in December. While Billy languished in Aberdeenshire, the schoolmaster was released at the promised time, but he had not learned the lesson that crime costs freedom.

22

ACTING THE GOAT

BILLY'S PAL WAS IN LOVE. We'll call him Neil Stobart. He had never met the girl, but swore she was the sun and moon to him. At just over 5 ft tall, he usually looked up to any dates, and now Neil had been given the chance to impress. A friend had persuaded a young woman to cheer him up by seeing him in Perth jail, and his excitement was growing. They would be sitting opposite each other in the visiting room, giving Neil the chance to look her in the eyes, and he was practising flashing smiles that he was certain would leave her swooning. However, he made the mistake of causing envy by giving a series of graphic descriptions of the girl's charms. As a result, his gleaming white false front teeth – covering an unsightly hole where the originals had been punched out in a teenage brawl – went missing.

His pal and hooch-drinking companion Billy Ferris was the culprit, sneaking into Neil's cell while he showered, then slipping the teeth into an envelope that he had hidden down his Y-fronts in case Neil accused him of theft and searched him.

'Ah've loft ma teef,' was the cry when Neil discovered the disaster. 'Haf onybuddy feen ma teef?' The thick Dundonian accent combined with the lack of teeth to drench anyone close in spittle and made his demands even more difficult to comprehend.

'Nobody would steal your false teeth, Neil, so calm down. Check your cell. They can't be far away,' Billy reassured him.

'Aye, yer right, but if onybuddy haf taken fem, Ah'll do him.'

The Glaswegian had concealed the envelope in his cell and there was no way he was giving the set back before visiting time. He spent an hour talking to friends in D Hall, feeling that the further he was from Neil, the less chance the toothless Romeo would have to grill him about the mystery disappearance.

When he reappeared, having retrieved the envelope, he discovered Neil sitting on his bed, his head in his hands and obviously feeling sorry for himself.

'I'm guessing you haven't found them?'

'No, Billy. Ah even got the fcrewf to let me check the rubbif binf.'

'I think maybe you should go to the surgery.'

'Whit fur? The dentift ifn't here fur anufer two weekf.'

'Aye, I know that, but you might have swallowed them when you were drunk.'

'No, Ah wid haf notifed.'

'Not in the state you were in.'

He knew from Neil's puzzled expression that he had created doubt. Could he have swallowed a set of false teeth without knowing about it?

'Aye, OK, Ah'll go after the vifit. Ah'm no lookin' forward tae feein' fif burd wi nae teef in. Ah dinnae want her tae fee me like fif.'

'Ah, you'll be OK, Neil, she might even like you like that,' came the reply, followed by a series of guffaws.

'It'f no funny, mun. If I had her phone number Ah wid haf put her off for a few weekf till Ah could get a new fet, fo Ah wid.'

At that, both men were called to the visiting room. Billy had the envelope back down his Y-fronts, knowing it would not be found there during the cursory search made by prison officers before visits. Billy followed his friend into the visiting area and saw him sitting two tables away facing a pretty, brown-haired woman, a hand covering his mouth as he chatted, while she leaned forward trying to catch his words. He waited ten minutes before calling, 'Neil!' As the love-struck inmate turned, Billy pulled the envelope from his trousers and threw it to him. In what seemed a millisecond, four prison officers were converging on Neil, assuming the package contained drugs. But before they could reach him, Neil had ripped open the envelope and was shouting with glee, 'It'f ma teef!' He held up the prized possession for all to see. The room erupted in laughter, even the prison officers joining in. Luckily, both Neil and his new girlfriend took the joke in good heart, but afterwards Billy was told, 'Ah'll never trust you again, you bugger. Ah'll get ma own back fur this.'

Billy had met Neil in August 1990 after being transferred south from Peterhead, where he had spent a miserable eight months. To him, Peterhead always felt like a landmine – just a clumsy action or wrong word could set off an explosion. When he arrived at Peterhead's punishment block, Billy was reunited with Ronnie Neeson. The pair spent many nights drinking home brew and discussing old friends and enemies, among the latter the much reviled Frank McPhie, who had been jailed that year for an especially sickening offence of running dogfights in which trained pit bull terriers tore one another to pieces while onlookers bet small fortunes on the outcome. He was caught with 31 others when RSPCA investigators, accompanied by police, raided a dogfight in Fife. But the initial satisfaction of animal lovers over his four-month jail sentence soon turned to disgust when it was replaced on a technicality with a thousand-pound fine.

Billy and Ronnie sang along as Ronnie strummed his guitar, trying to drown out the noise of other inmates who were unable to sleep and shouted curses at nursing staff, claiming their medication had been watered down. In protest, some began setting fire to their cells and were moved to the abandoned B Hall, which had been out of use since being badly damaged during the riots three years earlier. Those who were left, including Billy, Ronnie and Andrew Walker, followed their example simply in order to escape the smoke-reeking atmosphere. They found themselves in A Hall, where they were joined by Joe Steele.

In the constant war in which staff and inmates did their best to intimidate one another, Billy and Ronnie took to using their daily allotment of time in the exercise pens to train even in the very worst of weather. It meant they often endured freezing rain, biting winds and snow, but then so did staff who had to remain out of doors to watch them in case of an escape attempt. Other prisoners began following their example, and while inmates could keep semi-warm by running and jumping, the watchers had to stand about, stamping their feet in a hopeless effort to find warmth, leading to an outbreak of coughs and sneezes among the guards.

A young Glaswegian prisoner whom we shall call Charlie began training with another man, a homosexual nicknamed 'Tadger' who had at one time raped another inmate. Ronnie tipped Charlie off about Tadger's background. 'Watch your bangle,' he warned, meaning his backside. The young man was shocked, stole a teaspoon from the guards' office and sharpened it to a point on the sill of his cell window. Then, during the next exercise period, he stabbed his training companion in the head before being dragged off. Tadger was stitched up in hospital and returned to find that whenever he was seen in the hall cries of 'It's Mr Spoonssss' went up. Because of his complaints, metal detectors were introduced to check all inmates for hidden weapons before exercise.

It was shortly after this that Billy found himself at Perth. One day, on the football field listening to the sounds of traffic heading to and from the Fair City, Billy met up with two members of a well-known biker gang, with whom he often shared hash. 'Just the man we're looking for,' they told him. 'Want to swap some hash for angel dust?'

'Angel dust? I've never taken that before.'

'It's magic, man. Gives you the strength of ten people. Cops in America have to throw nets over you and use stun guns to get the handcuffs on.'

'Aye, right. I'll give you a bit of hash anyway. You just keep the stuff yourself.'

'No, man, a trade is a trade,' he was told, and a gram of angel dust was handed over in exchange for a lump of hash.

'How do you take it?' Billy asked.

'Up your beak, man, just like coke. Do a nice line and whoosh, man, it hits home and you feel like a fucking giant.'

Billy decided he would allow others to try this new delight first, and, as in a 'which is the butter?' taste test, he wouldn't tell his guinea pigs what they were taking.

He selected Neil and a mutual friend, whom we are calling Stan Wellington, for the experiment. Both men enjoyed their prison brew, a pipe of hash and a good laugh, but now they were about to experience an entirely new sensation. In his cell, Billy opened the pack of angel dust, spread half out on a mirror, chopped out a few lines and waited. When he heard Stan and Neil chatting as they approached, he leaned over the mirror, a rolled-up strip of paper held to his nose.

'Oh, coke,' they both said, entering his cell. 'Brilliant.'

'No, it's not coke, it's a surprise,' they were told.

'What is it?'

'Just take it and tell me if you like it. I've got another half gram in my pocket.'

'OK, let's do it,' said Stan, who snorted a line and was followed by Neil.

'How are you feeling, Billy?' they asked.

'Nothing yet. It's nearly time for lock-up. See you at six,' he told them as they went off to their cells.

Billy lay back to enjoy the hour-long break and had lit a hash pipe when suddenly a loud piercing shriek of 'Billy Ferrissssss' caused him to spill his smoke, burning the front of his shirt. He realised the maniacal scream was from Neil. 'Fuck's sake, he's having fun,' he thought, but gave no answer. There was no further shouting and he found it nerve-racking waiting for the cell doors to be reopened so he could discover what had caused Neil to yell out his name. When finally the locks were turned, he went to call on Neil, just two doors away, not knowing what to expect and apprehensive. He wondered if he might see his friends attempting to fly about the hall like Batman and Robin. Slowly pushing open Neil's door, he was greeted by the sight of two bulging eyes that looked as if they were about to pop out of Neil's head.

'Well, Neil, how was it?'

'Oh, Billy, this is heaving fucking stuff. I feel as if I could lift the cell door off its hinges. Whit the fuck is it?'

'Angel dust,' he was told.

'Whit? That gear gives you massive strength.'

'Oh, you've heard of it then?'

'Heard of it? I've been lying here terrifying myself with the things I've been thinking I might do. How are you feeling?'

'Me? Oh, I never took any. I just pretended to so I could see how you'd react.'

'Ya bastard. This isnae funny. It's scary.'

'Oh, it's not that bad, surely?'

'Not bad? It's murder. I can't look at my arms because I feel so strong I'm terrified what I might see. I think I've turned into Popeye.'

'Come on, let's see how Stan is.'

'No, no chance. I'm staying here.'

Billy had to wipe away tears of laughter. He found Stan, whose build would have graced the front row of any international rugby pack, sitting on the edge of his bed with a blanket draped over his shoulders. 'Oh, Billy, I've never been so terrified in my life. Is this stuff LSD?'

'No,' he was told, 'angel dust.'

'Angel fucking dust? You have to be kidding.'

'No joke. I never took any.'

'That's fucking out of order, Billy. You taking some now?'

'Am I fuck, after seeing the way it affected the pair of you. Neil wants to pull doors off their hinges. Come and see him.'

'Not likely. I'm staying put. How long does it last?'

Billy guessed. 'About twenty-four hours I think.'

'Twenty-four fucking hours? I'll never be able to handle that.'

'I'm only kidding, I don't have a clue. Try some sugar, that might make you feel better.' Stan began wolfing down handfuls of sugar from a bag used to sweeten his tea, unaware that Billy had also only been guessing at the effectiveness of this remedy.

'Want a hash pipe?' Billy asked.

'I'll never take anything off you again. Shut the door behind you.'

When Billy told Neil that Stan was gulping sugar, Neil followed suit, telling him, 'Put the light out and leave me alone. This has really scared me.'

The next morning, Billy gave them Valium after they both complained of having suffered a sleepless night. It was Saturday, which meant the start of a work-free weekend, and Neil and Stan announced they would spend it in bed. Billy was still finding it hilarious. 'That's jail humour,' he says. 'The crazier it is, the funnier it seems.'

During Billy's time in Perth, rumour spread among the inmates one day that something was going to go down. Those planning the trouble suggested that Billy and his friends go to the games room in the recreation area before it kicked off so that they would have an alibi should they be accused of involvement. It meant asking special permission, because normally inmates would be together having tea at the time. As an excuse, Billy asked if he and the others could watch the Prix de l'Arc de Triomphe, the most prestigious horse race in Europe, held each October at Longchamp in France. No sooner had they been locked into the recreation area than trouble began, with the targets being sex offenders.

Billy recalls, 'We'd smuggled in biscuits, cheese, bottles of juice and sandwiches and hidden them in the pool table so we had enough food to last us for a couple of days at least. We were in the telly room for two days before anyone remembered we were there. A few beasts' cells were smashed open and some of them slashed, but the jail covered up exactly how bad the trouble was. One of the officers asked what the result of the Prix de l'Arc de Triomphe had been. I said, "Riotous Behaviour first at 6–1 followed by the odds-on favourite Hostage," but he didn't appreciate my wit.'

In April 1991, Billy was returned to Dungavel, wondering how long his stay there would last this time. He remembered it from four years earlier looking from the outside like a five-star hotel but inside with dormitories where up to ten inmates shared a single shower and toilet. When he was taken for the standard introductory interview, he was pleasantly surprised to be told, 'Things have changed in here, and I'd like to think for the better, for staff and prisoners alike. Try to forget what happened in the past and give it a fresh start. How is your father?'

Billy told the man facing him across the desk, 'He's still ill and unable to travel or visit me because he had an accident and was knocked down a while ago.'

He was glad to be told, 'If you can get me a doctor's letter confirming that, I'll have one of my staff take you on an escorted leave visit.'

He mumbled his thanks, and thought how different the past four years might have been had he been treated in this way earlier.

The necessary paperwork arrived within a week and he was taken to see his family. The reunion helped him to settle and he was offered a repeat visit four weeks later. 'Thanks,' Billy said sheepishly, embarrassed at being treated with kindness and civility.

Later, when asked how he was settling in, Billy suggested developing an outside area where visitors could meet inmates in the open air.

'What have you got in mind?' he was asked.

'A fort where kids can play and a seating area attached to an aviary. I would get it filled with rabbits and budgies. It would be a tranquil setting for visitors, and the cons and the staff would feel more comfortable.'

He suggested cutting trees from the nearby forest to provide wood and promised other materials free from a company owned by family friends. Those same friends would supply the animals and birds and their food for free. Billy had discreetly spoken to the SSPCA, who had promised to advise on the welfare of the animals.

'You've sold it to me, Billy, but don't let me down,' he was told. 'I'll be watching your progress daily from my window. And good luck.'

Billy was delighted to be able to do something worthwhile for the visitors. In only six weeks, a team of volunteer inmates had built a wooden fort 20 ft by 30 ft, with four 8-ft-high turrets and a surrounding fence. A senior official provided a pet rabbit, a Californian grey as big as a Yorkshire terrier. It was christened Louis, and so the prisoners decided to call their structure Fort Louis. Over it flew the flag of the Confederacy, and when it was completed prisoners and staff alike agreed the venture was a magnificent success.

Billy spotted an advertisement in a local newspaper seeking a good home for a two-year-old pet Angora goat. It arrived one day complete with four bales of hay and a stock of food pellets. He thought its cries sounded like a moany person and named the goat Arty after Fatboy Thompson. Arty was like a big dog and had the run of the place. Kids loved him. Each day, Billy would put a dog collar and leash on Arty's neck and take him for a run through the woods.

Sitting on balmy nights watching cons and their families enjoy the sight of the pets running about their feet, he felt the efforts had been worthwhile and was proud of what he had achieved. One day, an inmate brought in a crow covered in oil and unable to fly. He was named Reggie and spent most days jumping about and squawking. Sometimes Billy would blow hash smoke into Arty's face. The goat appeared to develop a liking for the sweet aroma, and after a while Reggie and the budgies also started to creep towards him when he smoked.

Paul and two close friends from the east end of Glasgow, Joe Hanlon and Bobby Glover, would call to see Billy, bringing their sons, who loved Fort Louis and the animals. An open day was organised, at which Billy dressed up in a gorilla suit smuggled in by Joe and, with a chain around his neck, allowed himself to be dragged around by another prisoner posing as his trainer, while the children chortled their pleasure. It was all too good to last.

23

BULLETS AND ACID

THAT DAY OF LAUGHTER AND happiness was to be the last they would ever spend together. Within just a few weeks, two of Billy's visitors would be dead with a third facing a lifetime in prison. Mayhem loomed.

Arty Thompson was nearing the end of his sentence and, as a matter of routine, due to be moved to the relative freedom of an open or semi-open prison. It was suggested he be transferred to Dungavel, from where a series of weekend visits with his family in Provanmill would be arranged. Most prisoners would have jumped at such an opportunity, but then Arty discovered Billy Ferris was already in residence there. Memories of his recent beating were still fresh, and Fatboy asked to be taken off the waiting list for a place at Dungavel. He was overheard by a friend of Billy confiding over the phone to his father, 'I'd rather stay in a high-security nick. Why should I have to suffer? Why don't they move Ferris?'

Billy sent word that if Fatboy arrived at Dungavel, he would not be harmed. However, stupid as were many of his actions and utterances, young Thompson was not to be fooled by such a promise, one that Billy had no intention of keeping.

'That rat is blaming you for not getting here,' Billy was told one day by another con as they ate dinner. 'He's seething and badmouthing you, Paul and the rest of your family. He's accusing so many people of trying to whack him, and he's even drawn up a hit list of people he wants to be murdered.'

In the end, Arty was transferred to Noranside open jail, near Forfar in Angus. His first weekend at home was to be his last. On 17 August 1991, he ate an Indian meal in a Glasgow restaurant then returned to Provanmill Road, where, outside his parents' home – known locally, behind old Arthur's back, as 'the Ponderosa' – he was shot three times, dying shortly after midnight in hospital. The car used by the gunmen had been stolen earlier that day. It belonged to a police inspector.

Billy was asleep in his dormitory when a good friend, William 'Wullie' Barnsley, shook him awake. Wullie had been jailed for life in 1983 for the murder of his girlfriend Pamela Glen. A few years later, with release in sight, Wullie would decide to attempt an even earlier freedom by absconding from Penninghame jail in Wigtownshire after being given a week's leave to visit his parents. He decided to make for the Canaries, but luck was not on his side. As he was checking in for his flight at Gatwick Airport, a sharp-eyed police officer spotted that his passport was a fake, and he was sent back to a high-security nick.

'Wake up, wake up,' Billy heard, his friend now close to shouting.

'What's up?'

'Put the news on, quickly.'

As the picture on Billy's television screen slowly came into focus, there was a photograph of Fatboy, and he heard the newsreader saying, '. . . shot outside his house while on home leave from open prison'.

'Yes! Yes, fucking brilliant!' he screamed, waking up everyone else in the dormitory. 'Fucking brilliant!' He celebrated by lighting up a pipe of hash and was convinced it was the sweetest he had ever experienced. Friends joined him, and he could see how happy they were about the news of the murder; many had suffered over the year at Arty's hands, or at least those of his hangers-on.

One crook who had been hoping his ally Fatboy would opt for a berth at Dungavel was a convicted hash smuggler we are calling Michael Rutherford, a close friend of the Thompson family. Rutherford had claimed to be a ship's captain when he had been arrested with a group of smugglers from Merseyside, although it was popularly believed the title was one he had bestowed on himself. Much as Billy had been tempted on occasion to take out his hatred of the Godfather's son on Rutherford, he had held back, reasoning that an attack would only delay even further his release. However, he could not resist storming into Rutherford's dormitory shouting, 'Arty no more! Arty no more!'

When a startled Rutherford demanded, 'What's going on?' he was told, 'Your pal's dead, so I thought I'd come and give you the good news first.' Hearing no reply, Billy continued, 'Cat got your tongue? Don't worry, I'm sure if you ask the staff nicely, they'll let you out to call at the Ponderosa for a beer.'

Rutherford's dejection was more than matched by Billy's delight, and his misery worsened as inmates began dancing and singing shanty style, 'What shall we do with the drunken sailor now that Arty's gone?'

Billy believed justice had been done. Arty had bullied and terrorised those weaker than himself. Yet so many escaped their just deserts, he thought, reminded of Gordon Modiak, the bully whose crony he had battered at Saughton. Modiak had recently been in the news and was now regarded by good and bad in the prison system with loathing and contempt. Early in 1991, he had been revealed as the instigator of a terrible incident that shocked Britain. After being freed from jail, he had met teenage beauty queen and model Louise Duddy. They fell in love, married and had two sons. But Modiak was intensely possessive of his young wife and wrongly accused her of seeing other men. She suffered beatings and accusations but finally could take no more and demanded a divorce. His answer was to hire Kevin Greenhalghse and then watch as the monster ran up to Louise while she was with her children in a car and drenched her with sulphuric acid. She was blinded and hideously burned, and it was only by a miracle that the youngsters did not suffer the same fate. Modiak and Greenhalghse were jailed for 20 years and told by the judge, Lord MacLean, 'In the long catalogue of crimes with which this court has had to deal, it is hard to find one that is more cowardly, more wicked, more premeditated or more devastating.'

The next day, while Billy was outside feeding Arty the goat and the other animals, he was approached by a prison officer. 'I see young Arthur has been shot and killed,' said the screw.

'Aye, couldn't have happened to a nicer cunt,' came the reply, and he added, 'I bet Trumpet Arse regrets not coming here instead of sidestepping me. He might have been able to dodge me, but you can't dodge a bullet.'

Billy wondered about the identity of the killer, saying to himself,

'I'm sure he'll get away with it. Only a rat would want to finger whoever did it.' He worried that someone might assume Paul had been involved in the murder and take a shot at him. Then he discovered that his brother had been arrested, charged with kneecapping William Gillen and remanded in jail. Joe and Bobby visited Billy at Dungavel, and when he mentioned Paul they both told him, 'Stop worrying, Billy. Paul's in the Wendy House at Barlinnie. He can look after himself.'

The day after their visit, Billy had an accident and injured his knee. It needed a check-up by a specialist and he was taken to Hairmyres Hospital on the outskirts of Glasgow. The talk between his escorts was of Arty's funeral, taking place that day. When conversation petered out, the driver switched on the car radio and the first news item turned his passenger cold. It announced the discovery of two bodies dumped in a car abandoned outside a pub in Shettleston, on the route that the Thompson funeral cortège would take. He was sure that the dead men were Joe and Bobby.

'I felt a coldness in my heart, because I knew it was our pals. Going so suddenly from the euphoria of Fatboy's murder to what I was hearing didn't seem real. I felt as though my heart was squeezed and frozen in my chest, and I dared not cry in case the driver could see me in the mirror. It was Paul, too, who worried me, because I knew he would be demented. I thought of their wives, young lassies with kids. A kaleidoscope of thoughts and memories ran through my head. I was completely stunned. It hadn't been confirmed yet that it was them, but something told me they were dead. A worse feeling than that I could not imagine.'

By the end of the day, street gossip had confirmed the identities of the dead men. It would emerge that each had been shot twice. One pistol had been used to shoot them in the head, then a second gunman, holding a different weapon, had fired a single shot into each chest.

As the days passed, Billy was visited by the police, who had been told about his recent meeting with Bobby and Joe. He refused to cooperate on the grounds that he could tell them nothing. But he noticed others evidently talking to the police, including Michael Rutherford and Archie Steen, who had been jailed for life in 1975 for a Glasgow gangland murder. In June 1980, Steen and two of Joe Steele's brothers, Jim and John, had escaped from Barlinnie, partly in protest against abuse and appalling conditions at Peterhead, where they had served most of their sentences. All were eventually recaptured and given additional time. Billy wondered why Rutherford and Steen were with the police. If they had nothing to say, why not do as he did and refuse to say anything. And if they were telling lies, what was the point? He was distrustful of their motives in meeting the police, and the obvious conclusion that he and others drew was that information was being passed over, much against the spirit of the criminal fraternity.

The following day, at least one newspaper carried a story suggesting Bobby and Joe had been lured to their deaths hours after visiting Billy in Dungavel. The story was incorrect. It was true that Billy had been in the visiting room that night, but he had only sat in when one of his trusted friends received callers. He wasn't telling that to the police.

The dead men's wives, Eileen Glover and Sharon Hanlon, visited Billy. 'That was the saddest sight I ever saw. They were shattered, mentally and physically, their lives destroyed, the weans running around unaware that their dads were dead and gone for ever. I had no doubt that Bobby and Joe would have been proud of the way they were coping.'

He wrote to Paul at Barlinnie, feeling he was living in a nightmare from which he could not awaken. Rumours about who had been responsible for the three deaths were rife in Dungavel, with dozens of names put forward. The scenario worsened when Paul was charged with murdering Arty.

Then tragedy struck even closer to home. Willie Ferris, despite not being fully recovered from his accident and a subsequent stroke, disgusted by the behaviour of the Thompsons, whom he blamed for the murder charge against Paul, hobbled up to the Ponderosa on walking sticks and rattled on the front door. 'Ya fucking grass,' he screamed when nobody answered. 'It's not Paul you want. You're using your MI5 pals to keep him in.' This was a reference to the rumour that Arthur had collaborated with the security services in exchange for being allowed to continue running lucrative arms deals with Ulster terrorists. Willie raged, 'Don't get the police to do your dirty work. Get Paul out and sort it out like a man.' At that, three men ran from the house. Willie was pushed to the pavement and held down until Arthur arrived.

The Godfather produced a carpet knife and slashed the helpless victim several times before wandering off, leaving Willie lying in his own blood. Surgeons later had to use 65 stitches to hold his face together. 'He would never have done that to my da before the stroke and accident,' Billy says. 'Da was a proud man and had the courage to go on his own to see Arthur, who didn't have the guts to face up to him. My da never broke the code of conduct that you sort out your own problems and don't involve the police. Arthur had no code, no honour. He had broken all the rules.'

Billy was taken to see his father in hospital after the slashing. 'Whatever you do, son, don't do a runner now,' Willie begged him. 'That's what old Thompson is trying to intimidate you into doing, so he can have his police friends hunt you down. The publicity would be used against Paul when his trial starts.' Attacks on Willie would continue, but still he begged his older son not to try to escape.

Billy wanted to abscond and make his way to Glasgow, where he intended to exact a terrible retribution on the Thompson family. However, he realised the appalling effect this would have on Paul's chances of a fair and unbiased court hearing. He knew his dad was right and furthermore realised he had crucial information that could help his brother's defence, so he tried to sweat out the bad memories by throwing himself into training with a vigour that astonished those around him. The prison authorities, impressed by his restraint, allowed him weekly visits to Willie, and he was no longer embarrassed to give his thanks for the concession.

With other inmates' help, he organised a Christmas show for Dungavel prisoners' children, and set about raising money to guarantee a gift for each child and for youngsters in a local hospital. He collected over £3,000, more than enough to ensure sufficient gifts to go around. But not everyone was impressed. On the day of the show in the gym, where 500 presents were to be distributed, a sick caller rang the prison to claim a bomb had been planted. An emergency announcement asking everyone to leave was necessary. The hoax caused anger, and Billy took over the microphone and told everyone present to stay put. 'This is a joke,' he said angrily. 'Somebody wants to spoil our day, and we can guess who that will be.' There had been murmurings that some members of the prison service were unhappy about the publicity

Billy was receiving and the special treatment they thought he was given.

Repeated requests for the gym to be cleared fell on deaf ears. An army bomb-disposal unit was called in. With the help of police, it opened every one of the 500 parcels, but nothing suspicious was found.

Billy had arranged with friends for the entire proceedings to be recorded on video. The sight of so many children receiving their presents was, he felt, a tribute to Bobby and Joe whose memories had inspired the party.

24
• • • • • • • • • • •
DENNIS THE MENACE

PAUL FERRIS WENT ON TRIAL for murder at the High Court in Glasgow in March 1992. The trial lasted a record-breaking 54 days and cost the taxpayer between £750,000 and £4,000,000, depending on which broadsheet or tabloid made the estimate. More than 300 witnesses, including a notorious supergrass and the Godfather himself, were listed. Paul was charged with murdering Arty Thompson, attempting to murder old Arthur by repeatedly driving a car at him, threatening to kill William Gillen and shooting him in the legs and conspiring to assault Jonah McKenzie, as well as a number of other less serious offences. He denied all the allegations.

By the time the trial began, Billy had been in Dungavel almost a year. The case received blanket newspaper coverage, and from prisons all over Britain letters were sent to Billy asking that he pass on good wishes to his brother. Each night in the dormitory, prisoners would smoke hash, drink smuggled vodka and comment on the witnesses giving evidence for the prosecution. 'They're rats, every one of them,' Billy observed. 'The police have been working as rat-catchers, because most of this lot appear to have crawled out of the sewers.'

Prisoners are generally an unsympathetic lot, and the sight of Gillen on television hobbling on crutches from the court produced howls of laughter. In some cases, inmates were familiar with witnesses, having spent time in jail with them. Gillen rang a bell with Wullie Barnsley. 'I know him, Billy,' he said, as Gillen, described in court as a 'habitual criminal', was shown slowly leaving the precincts close to the River Clyde. 'I know that cunt.'

Gillen's evidence was among the most crucial presented by the Crown. If the jury believed him, then it would count as a major minus for Paul, and the likelihood was that it would sway them in favour of guilty verdicts, especially in the matter of the shooting of Arty. And murder, as Billy knew well enough, carried an automatic life sentence. He had already spent more than 15 years locked away with no prospect of an end to his imprisonment. Wullie's insistence brought him out of a reverie in which he had been visualising the worst possible scenario for his brother.

'Billy, honestly, I know the cunt,' persisted Wullie.

'Stop nipping my heid, Wullie, I'm not in the mood,' was the reply.

But Wullie was not to be distracted. 'Billy, I was a witness for him.'

While Paul's advocate, Donald Findlay QC, had been cross-examining Gillen, he had asked if he was a member of any paramilitary organisation and received an answer in the negative. Wullie said, 'Billy, I know him. I was a witness for him on a robbery charge. He was accused of bank robbery and asked me to go witness for him in court, to say he was doing a drug deal at Glasgow Central Station at the time. I was taken from Peterhead to Armley and from there to court as one of his alibi witnesses. The police interviewed me in the cells under the court. They commented on the Celtic tattoos on my arms. Then they suggested that the money from the bank robbery was for funds for the UDA. I was staggered when they said that, because Gillen never told me any of the charges were connected to the UDA. That was probably because he realised there was no way I would ever have gone along with giving him an alibi if I knew that. After hearing that at Leeds, I backed out.'

'Don't give me any shite, Wullie,' Billy told him.

His friend replied, 'I can prove it. I still have the production papers I was sent telling me I had been called to give evidence for him at court. They're in my property box under my bed in the cell. I'll go and get them.' Ten minutes later, he returned with the documents backing up his story.

Billy was ecstatic. He telephoned a member of Paul's defence team with the news. 'You sure about this?' he was asked, and he confirmed he had seen the documentary evidence.

He was then asked if his friend would be willing to be a witness for Paul. Billy knew he could rely on Wullie. 'Without a doubt,' he said.

'Then I'll get someone to Dungavel right away to get a statement from him,' came the reply.

The following day, Wullie was interviewed for the defence. Gillen had certainly been kneecapped, but not by Paul. The logical explanation that Paul's lawyers could now put forward was that the shooting was not the result of any gangland feud but a punishment for his involvement with the UDA.

When the prison authorities were notified that Wullie might become a defence witness, the police visited him while he was at the High Court to find out what he would be saying. He returned to Dungavel telling of being interviewed in the cells and warned not to give evidence amidst hints that doing so might adversely affect his chances of being released from prison. Lifers, he was reminded, could always be legitimately kept inside for ever.

He refused to be intimidated and stuck to his story. Although there was no proof that Gillen had links with any paramilitary organisation and Barnsley was not in the end called as a witness, his testimony gave Paul's defence team some of the ammunition it needed to tarnish Gillen's image as an innocent victim and create doubts in the jurors' minds.

Billy was sure that his days at Dungavel – he tagged it 'Dungrovel' because of the bootlicking, toadying manner adopted by many inmates towards staff in the hope of gaining favour – were coming to an end. He was due a move anyway but he was sure that, even had one not been in the pipeline, his days would have been numbered as a punishment for his efforts to help Paul.

Billy was confident of the outcome of the case, but there was still a long way to go before the jury went off to work out their verdicts. About two weeks before the end of the trial, he was allowed another visit home to see Willie. He did not know it then, but it would be his final home visit from Dungavel. Nor could he know that what began as a fairly run-of-the-mill trip back to Glasgow would end in hilarity and disgrace. But then his philosophy had always been 'What will be will be'.

He arrived at Blackhill in high spirits, but was shocked to

discover just what Jenny and Willie had been enduring at the hands of Arthur Thompson. 'I was crushed at the treatment dished out to my parents. I wanted revenge. My parents' suffering was unexpected, but I suppose the Thompson code of ethics made my family fair game. There was no rule book.' Their thoughts were not for themselves, but for Paul, and Billy tried to lift their spirits, and his own, by assuring them that all was going well. Still, their suffering made him angry, filled him with disgust and revulsion. It emerged that when Willie had been attacked outside the Ponderosa, he had been beaten with hammers before Arthur arrived with the carpet knife. Now his car had been torched outside the family home. In addition, petrol was poured through their letterbox and their windows smashed. Despite the intimidation, the couple refused to go to the police. Billy compared their attitude with that of the Godfather, who had not only given a statement about the shooting of his son but had also given evidence at the murder trial. He had not said outright that he believed Paul was the killer, but while in the dock he had pointed at the accused man and said, 'We know who did it.'

Billy was proud of his parents for refusing to be driven from their home, and even the prison officer escorting him told Jenny, 'I don't know where you get the courage from.' She smiled, and at that moment the officer's telephone shrilled. He placed it to his ear and in seconds his face was ashen. When the call ended, he said, 'My mum has just died.' Billy poured out a large whisky for him. The family were shocked and tried to find words to express their sympathy, although in such a situation nothing ever seems appropriate. Jenny in particular felt awful for the man. Her own mother was not long dead.

'Drink this and phone Dungavel to tell them what's happened,' said Billy. 'I'll go back with you straight away.' He had only been home for half an hour, a quarter of his allotted time.

'Are you sure, Billy?' he was asked.

'Aye, no bother. I'll get another visit later. Let's just phone and I'll go with you.'

The officer rang Dungavel but was told to stay with the Ferris family until a replacement arrived, when he could return home instead of first going back to the prison.

'Well, let's get this whisky down your neck,' said Billy, but the grief-stricken man refused the offer. 'Fuck it, I'll have it,' said Billy, and swallowed it.

While his parents continued to utter consoling words, Billy attacked what remained in the bottle. 'I'm getting steaming,' he promised himself. He liked the officer who had escorted him, but he was convinced that good fortune could not possibly strike twice, and that another friendly face was unlikely to arrive.

He was right – the replacement was clearly not in a mood to grant favours. 'Billy, you've 50 minutes left of your visit' was his opening shot.

'Aye, right, I know,' Billy replied. 'I'm only waiting on a fancy-dress costume coming. I'll have to phone and see what the delay is.' In answer to the man's puzzled expression, he said, 'It's my brother's son's birthday, and I've got permission to go to his party for half an hour before I go back.'

The officer was not convinced: 'I don't know anything about this. Nobody's told me.'

'Look, your pal's ma has just died. The last thing on his mind was to tell you that I was to go to a party. Fucking phone the jail to check if you don't believe me.'

Billy acted as if he had a right to be irritated and the challenger backed down, as Billy had been confident he would. 'I believe you. Calm down and I'll take you.'

Billy picked up the phone, dialled a number and pretended he was talking to someone, demanding to know what had happened to his fancy-dress costume. He was, in fact, speaking to a pal to arrange delivery of an outfit. When he completed the bogus call, he said the costume would be arriving in 20 minutes. The officer wanted to know the location of the birthday party and was told it was at a branch of McDonald's in the centre of Glasgow. Billy had been told about the party a couple of weeks previously. Initially, his idea had been simply that he wanted to give Paul junior, the youngster celebrating the event, a cuddle, regardless of the consequences. But the whisky was beginning to take effect.

Right on time, his friend arrived with a package containing a Dennis the Menace costume. Inside were tights, shorts, a striped jumper and a foam head, hands and feet. Billy had to strip to his underwear to get into the outfit, causing his parents to roar with laughter. His chaperone was not so chuffed. When he briefly left the gathering to use the toilet, Billy made the most of the opportunity to down another couple of whiskies.

'I didn't know you were going to the party,' said Willie.

'Neither did I, but I am now,' replied his son.

'You'll get into trouble,' warned his mother.

'So fucking what,' came the slurred reply. 'Paul can't be there, so I will.'

His friend took Jenny to the party. Willie, having little mobility because of the accident and attack, decided to stay at home. Billy said goodbye to his father, who was laughing at his son's antics. Billy's parting shot of 'Where's ma dug Gnasher?' had the old man in tears of laughter.

Billy was enjoying the discomfort of his escort, who was unhappy about the unforeseen developments. They walked to the party through crowded streets, the screw becoming increasingly unhappy as his charge, dressed up as the mischievous schoolboy, ran through the city centre charging up to girls and young women, grabbing hold of them and asking, through lips by now reeking of whisky, 'Seen ma dug Gnasher?' He ran into shops and even grabbed a policewoman, begging her for help to find the missing dog.

Eventually, they arrived at the party and Billy ran in shouting, 'Has anybody seen ma dug Gnasher?' The 30 children there loved it. Young Paul tippled immediately who Dennis really was. 'Oh, it's just my uncle Billy,' he said, laughing. Bobby Glover's boy Robert and his mum Eileen were there with Joe Hanlon's son Joseph and his mum Sharon. Billy's sisters and their children were there too, plus a few other family friends with their kids.

Billy's friend poured some vodka into a cup, and as Billy sipped it through a straw he could hear himself saying, 'I'm well out of it. The booze has got me.' The officer, realising he had been drinking, said it was time to go. Billy knew he would be disciplined when they returned to Dungavel, the most likely penalty being a transfer to another jail. But he'd been sure that was on the cards anyway.

'I'm staying till the kids go,' he said.

'Billy, I am ordering you,' said his minder.

'Good, mine's a double.'

The officer phoned Dungavel and, when the call ended, repeated his demand that they leave. The reply was, 'I want to have some fun with the weans. I'm enjoying watching them play while I sip away at my vodka. I was meant to be back at 2 p.m. and I've extended it to 5 p.m. What can they do to me for that? Give me the jail?'

He laughed, but minutes later the party was gatecrashed by police. 'Is that you out to spoil the weans' party?' Billy asked. 'Because if you are, and you don't leave, I'll set Gnasher on you.' After a short discussion with staff, the police left and Billy was told, 'Somebody telephoned them claiming a man in a Dennis the Menace costume was holding us up.' He suspected he knew who had made the hoax call, surmising that, with Paul on trial, his son and the children of his murdered friends at the party, it seemed likely that someone with a deep grudge against him and his family was responsible.

He made the most of the remaining time and wore his costume for the journey back to Dungavel. He was drunk and, with sweat pouring down his face, fell asleep. All he could remember later was arriving back at the prison and being unable to walk inside. To roars of laughter from his fellow inmates, he was helped by a team of officers to a cell in the reception area, where he was searched and allowed to fall asleep. Still sleeping, he was put on a stretcher and driven to Barlinnie.

In the Wendy House at Barlinnie, where Paul was being held during his trial, he was approached by an officer who told him, 'Your brother Billy has just arrived in reception on a stretcher.'

'What's wrong?' asked Paul. 'Is he ill?'

'No, far from it. He's fine.'

'Well, has he been fighting or what?'

'No, he's OK. Well, in fact, he's steaming drunk, wearing a Dennis the Menace costume and shouting out, "Buy every cunt a drink and make mine a double." We've taken him over to D Hall. He's going to Perth tomorrow.' At last, Paul had something cheerful to take his mind off the rigours of the trial, however briefly.

Billy woke up some time in the early hours. It was freezing cold and he was stark naked. He got out of bed and jumped up to look out of the window, expecting to see the trees and fields that surrounded Dungavel, but could see only the roof of another hall. 'Fuck,' he thought. 'I'm back in Peterhead.'

He found a blanket and had just wrapped it around his ice-cold body when the cell door was thrown open and a voice he thought he recognised asked, 'All right, Billy?'

Through bloodshot eyes, he found himself staring at a prison officer he remembered from his stint at Barlinnie. 'I'm fine. How did you get up here?' he asked.

'Billy, do you know where you are?'

'Aye, Peterhead.' He walked over to the door of his cell and found himself looking at familiar surroundings. 'Fuck's sake. I'm in D Hall, Barlinnie. I thought I was up the road. How did I get here?'

The only response was, 'You're on report, Billy.'

'It was worth it,' said the miscreant. 'Fucking worth it.'

Later that morning, he appeared before a gathering of senior staff and pleaded guilty to being under the influence of alcohol and refusing to obey a direct order to return to Dungavel. As punishment, he was told, he would lose his place at Dungavel and return to stricter security, this time at Perth jail.

25
REVENGE

BILLY NEVER DOUBTED THAT PAUL would walk free. 'I had no worries about Paul. I'd been gutted when he was arrested, but I knew he could take care of himself. And my confidence grew with the Barnsley statement. My biggest concern was the liberties inflicted on my da and ma by the Thompsons and their followers. That showed a total disregard for my parents and was completely out of order.'

Paul was found not guilty of all charges and released two weeks after his brother had arrived at Perth jail. There, Billy was told to begin work in the textile area, which at that time was being used to make uniforms for prison officers. 'I'm sewing fuck all,' he told himself. 'I'll make sure I'm not here long.' He hit upon an idea to have fun at the expense of the wearers.

During his time at Dungavel, a convicted rapist had been moved into his dormitory. Billy had suspected that some officers, irritated by his success with the animal park, hoped he would attack this monster and be shipped elsewhere as a result. He saw the potential trap, but his hatred of nonces and beasts meant he felt he had to do something. Taking fibreglass from one of the water pipes, he rubbed it into the rapist's bedding, the inside of his tracksuit, the toes of his socks and his T-shirt. For two nights, the victim scratched until his skin was red and bleeding, causing other inmates to demand, 'Get him out of here, he's lousy. Look at him scratching. He must have scabies.' To their delight, the rapist was transferred. Remembering that escapade, he encouraged inmates at Perth to sew small pieces of fibreglass inside the crotches of the uniforms and in the padding of the armpits. He imagined rookie officers scratching at their genitals and under their arms then showing their rashes to their respective medical officers. It was four weeks before his wheeze was rumbled, thanks to an informer, and he was told that his services in textiles were no longer needed. Still, he thought, 'Chalk another victory up to me.'

After that, Billy refused to work for the prison service, and thus earn a weekly wage, but he discovered he had a talent for designing and making wooden toys for kids. He began to build rocking horses for children's hospitals and sick youngsters. It developed into a passion, and over the years he has donated rocking horses to hospitals in Perth and Dundee, to Yorkhill, the Royal Infirmary and Stobhill in Glasgow and to Rachel House, the much praised and admired children's hospice in Kinross. Because of publicity instigated by grateful parents, newspapers began printing stories about his work, and he was inundated with requests for horses and toys from organisations and individuals.

For the first time in two decades, Billy believed he had found a measure of true happiness. But sorrow was never far away. Wullie Barnsley wrote from Dungavel:

> I don't know how to tell you, but our pals said I should write to tell you Arty the goat is dead. I went to feed him and he was lying dead. Everybody is choked because we all loved Arty. One day he was fine, the next gone.

Billy wrote to the prison suggesting that the goat, like his namesake, had been murdered. But a return letter said that a vet had examined Arty and concluded he had died of a cold. 'Fuck sake,' thought Billy. 'A mountain goat dies of a bad cold. Polar bears will be kicking the bucket from heatstroke next.' He was not convinced, and a further letter from Wullie only added to his suspicions that there were some at Dungavel who could never forgive him for what they saw as his takeover of the jail. Fort Louis and the aviary had been pulled down.

A third letter from Wullie brought even further dismay. It said that an officer with whom Billy had been on good terms and who had often taken him on home leaves had tried to commit suicide. It went on to say that it had been going about that the man was too much under Billy's influence and that unless he conformed to the prisoner's demands he would end up in the boot of a car and suffer the same fate as Arty Thompson.

One day, he had passed on these suggestions to Billy and asked, 'Everything will be OK, won't it?'

The reply was intended to reassure him. 'Of course there won't be problems. They're just trying to wind you up. Forget it.'

But the questioner persisted: 'My wife is worried sick over this. Could you reassure her?'

And so Billy had visited the family home to promise the woman nothing untoward would happen to her husband on his account. Willie and Jenny, too, had given words of encouragement to the officer when they heard of his concerns. Now, hard working, honest and decent, he had suffered a breakdown.

Life in prison took its toll on both staff and inmates. As Billy built his rocking horses in the joinery shop, working alongside him was James 'Jim' McAllister, much respected because he had won a silver medal for boxing at the Commonwealth Games in Edinburgh in 1986. In 1989, he was jailed for four years for indecently assaulting two women and a schoolgirl aged fourteen. McAllister was transferred to another establishment and when he returned a year later his appearance shocked all who knew him. 'He's like an old man,' Billy wrote to Wullie, 'not like the fit guy he was before they took him away.'

One day not long after Billy was moved to Perth, he learned in the exercise yard that William 'Tootsie' Lobban was in D Hall. The news brought an immediate surge of anger within him. Lobban was suspected by many of having lured Bobby Glover and Joe Hanlon to their deaths. In 1991, he had absconded from Dungavel and, after making his way to Glasgow, asked Paul Ferris for help. Paul arranged for him to stay in a flat in Finsbury Park, London, but in August he returned to Scotland and moved in briefly with Bobby and Eileen. The couple had fed and clothed him and given him money. But after Arty's murder, the word on the street was that the Godfather was offering £20,000 for the murder of Paul, Bobby and Joe, believing them to have killed his son. On the night before the funeral, Bobby received a call from Lobban asking to meet up. Minutes later, Bobby and Joe vanished in Joe's car and after the meeting with Lobban the two men were not seen alive again except by their killers. At the time, Paul was in jail accused of a shooting.

'Are you sure it's him?' Billy asked his informant.

'Aye, definitely. Why are you so interested?' he was asked.

'Because this sleazebag is a Judas who betrayed those who protected him. He is one of the most hated men in the Scottish prison system. Thanks for the news.'

Billy had only one aim: to entice Lobban, as he believed he had lured Bobby and Joe, to a meeting with retribution. The next day, he arranged for the delivery of a note asking Lobban to meet him on the football field, where he intended to stab him. Billy waited, with two friends acting as lookouts in case prison officers appeared unexpectedly, but Lobban didn't show. 'The cowardly bastard stayed in D Hall watching us from the safety of his window,' Billy told friends that night as they watched television. 'When he saw me, I drew my hand across my throat to leave him in no doubt what he was getting at the first opportunity. But he already knows that. That's why he bottled it and wouldn't come out to the field.'

Billy called at the cell of David Rafferty, who owed him a favour, and asked him to stab Lobban.

'I won't stab him, Billy, but I will do him with the leg of a bed I've got hidden,' Rafferty offered.

'Good. Tell him it's from me and he'll keep getting done until he comes out to face the music.'

Rafferty did as he had promised, with the result that Lobban ended up in hospital, requiring 18 stitches to a head wound. When he was returned to Perth, he vowed revenge, but after discovering that he and Rafferty were locked up next door to one another in the segregation unit, he had a change of heart. Instead, he manufactured a home-made weapon from a pen, sharpening it to a point, and took a warder hostage.

Billy heard the riot bell sound and hoped it was an indication that another inmate whom he had asked to stab Lobban had succeeded. Instead, half an hour later, he was summoned by a governor who told him that a member of staff had been taken hostage and said, 'I know you have a history with Lobban.' Before he could proceed, Billy interjected, 'I've no history with that king rat,' but the official continued, 'Be that as it may, he is asking to speak to you and wants an assurance from you that no one will attack him. If he has your word on that, he will release my officer.'

Billy recalled the faces of Bobby's and Joe's children. 'I'm not prepared to say that to him to make him feel secure. In fact, I hope he dies screaming in jail for what he's done. As for helping the screw, I've had too many beatings over the years to want to help. I'm not interested in making it easy for Lobban.' At that, he turned and went back to his cell. Lobban soon gave up. He was moved away and later had 18 months added to his sentence for misuse of his pen.

One afternoon, as Billy was returning from the joinery shop, an officer stopped him and told him, 'Take a look along the list of people in C Hall. There's a name there that might interest you.' When he looked at the list, Billy knew right away to whom the man was referring. 'Alistair Thompson,' he read. However, he soon learned the bearer had no connection with the Godfather.

During the 1960s, Thompson had murdered his grandmother. Now he was back in prison, waiting to be sentenced for another killing. This time, the victim was homosexual Gordon Dunbar. He had been murdered in a flat in Dundee, his body cut into pieces with a hacksaw, dumped into bin-liners and distributed throughout the city. His head was never found. Later, Thompson was ordered to spend at least 20 years in prison.

Another of Billy's fellow guests in Perth was Alexander Hall, a former policeman who had been jailed in 1988 for murdering Lorna Porter, aged 18, from Holytown, Lanarkshire, by cutting her throat. Hall had always protested his innocence. He was held in C Hall, and Billy was surprised that no one had slashed him. However, because of fears that he would be attacked, warders watched him constantly, and he repaid their vigilance by making them leather handbags, belts and moccasins. He never visited the television room, the most likely place in the jail for a stabbing.

Robert Mone, too, was careful where he trod. On 1 November 1967, while absent from his army unit, Mone carried a shotgun into his old school, St John's secondary, Dundee, took a classroom of girl needlework pupils hostage, indecently assaulted some and then shot dead their teacher, Nanette Hanson. He was sent to Carstairs, where he formed a gay relationship with Thomas McCulloch, who had threatened to kill a couple at a hotel just because there was not enough butter on his sandwich. In 1976, the pair escaped from the hospital, butchering three men in the process. Now Mone was at Perth. He looked to Billy like an older version of the Milky Bar Kid. His eyes seemed to be everywhere, watching, and he appeared constantly ready to leap out of the way if a full slop pot or heavy battery was thrown in his direction. Younger inmates especially hated Mone for his continual efforts to entice them into his cell for sex. He seemed to have protection from his guards, who invariably picked on one of his innocent victims if they scalded or attacked him while trying to defend themselves. Many believed they remembered that one of his victims at Carstairs had been a male nurse and that they were protecting him in order to protect themselves in case he decided to turn on one of them.

Sometimes Billy tried having a brief word with another fellow inmate, Vinko Sindicic, but his English was poor and as a consequence he was frequently ostracised, which meant that officers often had to explain to him an instruction or comment he did not understand. Sindicic, a Croatian, had acted on behalf of the former Yugoslav secret service when he shot exiled Nikola Stedul outside his home in Kirkcaldy, Fife, in 1988. The gunman was on the wanted list of police forces throughout Europe, suspected of involvement in a series of political assassinations, including that of journalist Bruno Busic in Paris in 1978, of which he would be acquitted in 2000. While doctors battled to save Stedul's life, Sindicic was arrested at Heathrow Airport trying to flee. He was jailed for a minimum of 15 years by a judge at the High Court in Dunfermline in September 1989 after Stedul recovered sufficiently to give evidence against him. Billy believed warders at Perth were terrified of Sindicic and enjoyed seeing their discomfort in his presence.

One of Billy's friends in Perth was Eddie Sweeney. In 1991, he and three others, including Martin Hamilton, became involved in an armed siege when police were tipped off about a raid on the Dunfermline Building Society branch at Anniesland, Glasgow. Heavily armed cops surrounded the building, watched by astonished onlookers, until the gang gave themselves up. They were later jailed by Lord Weir, who described them as, 'dangerous criminals and menaces to society'. Billy found Eddie good-natured, funny and game for a laugh.

The raider was pals with another robber, Willie Barbour, whom Billy liked and admired for his determination to prove his innocence despite many setbacks. Willie was convicted and jailed for life with a recommendation that he should serve at least 15 years for his part in a dramatic hold-up in East Kilbride in 1991. A gang had ambushed and abducted security guards delivering £2.5 million to a bank, forcing them to drive their armoured vehicle to High Blantyre, where the money was loaded into a waiting van. During the getaway, shots were fired at chasing police. Willie said he had been with his mistress, Anne Graham, at the time of the heist. Although his family produced love letters claimed to have been written by her to him, she denied having a relationship with Barbour.

26
. . . .
A FISHY TALE

LIFER DANNY WARD WAS HIV positive and depressed after a hospital consultant had spelled out what that meant. It was 1993, a time when the virus was still not well understood. There was little sympathy or understanding for those affected by it and virtually no appreciation of the fact that it could be transmitted through unprotected heterosexual sex. In Perth prison, Danny was offered little consolation. The officers were perhaps wary of him, wrongly believing that they could contract the virus simply through contact with him. Watching his decline left Billy irritated, angry and feeling helpless.

'They put Danny on report for refusing to go to work and would fine him one or two weeks' wages, so the poor guy had no tobacco. It was no use trying to explain that, for him, even getting up each day was a challenge. So much for claims of operating a humane system. The truth was they just didn't care about these poor guys. One died in D Hall the day after a screw put him on report for refusing to go to work. Had I been on the receiving end, I'd frankly have bitten a lump out of a few of them to infect them. Then they would have experienced the callousness and bigotry of their colleagues.

'Some screws thought these guys died without a fight, but in Danny's case they were wrong. He was forever being hassled and shouted at: "Get up and out of your bed, Ward, or you're on report."

'I'd tell them, "Leave the poor cunt alone." Whenever they fined him, I'd give him tobacco, because it would have been inhuman to let a sick guy go without cigarettes.

'Danny used to tell some of us it was all too much for him, that he wished he was dead. I'd say, "Nothing's that bad, Danny," but he'd reply, "Billy, you've no idea, you really haven't." I urged him to complain about his treatment, but Danny refused, saying, "That would be a waste of time, Billy. Besides, I intend getting my own back on them."

'"Danny, you're not fit to roll about with screws, is he, boys?" I'd say to our friends, who would tell him, "Billy's right, Danny."

'"Aye, I know. I'm not rolling about. But I've already done quite a few."

'"What do you mean?"

'He smiled and broke into a crazy laugh that was so infectious we were soon all at it. Then suddenly he stopped and said, "I wait and watch on the landing as the screws put down their tea or coffee on the landing desk to open some prisoner's cell door. Then I run over and squirt some of my blood into their cups and dive back to watch them drink it."

'Everyone gasped in horror. "What?"

'I told Danny, "You're fucking kidding."

'"No," he said. "I done three of them yesterday for putting wee Joe Steele on report for refusing to go to work. Wee Joe was only protesting his innocence."

'"Fuck's sake, Danny, that's heavy," said the boys. "Come on, Danny, you're joking, aren't you?"

'"No. On the life of my family, I'm serious. They're fucking about with what little life I have left. I'll fuck up their quality of life, then they'll feel the way I do."

'It was an argument I couldn't fault. You fight with what tools are to hand. And, by fuck, his was a psychological time bomb.

'Eventually, Danny did himself in, in a particularly brutal way, pulling veins out of his arms then cutting his throat. Everybody was late that morning, getting a slop-out, when Danny's body was found in his cell. The walls were awash with his blood. I thought, "What a way to go. No way could I have done that to myself. Danny must have been demented." I was opened up with the rest of the prison and everybody was talking about Danny. At last, people were taking notice of him.

'On my landing were three screws who I knew had been giving him a hard time. They were discussing Danny, and I heard one say, "Thank fuck he's off the numbers. He gave me the creeps. Turn around and he'd be watching you." As I listened, I was filling a basin with scalding hot water for a shave. Basin in hand, I fronted the three of them and said they were out or order for talking like that. They crapped themselves, expecting me to throw hot water over them. But I had different ideas. Other prisoners stopped and watched, not knowing what to expect but listening, not wanting to miss a word. I ranted at the screws, "Well, it won't be long before you're with him."

'"What do you mean?" one of them demanded.

'"Danny's legacy."

'"What's that?"

'"Punishment for fucking with guys who are ill and guys fighting their cases. You force them to go to work. Well, Danny used to put a syringe of his blood in your tea or coffee when you put your cups on the desk to go and open a door for the cons."

'The listening prisoners gasped and the screws turned chalk white. You could see their fear as they imagined themselves leaving their cups and opening doors while Danny watched and waited to pounce. One of them began to say, "I don't –" but I stopped him and said, "You're going to say you don't drink tea or coffee, only Coke or Irn-Bru. But he was putting it into whatever you left."

'The man stammered, "You, you can't get HIV that way."

'"No?" I asked. "Well, I certainly wouldn't like to risk it."

'I left them and when I reached my cell I turned and shouted, "You'll soon know if you're victims of Danny's legacy."

'Ten minutes later, one of the passmen prisoners, a cleaner, came to my door and said, "Billy, the screws are all talking about you. They're planning to take you to the punishment cells." I thanked him for the warning, hid a bit of hash I had and waited for them to drag me away. When the door opened, a female officer was there and she told me, "Ferris, punishment cells." I think maybe the others expected me to punch her so they could jump in and give me a hiding, but instead I jumped off my bed, kissed her and commented on her personal hygiene. The screws dragged me off, and by the time I reached the punishment block I had collected a few bruises. Other guys in the hall were banging on their cell doors and shouting, "Leave him alone, you bastards."

'The next day, I was given 30 days in punishment with 30 days' loss of pay for mutinous and inciting behaviour. It was worth it knowing that many of the people who had given Danny a hard time would spend years wondering, "Have I contracted Danny Ward's legacy?" And I hope that wherever Danny is he's found the peace and serenity he never found in life.'

Back in his hall, Billy knew the warders were wondering what he would do in retaliation for his bruises and punishment. He sensed that some of the more astute were making themselves out to be good guys, helpful, interested in his welfare, considerate, but he was, he says, 'too old a fox to be tricked by chickens'. Of his time in the digger, he told friends, 'I've had worse,' and in fact one of his fellow inmates, working on a gardening party, had managed to throw a lump of hash through the window of his cell block, with the result that he had been stoned for most of the 30 days.

Once more in general circulation, Billy became aware of a growing number of suicides at Perth. At one stage, the prison had a reputation among inmates for having one of the worst suicide rates of any jail in Britain. It was odd that men who had been placed in that environment because they had inflicted death could find the demise of other prisoners to whom they had become close so distressing. Some inmates saw in suicide the only way out, the only escape from the monotony and hopelessness that affected so many. Others died naturally, if not always peacefully.

One of Billy's friends, nicknamed 'Flyer', from Irvine in Ayrshire, went sick, complaining of pains in his chest. He was given codeine tablets but died as a result of a massive heart attack as he was climbing stairs one morning at nine o'clock. Everyone was locked up and Flyer's body was placed in the nearest cell. Inmates would later write home complaining to their families that it had been left there until three o'clock in the afternoon, when it was placed in a body bag and taken out by an undertaker. The delay caused anger and distress, and because of protests by Billy, a general meeting was called at which there were calls for bereavement counsellors to be brought in to the prison. This request was met, and although Billy did not take advantage of their presence, others did.

The tragedy left those who had known the dead man feeling morose, and Billy decided to lighten the atmosphere by playing a practical joke. Billy, Neil, Stan and an inmate we are calling Timmy would all take turns to cook meatballs, beans or tuna on toast in a microwave. Occasionally, Billy would complain, 'This is a pain in the backside. We have to hang about waiting to find out who has the tin-opener and then try to persuade them to hand it back.' One day, when it was his turn to do the honours, he found himself in his cell with two ounces of soft, black hash. Giving each of his friends a portion, and chewing another himself, he left them smoking joints and went on a tin-opener hunt. The friends had used their own money to buy tins of tuna and pilchards and were looking forward to hot snacks of the tinned fish. During his search, Billy caught sight of the E Hall fish tanks, full of new and exotic fish. Inmates in the hall had formed a fish club, breeding and then selling to local pet shops. It might have been the sensation of happiness and adventure inspired by the hash, but, chuckling under his breath, Billy wondered if his friends could spot the difference between goldfish and tinned fish. As the idea took hold, he considered whether to smother the goldfish in tomato sauce.

In the kitchen area, another of the prisoners, Ian from Glasgow, was halving an onion, and when Billy asked for a chunk he handed it over, not questioning why it was wanted. 'No problem, Billy,' was his only comment and, as a gesture of thanks, he was given a piece of Billy's diminished lump of hash.

'Watch out for screws, Ian, I'm going fishing,' Billy told him. At that, he pulled up the sleeve of his shirt and reached into the biggest of the tanks. The fish were slimy, but soon one was wriggling between his fingers, to be quickly followed by two others. He slid them into a food bowl and then popped it into the microwave, guessing that around four minutes would be sufficient cooking time. Watching through the glass door as the bowl slowly turned, he supposed the fish had lengthy names, probably Latin, but to him they were simply goldfish, admittedly bigger than those he had watched as a youngster swimming around tiny bowls in friends' homes. These must have been at least five inches long.

He turned to see Ian looking at him in horror and astonishment. 'Fucking hell, Billy, you're kidding, aren't you?' he stammered.

'Me, kidding? No way. They're fucking beautiful. I'll cook them for four minutes with an onion, cut off their heads and tails, smother them in tomato sauce and have them between a couple of slices of toast. A touch of salt and pepper and they'll be delicious.'

Years later, he was reminded of this incident while watching the game show *Can't Cook, Won't Cook*, in which two hopeless chefs cooked a meal and a blindfolded friend had to taste each offering. Billy thought his version would be titled *Can't Be Fucking Bothered to Cook*.

He rubbed in the horror by asking Ian, with an innocent smile, 'Any red or green peppers?'

His friend obviously took the request seriously: 'Naw, Billy, got none.'

Billy ordered Ian, 'Don't go telling anyone, otherwise every cunt'll be eating them.'

Just then the microwave sounded 'ping'. Billy reached in and took out the bowl containing the fish. Cutting off their heads and tails, he popped them on toast. 'Fuck's sake, Billy,' said Ian. 'They smell really nice.'

'Now you come to mention it, they do,' thought the illegal angler. 'But no fucking way am I eating these.' He settled for just toast. When he reached his cell, all three diners were stoned, the lights were out and the stereo was blaring. They tucked into the goldfish sandwiches. 'Mmm, mmm! Fuck, Billy, these are magic. That's what you call a Scooby-Doo sarnie,' they said, happily munching away.

He waited until they'd finished and told them, 'That was no Scooby-Doo sarnie, that was a tropical sarnie – tropical goldfish.'

'Ah, yer kidding!'

Billy's sides were aching from unstoppable laughter, tears running down his cheeks as one by one his pals bolted in the direction of the toilets. That only made him worse, and he lay on the bed howling with laughter. One of the trio returned to shout, 'That's the last time I ever take a sarnie off you, Billy. How could you do that?'

'Simple, I'll give you the recipe,' was Billy's reply, setting him off laughing again.

He had to admit that the tropical fish sarnies had had a sobering effect on the others. 'Come on, straight, did they taste good?' he wanted to know. At that, they shuffled off to their own cells, screaming abuse.

Billy went off to see Ian who asked, 'What did they say?'

'All of them thought it was the best fish they had ever tasted, the cat's whiskers, in fact,' he responded.

'They're not poisonous, are they?' Ian wanted to know.

'Naw, the only side effect'll come when they go to the toilet. They'll be passing tiddlers.'

Just then the bell rang. 'Time for lock-up' was the shout.

'Talk about life in the goldfish bowl,' thought Billy, and wondered how long it would be before an investigation into the stolen fish began.

27

GRAND FAREWELL

A YEAR AFTER DRESSING AS Dennis the Menace and going on a bender, Billy decided to play truant. Willie's health had deteriorated, and when Paul visited his brother at Perth, Billy could see he was upset. What Paul had to say made him determined to abscond: 'Billy, you'll have to see the governor about visiting Dad. He's really ill.'

'Oh, he'll be fine, Paul.'

'No, Billy, he won't.'

He knew then it was serious, because Paul's customary confidence was gone, but he was too afraid to ask for the truth, for fear that what he was told would scare him into showing weakness. Over the years, he had watched strong men broken simply for showing a hint of fragility. A flaw in a previously hard exterior could, he knew, be pounced upon by staff and used to blackmail a man into submissiveness. In such circumstances, the mere threat of stopping a longed-for home visit could be enough to subjugate the most troublesome inmate. It would be worse, even dangerous, if an enemy discovered a weakness in a man's character, because he would then face humiliation. Once that happened, there was no way forward for the victim except an even greater loss of dignity. Prison life was raw and all about confrontation among prisoners, and between prisoners and their keepers.

Billy was determined that, after 17 years, he was not going to allow himself to fall apart, even though he was in turmoil at the thought of his father dying. He wanted to see Willie but knew that might never come about if he allowed anyone to discover the terror over his father's health that was tearing him apart on the inside. He was sent a medical report in which a doctor held out no hope for his father's survival. Now he realised that his next visit home would surely see the last reunion between father and son. It was to take place on 19 April 1993.

On the 18th, his regular parcel of hash arrived. For months, he had been receiving four ounces for himself together with a further ounce plus a hundred pounds for the smuggler. Its arrival normally put him in an ecstatic mood, but now he felt only numbness. He invited three of his closest friends into his cell and told them, 'My dad is dying. I'm seeing him tomorrow, but I'm not coming back.' It was obvious they were about to protest, but he held up a hand and added, 'Divide this hash amongst yourselves. Have a party on me. Tell no one until you hear it on the radio. I'm going AWOL.'

'Billy, for fuck's sake, you've done 17 years. It's crazy to fuck off now,' all three agreed, but he was not to be dissuaded.

'Look, the people running this place know how ill he is and expect that after the visit I'll come back here and plead to see him once more. I will not give them the satisfaction of seeing me beg just so they can refuse me. I couldn't handle that, or being prevented from going to his funeral. The bastards would have won. They'd have crushed me. I've not done all this time just to end up an emotional wreck for screws and enemies to gloat over as I fall apart. Now, I don't want to talk about it any more. Just do as I ask and enjoy yourselves.' He ended his little speech by adding, 'I'm off tomorrow, so I'll say goodbye now.' He left and went to his cell, where he endured a miserable, sleepless night, imagining how his sick father would look and dreading having to see that sight.

Next morning, when he heard shouts outside in the hall and the rattle of keys unlocking cell doors, he realised his stomach was churning just as it had before his first fight as a boy. Now he believed he faced the biggest battle of his life: acting the role of a man despite looking into the eyes of a dying loved one. Two officers drove him the sixty-five miles to Hogganfield Street, and during the ninety-minute journey he feigned sleep, having no heart to join in the conversation. At one stage, he felt sick, choked back bile and wondered if the nightmare trip would ever end.

Finally, they were pulling up outside the home where he had known such happiness as a boy. Neighbours were in their gardens, alerted to Billy's impending visit by the arrival of two police cars, one parked around the corner from the Ferris home and the other at the opposite end of the street. When he climbed out of the rear seat, a handcuff was clamped around his wrist, joining him to one of his escorts, while the driver announced that he would remain in the car.

'Like most sons, I thought my dad would always be there for me. I got my strength from him. I was afraid that without him to guide me I would let him down by being weak. I was thinking, "How do I tell Da I'm struggling to cope with his worsening health and how do I gain his support and understanding for fleeing?" I had decided to fuck off the minute I saw the strain on Paul's face when he told me how ill Da was. From then on, I'd never had any doubts, even though I was under no illusions and knew escaping would mean that if I was recaptured before his death I would not be allowed to attend his funeral. I'd told myself, "I'm off. Fuck letting these bastards see me fall apart after all this time."

'Screws had given me doings galore over the years, but they couldn't beat me into submission. Yet being battered in the heart by Da dying fairly tore me to shreds. My whole life's breath was my family, who had been, and always would be, there for me. I'd never imagined my da wouldn't be there any more. I was fragmenting, ready for meltdown, and it was the worst feeling I had ever experienced. When I walked into my parents' home that day, my mind was a blur. I was dreading it. It was the only time I have been truly afraid.'

As he made his way up the garden path, friendly faces paused while cutting lawns and trimming hedges to shout greetings. 'Hello, Billy,' they called, but he was anxious to get indoors. He noticed that his mother was pale and subdued. 'Ma looks so old and frail,' he said to himself. He was terrified by the change in her. Mother and son clung to one another as the handcuffs were loosened and then removed. He choked back an ocean of tears and realised he was in danger of falling apart, drowning in the emotion of the reunion he was about to experience.

'Where's Da? In his room?'

'Naw, son, he's in the living room waiting for you.'

Billy was immediately shocked by how very old, how thin and how ill his dad looked. Yet, through the pain, Willie's eyes sparkled and soon he was holding his son. 'William, son, it's so good to see you.'

Tears were streaming down his face and Billy felt his own eyes fill with tears. Looking at his escort, he said, 'Come on, Da, you don't want this guy to go back and tell his pals I was crying, do you?'

'Naw, naw, you're right, son. You live where others would just curl up and die,' said Willie, and Billy thought, 'That's my da of old.'

Father and son sipped coffee while Jenny fussed in the kitchen. The men exchanged small talk, skirting around how ill Willie seemed, the subject hanging like a black cloud over them.

'Look, your ma's not too well because she's worrying about me, but I'm fine, son,' said the old man.

At that, Billy turned to his escort, pointing to an adjoining room as he spoke: 'I want you to go and sit in that room there. You'll still be able to see me and I can't leave the room without passing you.'

'Aye, sure, Billy.'

'My ma'll give you some dinner shortly.'

Now Billy and his father were alone, both abandoning the struggle to hold back tears. 'You know I'm dying, son. This could be the last time you ever see me,' whispered Willie.

'I can't handle this, Da. I'm not going back to jail.'

'Ah, I knew you would feel that way, son. Here, take this,' Willie said, slipping Billy a brown envelope he had retrieved from his pocket. 'There's a thousand pounds in there. Just let your ma and me know you're safe, that's all, son. OK?'

'Aye, Da. I'm going to see you again, Da, believe me I am.'

'I know you will, William. I know you will.'

'My ma'll be really upset.'

'Don't worry about that, son. I'll explain to her.'

'I'm going now, Da. If I stay longer, I'll fall apart.'

'No, we can't have that, son.'

He wiped tears from Billy's face, they cuddled and the younger man said, 'I love you, Da.'

'I love you, son. Watch yourself, OK?'

Billy thought to himself, 'No cunt will stop me now,' and he told the prison officer, 'I'm going into the kitchen to talk to my ma.'

She was cooking when he went in.

'So you know, son?'

'Aye, Ma, I know.'

He kissed her and said, 'I love you, Ma.'

'And I love you, son.'

At that, he told her, 'I'm off to straighten myself up.' He gestured to the guard and called, 'I'm going in here,' pointing towards the toilet.

Inside, he locked the door, opened the bathroom window, shimmied down the drainpipe and was about to vault a fence, when there, looking up at him, was a massive black Alsatian dog. For a tick of time, he thought it was a police dog and then, with a sigh of relief, thought, 'Thank fuck. It's Sheba, the neighbour's dog.' He calmed the dog down and kept running, watched by a couple of neighbours who wished him luck, one telling him, 'No afore time son. Run like fuck. Nobody's about.' He flagged down a taxi and gave the driver an address in Dennistoun, a ten-minute drive away, where he used a telephone kiosk to call a friend. Within minutes, a car had pulled up alongside, a friendly face was waving him in and they were driving south. He was free at last, but as the miles sped by, Billy was increasingly tempted to beg his driver to turn around and head back to his dying father.

The disappearance of her son astonished Jenny, who had no inkling of what was to take place. 'William went to the toilet and had been in there for what seemed to be ages, so I kept tapping on the door telling him, "Hurry up, William, there's somebody wanting in there." Suddenly, the officer in the house stood up and asked, "What's going on? What's wrong?" He started banging on the toilet door and when there was no answer he tried to force it. When finally he managed to get it open, the bathroom window was wide apart and the room empty.

'All of a sudden, there were police everywhere in the house. Never in my life had I seen so many. I must have fainted, because the next thing I knew I was lying in my bed with a policeman telling me I must have known what was going to happen because the bathroom window was open. The more I tried telling him I hadn't a clue William was going to escape, the more suspicious he became. What I kept asking myself was, "How on earth did he open the window without making a noise? It was painted up."'

Never in a million years did I imagine he would run off. Willie was so calm about it, but I was going mental. The police gave us a very hard time of it, trying to say we knew what was going on, but I honestly knew nothing. All the same, they would not give up calling and demanding to know whether William had been in contact.'

On the drive south, while police cars set up roadblocks around Blackhill and a helicopter circled the area, Billy cut his hair and shaved off the bushy prison beard he had grown. While he was doing his best to change his appearance, Eileen Glover had called at his parents' home, hoping to wish Willie well and have a brief chat with Billy before he returned to prison. She was surprised to find the street swarming with activity, and even more astonished when she was hustled into a police car and driven away to be questioned, her interrogators evidently, but wrongly, suspecting there was a connection between her arrival and the escape.

Meanwhile, the man who was the subject of the search and his driver broke their journey at Preston in Lancashire, where he used some of the money in the brown envelope to buy a new set of clothes. He telephoned a friend from the Manchester area, with whom he had served time in prison, to tell him he had escaped and ask if he would book him and his companion into a hotel. 'Don't come to Manchester, Billy,' he was told. 'It's too risky. The police'll be nosing around anybody who's known to be friendly with you. I'll check you into somewhere in Blackpool. The holiday season is just starting, and there'll be loads of visitors with Jock accents.'

Nearing Blackpool, Billy rang again and was given the name of the hotel he'd been booked into. 'It's brilliant you've done a runner, Billy,' said his contact. 'A few of us'll come round tonight and have some beers with you. We'll take you clubbing. Nobody's going to expect you to be whooping it up.'

An amazing adventure was about to begin.

28

MOST WANTED

BILLY CHECKED INTO THE BLACKPOOL hotel and telephoned friends in Manchester who promised to meet up with him. That night, the group boldly went out on the town and headed for Stix, the popular nightclub in Blackpool greyhound-racing stadium.

They were hoping to meet up with Steve Sinclair, a successful businessman who was, and still is, well known, liked and respected on the club scene. Failing to spot him, one of the group approached an attractive young woman chatting to a girlfriend. She was Lorraine Casey, Steve's sister, and the memory of that night would remain with her for the rest of her life.

'A guy I knew came over and asked where Steve was. He said some guys from Glasgow were looking for him. I said Steve was overseas and told him when he was due back. Then he introduced me to a dark-eyed man who told me, "Hi, I'm Billy," and it was obvious from his accent he was a Scot. He said, "I'm really sorry if I'm pestering you, but you were pointed out to me as being Steve's sister, and a very close friend once told me that if I was ever in Blackpool I should meet up with him." He had another Scot with him and we chatted over a few drinks.

'They invited us to their hotel, where we had another drink and were treated with the greatest respect. Eventually, it was time to go. Billy called us a taxi and said, "I've really enjoyed tonight, Lorraine. Fancy meeting up again?"

'I knew I wanted to, but I told him, "Give me your phone number and I might give you a call."

'On the way home, my girlfriend told me, "You really took to him, Lorraine. You're going to call him, aren't you?" and although

I told her I'd think about it, I knew she was right.'

Billy was equally enamoured of Lorraine. 'The first time I saw her, I thought, "She's really nice. I'd like to get to know her." And when I did, we started a whirlwind romance. It was like a dam bursting as my emotions poured out. I had been cooped up for so long, and she helped me fall in love with everything on the outside.'

The following morning, Billy was on his way to buy a newspaper when he reached the front door only to discover armed police were patrolling outside the hotel. Rushing back to his room, he awoke his Scottish friend, who quickly threw on some clothes and went off to find out what was going on. He was back ten minutes later, roaring with laughter. 'Billy, you couldn't have picked a safer spot. A load of MPs are staying here for a convention at the Winter Gardens.' The real reason why police were there in such force would soon give Billy cause for concern: there were genuine fears of an IRA attack on the politicians. Still, he was so relieved to know the police had not picked up his trail that he celebrated with a pipe of hash, and rarely before had he enjoyed a smoke so much. That was followed by a call to room service for brandy and beers. Then Billy showered and went off to meet up with his Mancunian friends.

Later that day, following a series of phone calls, he visited an address in Blackpool where he was given a false passport and driving licence in the name of Michael William Raynor. His head told him he had been lucky thus far and that if he remained in Britain, the odds were that he would be recaptured, so he decided that within the next few days he would pay another visit to his father and then head for Spain. 'Viva España,' he told himself, trying to feel excited. But he could not rid himself of the memory of the girl in the nightclub and found himself hoping she would call.

Word had been discreetly spread among former fellow prisoners that Billy was on the run, and some arrived in Blackpool with offers to help with his plans for a move to Spain. Having their support and companionship meant he was out and about during the daytime, while at night he slept surrounded by armed police patrolling the hotel corridors, a situation he found bizarrely reassuring.

To fill in time, friends took him drinking and then on to a fortune teller on the North Beach. He sat in a reception room feeling drunk and woozy from hash, while all around were walls covered with photographs of actors and celebrities, presumably some of her clients. After a wait of ten minutes, he was invited into a darkened room and found himself facing a middle-aged, dark-haired woman, seated behind what he presumed was a crystal ball. It turned out to be a typewriter. He thought she was the psychic, but he was then shown into another room, where he was met by a woman who looked like Mystic Meg, a crystal ball before her.

When she spoke, it was in a foreign accent. He suspected he detected a trace of Glaswegian. She asked to examine his palm, and he had to stop himself from laughing out loud.

'Are you in the forces?' he was asked.

'No.'

'I see a number of men in uniform carrying guns.'

'Are you sure?'

'Definitely,' she said.

'I'm off,' I told her. 'It's a wind-up arranged by my pals.'

'No, no, I don't know your friends.'

'Thanks, anyway. I'm off,' he said, leaving her looking puzzled.

He thought, 'If that wasn't a set-up, she's too close to the bone. I don't want to hear any more.'

Outside, his friends told him, 'Fuck, Billy, you weren't in long. What did she say?' When he told them, their howls of laughter brought looks of curiosity from passers-by. 'What was she like, Billy?'

'Spooky, fucking spooky. She spooked me.'

That evening the telephone rang and when Billy answered a female voice he had hoped to hear asked, 'Hello, Billy. Your offer of a drink still on?' His heart was about to overrule his head. Later on, as dusk approached, he ordered a taxi and collected Lorraine. They went to a pub appropriately named Promises, where they chatted about themselves and Billy told her about his background and that he was on the run. Lorraine has a special reason for remembering that night. 'He was so honest and I really don't know why it happened, but that's when I fell in love with him.'

She, in turn, was honest with him, explaining that she had two children but had split from their father. 'She's lovely, bubbly, funny and good company,' he thought. 'Anybody would fall in love with her.'

Lorraine met up with her brother Steve, who had returned from his trip abroad. 'I told him I'd met this guy from Glasgow and that I really liked him. Steve said, "As long as he's not called Ferris. The police are looking for him."

'I said, "I'm afraid that's him." The look on Steve's face was a picture. But when I took Billy to meet him, Steve really liked him, as did all my family.

'Billy told me he had headed for Blackpool because he had friends there who had arranged transport and a passport so he could get overseas. But he said after meeting me he'd changed his mind and no longer wanted to go. I truly believed him and knew beyond any doubt that he loved me.

'After we fell in love, he woke me up one morning with a coffee and a newspaper and told me to open it up. I nearly died when I saw a headline about "Britain's Most Wanted", and there was the man I loved staring at me from the pages.' The accompanying article told that he was an escaped murderer and that armed police all over Britain were hunting him.

'It looks as if they want to shoot you, Billy,' said his friends when he saw them later in the day.

'Aye, right, thanks for cheering me up, boys,' he told them.

Billy recalls, 'I had been described as most wanted. Now I really was – not by the police but by Lorraine. It felt unbelievable that love had come despite such adversity. It seemed to me that our love put even Blackpool Tower in the shade.'

Billy took the publicity lightly, too much so for the comfort of his friends, who warned him it was time to get out of the country and advised that until that was arranged he should move to a safe house. He agreed that, for the time being anyway, it would not be safe to go through with his plan to visit Willie. Lorraine sensed the panic of his friends, who decided to take him north, with one suggestion being that once the heat died down he could move to Northern Ireland. They promised her it would be only for a short time, and under cover of darkness they set off.

Less than a day later, though, Billy rang Lorraine from Carlisle.

'They've left me here in a safe house and told me to stay for a few days, but I miss you too much. I'm coming back.' He hired a taxi to return to Blackpool. From that day, every time Lorraine heard 'I Drove All Night', the song made famous by Roy Orbison, it reminded her of Billy. When he arrived back, they hugged and he admitted, 'The last straw was not being able to work out how to use their fucking microwave. I nearly chucked it through a window. That's the trouble with being in prison so long. You lose touch with how to operate newfangled gadgets.'

Friends in Glasgow called on Jenny and Willie to pass on Billy's love and tell them not to worry and that he was safe. It was true that he was being well looked after, but he had escaped in the middle of an IRA bombing campaign. Just three weeks before he'd wriggled through the bathroom window at his parents' home, the entire world had been shocked and disgusted when a bomb planted by terrorists in Warrington exploded, killing three-year-old Jonathan Ball. Days later, Tim Parry, aged 12, died as a result of his injuries. It was not only their deaths that caused public outcry but also the fact that a cynical warning had been telephoned in on behalf of the Provisional IRA claiming that the bomb would be going off in Liverpool, 15 miles away. Security was heightened, and anyone with an Irish connection was regarded with suspicion. The situation worsened on 24 April, when a massive bomb exploded in the City of London, killing freelance photographer Ed Henty, aged thirty-four, married with two children. Elsewhere, there were threats to bomb railway stations.

Billy became paranoid about his passport. Raynor was an Irish name, as was Michael. He was convinced that should he be stopped for even a routine police check, a thorough investigation would be made into his background and his real identity discovered. His friends warned him it was time to get out of the country, but he had major reservations about trying. He could not bear the thought of leaving Lorraine, he desperately wanted to see Willie once more and he dreaded having to show the passport at airport or ferry checks. When news bulletins began carrying items stating that there were to be spot checks on vehicles around London and that anti-terrorist police had placed rings of steel around major cities, ports and airports, he decided there was no chance of him going anywhere.

His paranoia intensified during a chat with a hotel chamber-maid. 'We're approaching the busiest time of the year,' she replied in answer to his casual enquiry about the level of business.

'Oh, why's that?' he asked.

'Well, next week we have a Police Federation conference followed by one for the Prison Officers Association.'

'Really?' he asked, almost choking on his brandy.

He had visions of being joined in the lift by the chief constable of Strathclyde Police or having the chief prison officer from Barlinnie in the next room and decided he had to go, and soon. Friends arranged for him to shuttle between two hotels in Blackpool owned by a leading London crime family and also organised a visit to the resort by his parents. It would be a final chance for them to be together as a family before he moved abroad. Many younger family members arrived, nephews and nieces, some staying in the same hotel as him. It was a special time for Billy, because many of them had been born while he was in jail and the only places where they had met him before were prison visiting rooms. In one or two cases, he had not even met the children yet, and was eager to spend time getting to know them.

Later, he would look back with much happiness on that interlude, knowing that Lorraine's presence had added to the joy of finally being able to act like just another member of any normal family. One day, Billy took her into the centre of town and bought her a diamond engagement ring, an action that thrilled her and delighted her family.

He regularly took half a dozen of the children, all aged 12 and under, to the world-renowned Pleasure Beach, sometimes feeling, as they trailed behind him, as though he were the Pied Piper of Blackpool. He liked having the kids about, sometimes feeling he was able to relax better in their company than in that of adults, who, in his view, tended to ask too many awkward questions about prison, an aspect of his life he was trying to forget. The youngsters loved donkey rides, and on their first experience of this treat, Billy gave the young woman in charge of the animals £20, telling her, 'Give me a shout when the money's used up.' He sat smoking a hash-filled pipe, watching the youngsters laughing and happy, and when the woman told him the money was gone willingly gave her another £20.

Some time later, when she approached again, he reached into his pocket for more cash only to be told, 'No, sir, I've not come for more money. Will you take the kids to the donkeys further along the beach? Mine are tired out and need a rest.'

He burst into laughter. 'Aye, OK,' he said, and shouted to the kids to let the donkeys rest.

He smiled at the prospect of telling his parents, when they arrived, that their grandchildren had ridden the legs off the donkeys at Blackpool. When it was time for the short walk back to the hotels, he decided to give the kids an extra treat by hiring one of the horse-drawn carriages waiting close by. As they clambered in, he gave the name of his hotel and asked the driver, 'How much?'

'Fifty pounds, mate.'

'Aye fucking right! Fifty quid for a three-minute drive for six kids under twelve years of age? You're kidding?'

'No, it's fifty pounds, mate.'

'I don't want to buy the fucking carriage. Stuff it up your arse, pal,' Billy told him.

The children climbed out, burst into laughter and mimicked him, shouting, 'Stuff it up your arse, pal!'

'Come on, kids, let's get a couple of taxis,' he said.

'Yesssss!' they shouted, and he realised how easily pleased children can be.

Later, Billy watched his parents step from their taxi and waited an hour before knocking on their room door. He was itching to tell them about the fun he was having with the children, but he could see they were exhausted after the journey from Glasgow.

'Having them in Blackpool was a dream come true, but when they arrived I thought they looked like my grandparents. For the first time, Ma and Da really seemed old. Through lying in jail so long, I hadn't had time to study them as the years went by. You don't look for frailties in your parents until one day you realise they're ill. Then, if you don't have your freedom, it blows your mind because you become aware of just how helpless you are. That was one of the reasons why I lived each day on the run as though it were my last on earth.'

He treasured the experience of being free to be with them. Until they returned home, he spent time with them each day, slowly walking along the sea front or relaxing over a meal. He thought he had the best of many worlds, having his parents close by, the children to spoil, Lorraine to love and her to love him.

Sometimes Billy, Jenny and Willie would be joined by a man we are calling Dai Wells, an associate of Howard Marks. Welsh-born Marks was a legend in the murky world of international drugs. In 1981, he was acquitted of smuggling 15 tons of cannabis from America into Britain through Scotland. He spent seven years in the Federal Correctional Complex, Terre Haute, Indiana, after a long and expensive operation by the US authorities to trap him. Following his release, he published his autobiography, *Mr Nice* – one of his numerous aliases. Dai was booked into the same hotel as Billy, who did not ask what he was doing in Blackpool. Jenny and Willie took to the Welshman, and the hotel owners would sometimes join the little group for a session of drinks and jokes.

'It was one of the best times I've ever had,' Billy reflects. 'I won't forget the beaming smiles of my mum and dad during that time we had together. But the time flew by too quickly, because I knew it was unlikely I would ever see them together again.'

Billy's brother also came to see Billy and became acquainted with Steve Sinclair. Steve had liked Billy from the outset, not least because the Scot was kind and respectful towards Lorraine. In his excellent book *The Blackpool Rock*, Steve remembers his first meeting with Paul.

> One night, as I was working on the door of the High Society club along with my pal Steve Daley, a taxi pulled up outside. The door opened and two men in suits climbed out. The first one looked like an accountant and the second one like a bank manager. I thought I would be better letting them know that the club was full of young tossers before they let their taxi leave.
>
> Stepping down a step, I said, 'Excuse me, gents, I don't think this club will suit you.'
>
> The accountant turned and looked at me and in a pleasant Scottish accent said, 'Hi, we are looking for Steve Sinclair.'

I looked the pair of them over. They definitely weren't the Old Bill and they didn't seem to be much of a threat.

'I'm Steve Sinclair. What can I do for you?'

The accountant put his hand out to shake mine. 'I'm Paul Ferris and this is Rab Carruthers. I believe you know my brother Billy.'

Paul became a regular visitor to Blackpool, and recalls a family get-together with Billy while the older brother was on the run in the resort. 'A crowd of us, including my sister Carol, my nephew Gary and my son young Paul, decided to visit my younger sister Maureen in Puerto Rico. It was a sort of exodus of the Ferris clan. We were flying from Manchester and had an overnight stay in Blackpool. Billy obviously got wind of where we were and came to have a meal with us in an Italian restaurant. All of a sudden, a camera was produced, photographs were being taken, we were asking one another, "How you doing?" and that sort of thing, then the next day we flew off to Puerto Rico.'

Knowing that Billy was making the most of his freedom gave the holidaymakers an extra reason to enjoy themselves. But for him, the good times were about to come to an end.

29

THE INFORMER

On THURSDAY, 24 JUNE 1993, Billy was daydreaming as he sat in a car driven by a builder friend, Robert 'Rab' Florczyk. They had been parked close to a Blackpool branch of the Bradford & Bingley Building Society. Now, as they waited for traffic lights to change, the Scot glanced in the passenger-side wing mirror and to his alarm and astonishment saw strangers holding guns moving up to the rear and side of their motor. Suddenly, men were screaming, 'Armed police! Don't move! Hold up your hands where we can see them!' and pistols were pointed at their heads. They were dragged out, forced to lie spreadeagled face down on the road and handcuffed before being taken away to a police station.

'I was telling myself, "Here we go back to jail, Billy boy." I had loved every stolen second of being free, and I was never afraid of recapture, because it was inevitable. Nor had I worried about being grassed up, because I believed I had good people around me. Yet at the moment of recapture every emotion went through me, shock, horror, feelings that can be summed up in a single word – dread. I wasn't worried about any charges they'd make against me. My fear was for my ma and da, knowing he was dying. That mattered more to me than spending the remainder of my life in jail.'

Over the next few days, Billy was held in cells at Blackpool police station. He was eventually charged with conspiring to rob the Bradford & Bingley Building Society, possessing firearms, ammunition and controlled drugs, conspiring to rob a mail train, possessing keys for railway cages containing mail, and possession with intent to supply controlled drugs. After hearing the increasing list of charges, Billy told one of his captors, 'This is pure fantasy. These won't stick and you know it. You'd better check Blackpool Tower is still there and I haven't stolen it too.'

When he met up with Rab as the pair prepared for their initial court hearing, he was given news that bewildered him. Guns had been discovered in the car. Rab told him he had found them in an old house he was converting and intended selling them to two Gypsies he had arranged to meet after dropping Billy off. He also said the police had shown him photographs, taken from Lorraine's house, of a man wrapped up in a carpet, his face covered with blood, and asked what he knew about him. Rab told Billy that the police had said that was what Paul would do to him if he didn't take the blame.

Billy told him, 'You've nothing to worry about, Rab. Stick to what you've told them. I know all about the man in the carpet.' He could see terror on the face of the big builder, who was horrified at the prospect of being labelled a gangster. 'Rab, stop worrying. The guy in the carpet isn't being eaten by the fishes off Blackpool pier. He's alive and well. Let them think you're a major-league criminal. I promise it'll pay off for you in court when they can't prove it.'

Both men were remanded to Preston jail. It was Rab's first experience of prison, and his initial impression was that the intention was to starve inmates into submission.

'I'm fucking starving, Bill. Do we get fed?' the 16-stone Lancastrian asked.

Billy joked, 'No chance of grub, Rab. We get bread and water until our visitors bring food up for us. It's because we're on remand. So forget about food for at least 48 hours.'

'Surely not, Bill. I wasn't able to eat during the three days we were at Blackpool police station.'

Billy began shouting, 'A hungry man's an angry man, and we're fucking starving.'

The warders couldn't understand his accent and were asking one another, 'What did he say?' Suddenly, Rab charged towards them. Officers were shouting, 'Calm down, big fellow, calm down,' and Billy told him, 'It's OK, Rab, they'll feed you now.' Turning to the staff, he said, 'My big mate is a diabetic. He needs food to get his sugar level up, otherwise he goes nuts.'

The reply – 'Jock, nobody told us that' – annoyed Billy. He hated the term 'Jock' and shouted back, 'My name is Ferris, not Jock, and it doesn't matter if you weren't told he was a diabetic, this is fucking diabolical. So what about something to eat?'

'Will an omelette do you, big fellow?'

'An omelette, for somebody his size? Don't wind him up,' said Billy, who felt so hungry he'd have been prepared to take a warder hostage up on the roof if it would get him an omelette.

'OK, maybe two of them.'

'What about Bill?' asked Rab.

'Oh, you mean Ferris? He can have the same.'

Rab recovered after eggs and an insulin injection, but was unimpressed by his friend's continued laughter. 'How can you laugh at a time like this?' he demanded.

'Easy – because we're innocent. If there was any truth in the charges or if somebody was dead, I would not be laughing. But there isn't and I am.'

Rab was kept in the remand block of Preston, but because he was on the run Billy was held in the convicted section of the jail. There he met up with a tall, grey-haired, friendly man whose accent reminded him of the famous Goon, Welshman Harry Secombe. 'I was told you had been arrested and to watch out for you. Anything I can do for you, my friend?' he asked.

'I could really do with a pipe of hash.' The newcomer produced an ounce of soft black from his pocket. 'Who do you want murdered?' asked Billy, joking but delighted.

'No, no, no one. It's a present to help you get back on your feet.'

'Back on my feet? I'll be on my fucking back for a fortnight with this.'

He later discovered his benefactor was a good friend of Liverpudlian Stan Carnall, a pal of John Haase and, like Paul, one of many victims of supergrass Dennis Woodman when he was jailed for a drugs offence in 1984. In 1999, Stan was jailed in Scotland for supplying heroin worth more than £663,000. His initial six-year sentence was later extended by appeal court judges to ten. At one stage, he went on hunger strike at Kilmarnock jail in Ayrshire as a protest against the standard of prison food. Billy liked most of his fellow inmates, especially the Welshman who had given him hash. When this man was beaten up by staff, he protested, received a beating himself and was then transferred to Walton jail, Liverpool.

In court, Rab and Billy were joined in the dock by Lorraine, who was charged with harbouring her lover. She will never forget the day of her arrest. 'My friend Diane had called with her daughter, who was playing with a toy elephant and began screaming when we tried to take it from her. Billy had just said he would go out and buy her one when his mate Rab came round with the car. Diane and I decided to go out for lunch to the Welcome pub. We had just ordered a meal and were talking when three men came in, glanced at us and then went to the bar. I don't know how I knew, but I said to Diane, "I think they're CID."

'She said, "No, they're probably businessmen having a pub lunch."

'Two minutes later, one of them came over, asked me if I was Lorraine, showed me his police badge and asked me to walk round the corner with him. I did and he said, "We've got Billy."

'I remember keeping real cool and asking, "What do you mean? What has he done?" My dad and Billy had drummed into me how to act if I was ever arrested and what to say. I was to tell them I thought he was on parole and had no idea he was on the run. The police went on to tell me he was on the run from prison and had killed a guy. Billy had never kept anything about his past a secret from me; I reacted appropriately with mock horror. I then had to tell my friend I was being arrested and ask her to contact my ex-husband so he would pick the kids up from school and kindergarten. She just stared at me with her mouth open.

'They drove me to the police station, where I saw my son in the back of a police van. I went straight up to him, and he told me the police had cordoned off the street and arrested him after knocking him flying when he opened the door. They asked him where Billy and I were and said they had been tipped off by someone who knew he was with me. While they were arresting him, they had been watching Rab's car, which was parked outside the building society in the middle of town. Billy had stupidly asked Rab to wait while he went over the road to the toyshop to buy the bloody elephant. The police searched the car and found a shotgun in the boot. I persuaded them I knew nothing and was told I could go soon.'

Lorraine told police she had only discovered the truth after confronting Billy with newspaper articles about him being on the run, that he'd admitted escaping from prison but that by then she was too much in love to turn him in. She was held in a cell overnight, but then given bail.

'When they let me out of the cell next morning, I was given a throwaway toothbrush and allowed to wash and clean up. A girl was in the washroom and asked what I was in for. When I said, "Harbouring an escaped murderer," she said, "Oh, you'll be on the bus with me to grisly Risley." I'd heard terrible stories about Risley remand centre at Warrington, and my legs felt like jelly. Fortunately, the magistrates allowed me to go home. I was about to leave when the nicest one of the detectives who arrested me said he would let me have a minute with Billy, who was going to be moved to Walton. Billy cuddled me and told me not to worry. "Everything'll be OK," he said, and I believed him.

'The night after my court appearance, I went out to wind down with a few drinks in Stix. The same friend who'd been there the night I first met Billy was with me. A man who had also been there that night introduced us to a Spaniard who came over and joined us. He explained he was on the run from Spain and was wanted for murder. I couldn't believe it. There was me on bail for harbouring a murderer and here I was sitting with another escaped killer. What are the chances of that happening? I began to wonder if every other stranger in Blackpool was an escaped murderer. As you can imagine, we made our excuses and left. Later, I told Billy about it and he found it quite amusing.'

Paul remembers news of the arrest being telephoned to him in Puerto Rico. 'What I didn't know was that when he was arrested he had all these photographs of us on him. When we came back, we touched down at Manchester Airport and, passing through control, a man approached me and asked, "Mr Ferris?" I answered him, "Yes," and he said, "I'd like a word with you." It was the police, who said they were intending to charge me with aiding and abetting an offender and stuff like that. They asked, "When was the last time you saw your brother?" and I gave a non-committal reply such as "No comment" or "Can't remember". It was one of these situations where the guy asking the questions must have felt like a good poker player, knowing he has a winning hand and wanting to flash it but saying nothing. In this case, the winning hand of aces was the photographs of Billy and me with our arms around each other. When he showed me them, I could only say, "Oh, *that* last time I saw my brother."

'I told them, "That was in an Italian restaurant in Blackpool. We had to stop off in Blackpool to give the kids a rest after the trip from Glasgow before the flight from Manchester."

'The police asked, "What did you say to him?"

'"Oh," I said, 'Oh, Billy, what are you doing here? I think you should go and hand yourself back in.'"

'There was a look of astonishment on the guy's face as he slammed his notebook shut. He said, "So it was a case of, of all the restaurants in the world, he happened to walk into the same one where you were?"

'I thought, "Well, you said it," and told him, "Probably, aye. That was it. I'm just glad I gave him that advice. Whether he took it I don't know."'

Billy was in no doubt that he had been the victim of an informer, and that he knew who that was. 'A mate who had come to Blackpool with me had been visiting friends in London, Manchester and Sheffield, and wasn't too pleased with me because I was wanting to stay in most nights. I said to him it was time he returned to his family. I knew he wasn't happy, but I didn't realise how annoyed he was. He loved the nightlife, the women, the drugs and being with villains. He wanted to be an Italian don. We had many a laugh at his Mafia dress sense. But I liked him and was really shattered that he was the one who stuck me in. I never thought he was an informer. In fact, my whole family trusted him, until he betrayed me.'

In a letter to Lorraine, Billy told her that being free and meeting her had altered his outlook on life:

> These experiences have been exhilarating and now I have replenished my whole thoughts on what life is all about. I see things so differently. When strangers speak I no longer suspect they have some ulterior motive for doing so. In prison nobody talks to you without having a reason, while outside you take for granted the ability to chat to someone without having to watch your every word. All

these suspicions have started to disappear, along with the sensation of being institutionalised. It has been refreshing to think nice thoughts, and after our meeting, I dismissed any thoughts of going to live in Spain. I have had a chance to recharge my batteries and feel better equipped for the rest of my sentence.

Lorraine, I always knew I would eventually be caught and taken back, so when that happened it didn't especially bother me. I'd had my memories and a few moments of freedom. Before escaping, I could never imagine what it would be like to be released, and frankly I had lost hope. For so long I have lived like an animal in the jungle, bitterness and hate eating away at me, but now prison has no fears because I've tasted freedom and know what to look forward to. I've cast out my demons.

What of Lorraine? She is now married and living happily in Australia, but her memories remain crystal clear and joyful, despite her night in the cells and receiving an 18-month conditional discharge with a £35 fine for harbouring Billy. 'The six weeks he lived with me were the happiest of my life. He treated me and the kids wonderfully and they adored him. My mum and dad thought the world of him as well. Of the boyfriends I had introduced to them, he was the only one that they liked. There was never a dull moment with Billy. After only a couple of days, I was hooked on him, and I remember telling my mum that I thought so much of him that if the police turned up and tried to shoot him, I would stand in the way because I wouldn't want to live without him. In court, the judge said it was a crime of passion. I think he felt sorry for me because I had never been in trouble before.'

Lorraine visited Billy in Walton jail, and after he was transferred to Perth she often travelled north with help from Paul, Steve and members of Billy's family. Occasionally, she stayed with Willie and Jenny or one of Billy's sisters. 'They were all lovely people. I carried on visiting Billy for more than four years. During that time, I was often visited by the drugs squad. They never found anything because I wasn't into drugs at all.

'Eventually, though, I had to tell Billy that I had met somebody else. When I heard he had been released and was married, I was happy for him. But I was devastated when I learned he had been accused of murdering a teenager, because Billy absolutely loved kids of all ages, and my instinct was that he had been set up.'

Billy, waiting in Walton jail to be returned to Scotland, would ultimately be proved right when he scoffed at the charges police proposed pressing. But before then, he had a visit from police who had travelled from Scotland suspecting another murder had been added to their list of unsolved crimes.

30

THE CARPETBAGGER

BILLY KNEW POLICE WOULD BE desperate to discover what lay behind six Polaroid photographs found in Lorraine's home, apparently showing a blood-covered man, dead and wrapped in a carpet. So the arrival at Blackpool police station from Glasgow of two senior detectives was no surprise. They introduced themselves, but Billy failed to catch their names and in any case instantly decided to nickname them Hoddit and Doddit. He could see they were keen to get their questioning of him under way, and had the look, he thought, of punters with a huge bet on a horse guaranteed to win. He was convinced they were sure that before long they would be charging him with a murder on evidence no jury could reject.

'Billy, we are here to ask you about photographs found in your case in a house where you were staying in Blackpool,' said Hoddit, pushing the brightly coloured snaps across the interview-room desk. He received no reply and carried on with the interrogation. 'The man in the photographs – who is he?'

'I'm not prepared to say.'

'It's OK, Billy, we know who he is.'

'Fine, then. Why ask me?'

The detectives gave the correct name. We will call the man in the carpet Ronald Burns. Then they asked, 'Is he alive?'

'Why ask me? If you know him, ask him.'

'That's just it, Billy. We can't find him.'

'Well, I don't work for the missing persons bureau, so it's a waste of time asking me.'

'Would you agree he looks injured and in a very bad state and is rolled up in a carpet?'

239

'No.'

'No? It certainly looks that way to us. In all six photographs he appears to be dead.'

'Maybe he's a pervert who's into carpets and has just spanked himself to sleep.'

'Billy, this is a serious matter. This man appears to have been tortured. His face is covered in blood. Don't you agree?'

'No. Pictures can be deceiving.'

'Did you take these photographs?'

'No. I'm not Lord Lichfield.'

'Will you tell us where the camera is that was used to take these photographs?'

'Aye, Boots. You can buy one of them at any Boots branch.'

'Billy, we're not getting anywhere, so let's cut the crap. Is this man dead or alive?'

'Why do you want to know?'

'So we can determine if it's murder or abduction.'

'Has he been reported missing?'

'No, not yet.'

'Not yet? What kind of answer is that? Either he's missing or he's not.'

'We cannot find him and these photographs give us cause to be concerned about him.'

'Ronald's a crook and you don't give a fuck if he's dead or alive. Photographs can be deceiving, depending on how you look at them. My theory is that he might be a carpet pervert. I could give you more ideas, but you seem stuck on the view that there's something sinister about the whole thing.'

'That's not our view, but the view of the police in Blackpool who found the photographs. It's at their request that we are here to interview you.'

'Well, then, you'll be pig sick when he turns up on his flying carpet. Maybe he's rehearsing *Sinbad the Sailor* and fell off at the Pavilion Theatre. Have you looked there?'

'Billy, you're doing yourself no favours with this attitude. The forensic team are confident it's only a matter of time before they identify the house where the photographs were taken.'

'Good, then you'll be gutted when you find out they're souvenirs of Ronnie the Carpet on a dirty weekend in Blackpool.'

'You should think very carefully over the next few hours. Clearly you don't realise the seriousness of your situation.'

'Hey, I'm not the one wrapped up in the carpet playing hide and seek with you. Ronald's a crook and it's obvious he doesn't want to see you.'

'One last thing – are you friendly with Ronald?'

'Am I friendly with him? He has no friends.'

He was taken back to his cell, determined to keep the farce going. The next morning, he faced the two detectives again.

'Billy, things are not looking too well for you at this point. So help yourself and cooperate by telling us where we can find Ronald Burns.

'Do you know Blackpool's North Pier?'

'No, but we can get a local officer in who does. Do you mind?'

'No, the more the merrier.'

'Coffee or tea, Billy?'

'Aye, coffee. And a roll and sausage. I'm hungry.'

Minutes later, a mug of coffee in one hand and roll and sausage in the other, he and the two Glasgow policemen were joined by an officer from Blackpool whom we will call Sergeant Crook.

'Billy, he's here because he knows the local area.'

'OK, but is that his real name?'

Sergeant Crook confirmed that was the case but did not look amused by Billy's grin. Hoddit and Doddit resumed. 'OK, Billy, when we asked you to tell us where we could find Ronald Burns, you asked if we knew the North Pier, intimating that you might be trying to suggest an area where we should look. Is this correct?'

'Yes.'

'Tell Sergeant Crook precisely where you mean.'

'The North Pier of the Pleasure Beach. Just before you go along it, there's a fortune teller who does readings for the stars. She has loads of photographs of celebrities on her walls. Do you know where I mean?'

'Yes. Go on, Billy, I know that place.'

'Well, do you know her?'

'Yes, go on.'

'And you know the front of her premises?'

'Yes, yes, carry on.'

'And you know how you pass her receptionist to get into the room where she operates?'

'Yes, yes, come on.'

'You've definitely got the woman I'm talking about?'

'Yes.'

'Well, go right into her office.'

'Yes.'

'And ask her . . .'

'Yes, yes.'

'. . . where he is, because she has more chance than me of knowing.'

His laughter infuriated the three policemen. Doddit screamed at him, 'This isn't funny, as you'll find out,' while Crook kicked over his chair and stormed out of the interview room.

'Can I have another coffee and a roll and sausage?' asked Billy, before he was dragged back to his cell.

So what was the truth behind the photos of the man in the carpet? 'Strathclyde Police knew as soon as they saw the photographs that the head sticking out of the end of the carpet belonged to Ronald Burns, 'Ronnie the Fence'. He was a career criminal, well known throughout the underworld and to the police. When he hadn't been seen for a while, police began door-to-door enquiries and that set off gossip to the effect that he was off the numbers, murdered. His description was circulated to other forces, and somebody in Blackpool remembered seeing his face in the carpet photographs. So they had a missing person and photos of an apparently dead man wrapped in a carpet, his face covered in blood, in the house where an escaped murderer was living. They reckoned it was only a matter of time before the body turned up.

'What really happened was that while I was on the run in Blackpool, I was having a drink with some good pals from Manchester when the phone went for one of them. I heard him say, "I'm in Blackpool with an old pal from the jail. When are you going up north? OK, yeah, sure thing." After he hung up, he said, "Sorry, Bill, that was my partner. A prick from your neck of the woods pulled a fast one on us for a few thousand pounds last year. Now we've got an address for him and he's going to pay big time for fucking us." I asked him for the guy's name and he said, "Ronald somebody. I'll phone my mate back to get his surname," but I said, "No need. It's Burns. I know him."

'Then he asked me, "Bill, could you do us a massive favour?" and I said, without knowing what it was, that whatever they wanted done they should consider it carried out.

'He said that after finding out about the sucker stroke they telephoned Ronald, who told them two guys called Joe Hanlon and Bobby Glover had just been murdered. According to him, Glasgow was in the middle of a war and if any of them arrived sniffing about and asking questions, they would not be going back down south alive. He had hung up and then changed his number, and it took them more than a year to find out where he was.

'I said, "I'll phone a pal and find out how Ronald is for money. If he's skint, there's no use going to Glasgow to try getting cash out of him." However, my pal told me Ronald was flush and agreed to help lure him to Blackpool, provided nothing heavy was going to happen.

'My friends booked me into the Piccadilly Hotel in Manchester and introduced me to the guy Ronald had bumped for money. He was really angry and said Ronald would pay his dues in cash and flesh. I said I could have him tricked into travelling to Blackpool, where I'd meet up with him and shock him with as little violence as possible into paying up. And I told him, "Once you have your money, you can visit him in Scotland if you're still in a mind to do him damage." He asked my friends what they thought, and they told him, "Billy will get you a result."

'The next day, I called Glasgow. I was going fishing for Ronnie the Fence and I just hoped he would take the bait. Our story was that a drug dealer from Fleetwood had been jailed and faced losing his assets, which included a brand-new £40,000 speedboat, and that his wife was willing to sell the boat for a fraction of the value before the police discovered it. We made sure this tale reached Ronald, who, immediately he heard about the chance to make a quick fortune, was hooked. He promised to be in Blackpool later that same afternoon.

'Before he arrived, I rehearsed with the others what would happen and their roles in it. I met him and took him to a house in Fleetwood, where he was shocked to find four guys waiting, not realising that among them was one of the victims he had ripped off. All he could say was, "Billy, Billy, what's this all about?" Then he was grabbed and tied up. He was too shattered to resist and blurted out, "Billy, I've done nothing to deserve this."

'I told him, "Ronald, you're a conman to the end, but you won't talk your way out of this one." Then I told the others, "Roll him up in the carpet." When they did, I pulled the carpet down from his head to let him speak. He looked like an Eskimo. I said, "Now listen, Ronald, your car will be driven back to Glasgow and parked outside your house. The only person who will miss you will be your wife and by the time she realises you've gone nobody will know where you are."

'We'd arranged that only I would speak to Ronald and there would be no violence. I'd bought a bottle of sauce – HP, which I thought was appropriate as this was all about a debt – and I threw some over Ronald's face and took Polaroid photographs, which I showed to him. Then I told him, "Cut the crap about not knowing what this is all about. I'm going to give you some time to think and then you had better be prepared to do the right thing and return the money with interest, otherwise this is how you will look. You let these guys think you were involved in a war and threatened they would get done like Bobby and Joe, two friends of mine." He begged to speak to his wife, but I refused to let him talk to anybody until the money was repaid.

'I gagged him and pulled the carpet around his head. One of the others had been primed to ask why he had to be wrapped up in the carpet, and I raised my voice so Ronald could hear and said, "Simple. If I shoot him through the carpet, it'll absorb all the blood and save us the trouble of cleaning up afterwards." Ronald was wriggling about like a giant caterpillar, moving up and down the room. We had to go into the kitchen so he wouldn't hear us laughing.

'After ten minutes, I pulled the carpet back down. He was drenched in sweat and gasping for air, and I told him I wanted an answer immediately. Was he going to pay up? He asked to make a phone call. We agreed and when it was made he promised the money would be handed over within an hour to one of our friends in Glasgow. I said he would only be released once the money was in our hands. Just under an hour later, we had a phone call from Scotland to say the money had been delivered and our friend was driving to Blackpool with it. When he arrived, I gave Ronald £200 for a taxi back to Glasgow. The others said I'd been over-generous and that he should have been given 200 stitches, until I pointed out it was counterfeit cash that a friend had bought months before. Later on, we heard Ronald got home and kept his head down for a few weeks before reappearing with some cock-and-bull story about where he had been.'

31

. . . .

THE FERRIS GOLD EXPRESS CARD

SHORTLY AFTER BEING MOVED TO Walton, Billy was told that his father was in intensive care in Glasgow. He was allowed special permission to speak to Willie by telephone. As the phone was held to his mouth, Willie whispered to his son, 'I love you, Billy.'

'Da, don't leave me,' begged Billy, but Willie had the strength only to say, 'I'm tired, son, really tired.' They were the last words spoken between father and son. In the early hours, Willie passed away. Prison authorities in Liverpool offered to arrange for Billy to attend the funeral. But then came a bombshell. Both the Scottish Office and Strathclyde Police refused to allow him to be there. The funeral was delayed while Paul fought for a change of heart, but eventually Jenny had to ask Billy, 'How much longer must we keep your da in that cold mortuary?' He knew the right thing was to allow the funeral to go ahead, but he would never forgive or forget being kept away.

The death of his father still hurts. 'Da had the heart of a lion and never hurt anyone. He treated people as they treated him. He is forever on my mind, forever in my heart. He travelled thousands of miles to see me, sacrificed his last pound for a visit. There were so many ways in which he showed his love. I could never stand in my da's shoes. He epitomised all that was good in my life, and when he died I lost not just my dad but my best friend. When I ran away, the motive was solely so that I could spend time with my parents. Only a fool would run away after 17 years without a good reason. After such a long time locked up, most men would be glad to know they were on the verge of freedom. I saw no light at the end of the tunnel, though. I was in the pits of despair. There seemed no way out and I wanted new memories because spending so much time in solitary thinking about the past meant I had all but exhausted the ones of our early family life together. At least those memories had helped me get through.

'Had I still been on the run at the time he slipped away, I would have made sure I was at his bedside even if it meant being recaptured. I realised escape meant my chances of being allowed to go to his funeral were zero, so I never really looked for sympathy or decency. I knew there would be none, for I had seen none when Billy Armstrong was not allowed to go to the funeral after the death of his father.'

Billy remained at Walton while the investigation into claims that he had been planning an armed robbery on the building society continued. In April 1994, he was returned to Perth jail.

That year, he learned on the grapevine that escapee John Bowden had been recaptured when a giro-cheque scam with a former prison friend was uncovered. Bowden had been jailed for life in England in 1982 with a recommendation that he should serve at least 25 years for killing and beheading a London park keeper. A year later, he was given a further ten years for his part in an incident in which the assistant governor of Parkhurst prison, an establishment well known to Billy, had been taken hostage. In 1992, he went on the run from Maidstone, another of Billy's former prisons, during a home visit to see his sick father. He made his way to Edinburgh, where he called himself John Harvey, met secretary Alice Still and apparently vanished into thin air. The authorities had vowed not to stop searching for him.

On his recapture, John ended up at Perth with Billy. He and Alice were married in the prison. Paul Ferris arranged for flowers and a cake for their big day, and even a piper to pipe in the bride from the gate. Prison authorities put a block on that, but the wedding went off without a hitch. Although John was eventually sent back to prison in England, he later returned to Scotland.

In March 1995, almost two years after his escape, Billy appeared at Glasgow Sheriff Court where he was convicted of attempting to defeat the ends of justice and jailed for two years, to be served alongside his life sentence. Nothing further was heard of the other allegations. Rab was not so lucky. Despite telling the truth about the weapons, he was jailed for five years. He earned considerable respect for not having tried to pin the blame on Billy.

As Billy was driven from court, he reflected on having been in prison almost 19 years. He might with some justification have felt rueful and wondered about justice after reading of the further exploits of Brian Doran. In 1993, while Billy was on the run, it was discovered by accident during an undercover drugs investigation that Doran was in Colombia, the cocaine-producing capital of South America, where he was known as 'El Jock'. The result was a major surveillance operation – Operation Stealer – on him and his associates, including Tony White, whom Billy had known in Maidstone. In 1995, Doran and a Scottish pal, Kenneth Togher, were jailed for 25 years. White was sentenced to 11 years. Good fortune favoured them, however, when the convictions and sentences were quashed because it was ruled that customs officers had illegally bugged a hotel room used by Togher.

Doran's one-time employer Walter Douglas had also been busy. In 1994, he was arrested in Holland and given four years for smuggling after the discovery of one of the biggest ever hauls of hashish – eighteen tons – when customs officers intercepted the ship *Great Alexander* off the coast of Africa. He appealed and was bailed but did not hang around to await the outcome of any hearing, heading to Spain, where he settled. Two years later, Spanish police were tipped off that Walter was living in Fuengirola and turned up in force to arrest him. Unfortunately, they arrived at the wrong house, and by the time they realised the mistake their quarry, hearing shouted commands and the din of doors being battered in, had made off. These were men who had travelled the world as a consequence of criminal enterprises. Billy's journey was less exotic. Approaching his 45th birthday and reckoning it was time he returned home, he became a model prisoner.

In November 1995, he was transferred to Gateside jail in Greenock, where he was reunited with many old friends and others not on his list of favourites. Among the former were Ronnie Neeson, a friend we are calling David and Paul McGovern of the well-known Glasgow family, a friend of Paul.

On one occasion, David was allowed a home leave, and when he returned told them of having spent an hour on a bouncy castle. Because of the length of time they had been in prison, the others had never seen a bouncy castle. They thought David was boasting about a marathon sex session with a well-built girlfriend.

'Aye, right. Away wi yerself,' Ronnie said.

'No, I was on and off about 15 times,' David protested. 'Honestly, I've even got photographs.'

'For fuck's sake, she's not shy, is she?' asked Billy.

'What do you mean?'

'Your girlfriend, letting you take pictures.'

'Billy, she wasn't there.'

'What! Not there? Well, who was it you were shagging?'

'I wasn't shagging anybody.'

'Well, what the fuck is a bouncy castle if it isn't your girlfriend?'

David was annoyed. 'That's out of order, calling her that.' From then on until he and the girl split up, she was always referred to as 'the bouncy castle'.

Billy also renewed his friendship with Donald Forbes, the recipient of the last-minute reprieve whom he'd met in Peterhead, and made the acquaintance of Tony Quigley. Tony was serving life for murder, but there were many who argued he should not have been in prison. In 1984, Glasgow-born antiques dealer John Ward had been shot dead. After the killing, Tony's brother Desmond went on the run. In his absence, Tony, despite producing witnesses who said he had been elsewhere at the time of the shooting, was convicted and jailed. Desmond gave himself up and, after admitting he was the killer, was sentenced to life imprisonment. He swore an affidavit saying that Tony was innocent.

Billy wondered at the inconsistency of the law. John Haase had been the beneficiary of a remarkable judgment. In 1995, he and his nephew Paul Bennett were each jailed for 18 years for running a highly organised international gang that smuggled millions of pounds' worth of heroin into Britain. The trial judge said, 'It is rare that courts deal with people so high up the ladder as you, and it must be marked by a heavy sentence.' But only 11 months later, the pair were free, released by then Home Secretary Michael

Howard after he received a letter from the judge saying customs officers had had enormous help from the pair, who had tipped them off about major arms stashes. In fact it later emerged that the weapons had been planted by their pals.

Billy began home leaves, and during the first of these his life changed dramatically. A friend nicknamed 'Versace', because he was always nattily dressed, and his wife took him along to a club in Irvine. Versace, a one-time safe-robber, was a well-known party animal who blew a fortune in his search for fun. As Billy made his way to the bar, his eye fell on a tall, dark-haired young woman chatting to friends. He was instantly struck by her smile, which seemed to broaden whenever their eyes met. He had never seen her before in his life but knew he had to meet her. He found an excuse to be near her, and when they began talking it was as though no one else existed. He felt as if he had been in a coma and had suddenly come to life to find her smiling at him. That night, Billy fell in love. 'I loved her the minute I first saw her and told her within the first minute of our meeting that she was gorgeous. I knew we'd meet again, and from that moment I spent every leave with her.'

The spark that became love's flame burns equally fiercely within Carol-Anne, and her memories are just as vivid. 'He bought all my friends a drink, but when he asked if I would like one I told him, "No, thank you." I was single, divorced with two boys, and felt men who wanted to buy you a drink really wanted something else. But we exchanged phone numbers, and later that night when I was at home he rang me. He has telephoned me every day since.

'I didn't know who he was and had never heard of Paul. But as we got to know one another Billy told me everything about himself and Paul. My family was wary, and when I told them who I was seeing they warned me, "Don't go down that road." I could have walked away at the very start. I had never been in trouble, never set foot inside a courtroom, and nor had my family. But I was so attracted to Billy, because of his honesty about himself, his laugh and the way he constantly cracked jokes.

'I visited him in Greenock, but only once. He said he had a half-day on the outside, so I went to meet him. We had a few drinks and then booked into a hotel. After a couple of hours, Billy said he had to get back to prison. I said I'd go with him but he told me, "You'll need to walk ten paces behind me." I asked, "What do you mean?" and he said, "I'm overdue. They'll be out looking for me now. If they catch the two of us together, they'll pull you in." I never went back to visit him there again.

'Later on, I found out that before joining me he had been told his latest parole application had been rejected on the grounds that he was an alcoholic. A man who had been in prison 20 years told he had a drink problem. That didn't make sense, but what did was that had Billy been freed, it would have meant him being able to rejoin Paul. It seemed to me that the police didn't want them on the streets at the same time.'

In any case, the possibility of such a situation arising was about to be extinguished. Paul had been under sporadic surveillance ever since his acquittal at the Arty Thompson murder trial. Was it coincidence that now, as reasons for continuing to imprison his brother crumbled, the level of that surveillance was stepped up? Whatever the motive for the increasing police interest in him, he was arrested in London in May 1997. Following a tip-off, guns had been found in his car.

Billy was distraught at the news but helpless to do anything. He felt he could best aid Paul by being on the outside, so persisted with his pleas to be freed. He was even backed by a prison-service supervisor, who, in an official report on prisoner 6891's progress in 1996, said, 'Nineteen years would seem to be an inordinate length of time to serve for a murder when the prisoner would appear in recent years to have been of reasonably good behaviour.' It was clearly a view shared by others. Another report, this to the Parole Board for Scotland, sympathised with Billy's view that he was known as 'the Ferris Gold Express Card'. It said that he felt enemies of Paul made outrageous allegations against him to curry favour with prison staff and get transfers to other jails on the grounds that when the brothers discovered the identities of informers, they would cause the culprits severe grief. The same report also pointed out that parents of disabled children had written thanking Billy for the furniture and toys he had made, including an ingenious feeding table and chair for a child with no arms.

Finally, a glimmer of hope appeared. In November 1997, Billy was transferred to Noranside open jail, the same prison from where Arty Thompson had made his final journey more than six years previously. The move, usually a precursor to freedom, had been delayed because of allegations made by Toe Elliott against Billy and Paul. There were many who felt Toe had been slow in trying to help Ronnie Neeson by clearing him of involvement in the murder for which the two men were serving life. The Ferris brothers were known to be friends with Ronnie, and Elliott said that he was afraid of reprisals from them. Toe was already at Noranside, and Billy was forced to wait until he could be moved to Penninghame.

At Noranside, he met former public schoolboy Paul Macklin, jailed in 1994 for eight years after being convicted of conspiring to rob employees of Aberdeen District Council's contract services division of their wages. Macklin had once been a pupil at Gordonstoun, the world-famous school near Elgin, Moray, where Prince Charles had studied. That had earned Paul the nickname 'the Yuppie Robber'. Billy took Macklin and a group of other inmates out for a run one evening during a blizzard. The younger man put his foot in a rabbit hole and instantly his ankle began swelling, giving rise to fears it was broken. 'It's as well it happened now, Paul,' Billy told him. 'There's no shortage of ice to put on the swelling.'

In July 1998, Paul was sentenced initially to 15 years until it was pointed out to the judge that he had exceeded his powers. The sentence was reduced to ten and then further lowered to seven on appeal. Among Paul's fellow accused was Henry Suttee, the father-in-law of Ben Alagha. Paul was initially held at Belmarsh jail in London, where other major-risk inmates included Charles Bronson. He was then moved to Full Sutton near York before ending at Frankland.

As liberty loomed large for Billy, so also it did for Alexander Hall, his fellow inmate at Perth, who, astonishingly considering the vile nature of his supposed crime, had survived prison relatively unscathed. There had long been doubts over the reliability of the evidence of a crucial Crown witness, and Hall, who had been imprisoned in 1988, was finally granted a retrial in May 1999. He went free when the jury returned a not proven verdict.

Billy was by this time firmly established in a loving relationship with Carol-Anne, and enquiries on behalf of the Parole Board had confirmed that she looked forward to welcoming him into her home when he was freed. Paul was in Frankland prison on 1 June 1999, when Billy was finally released. He was still on licence and therefore liable to be hauled back to jail for the slightest infringement. But he was free.

He ruefully reflected that the same was not true of many men he had known during the past 23 years, among them the railway-depot robber Alan Brown. Like Billy, Brown had found he could not rely on the judge's tariff as a reasonable guide to his release date. His target date was 1999, but he had discovered that hope could be a futile sentiment for those in jail. Disheartened at being told by the Parole Board that he would not be given parole until 2003 at the earliest, he went on the run three months before Billy walked to freedom. While working on day release from Saughton prison in a café in Edinburgh, he absconded and headed to Brighton, changing his name to Power and masquerading as a wealthy businessman. His freedom lasted just eight months. By chance, his fake name cropped up during a police investigation into a car-ringing gang, and when he was forced to give his fingerprints his true identity emerged. Billy found it hard to suppress a grim smile when he heard that Brown was held at Lewes jail, the scene of so many varied memories, to await his sentence. He would find nobody in any hurry to decide his further punishment.

Billy liked Brown, who, he knew, harboured a desperate desire for liberty and happiness. Billy now had the first and was about to embrace the second. Four and a half months after he walked to freedom, he committed himself to life with Carol-Anne.

32

. . . .

THE SPY

MEN AND WOMEN WHO HAVE served long prison sentences can discover that freedom only brings more problems, not the least of which are finding a home and a job. In this respect, Billy believed he was lucky. Not only did he have the love and support of Carol-Anne but he had too the promise of work from Ben Alagha, who was managing the Watermill Hotel in Paisley and Rico's Restaurant in Glasgow. 'I owe you my life, brother,' Alagha said. 'What's mine is yours. I am here to keep my promise to you.'

Such a proposition from a man Billy trusted and in whose sincerity he believed was manna from heaven. The job was to act as an assistant to Alagha. On one occasion, he accompanied his new boss to a meeting with representatives of the Teamsters union in Las Vegas to discuss marketing a newly invented form of identity card. Then, in 2000, Alagha and a group of associates including a wealthy and well-known English entrepreneur became interested in research into a means of eradicating mosquitoes. A scientist believed he had discovered that by spraying a chemical used for breaking up oil slicks over marshes where mosquitoes were known to incubate the malaria-carrying insects could be wiped out. One government showing interest was that of South Africa, and to impress the authorities there a number of well-known figures in business and politics were invited to a conference at the Bridge Hotel in Epsom in the hope of involving them. Later, the anti-malarial scheme came under scrutiny from South African police.

If it all seemed too good to be true, it was. Alagha was spying for UK law-enforcement agencies, and his targets included the Ferris brothers. Ignorant of this deceit, Billy worked on and found time to keep up with the comings and goings of some of those he had known in the past. He seemed to be forever reading of the further downfall of someone he had known in prison. Mostly, the news saddened him, but not always.

One exception was Frank McPhie, Arty Thompson's one-time bodyguard. In 1997, McPhie was in Perth prison, nearing the end of an eight-year stretch for drug dealing, when he was accused of involvement in the stabbing dead of lifer William 'Worm' Toye. A jury returned a not proven verdict, but just three months later, McPhie was again accused of murder. The victim this time, Christopher McGrory, was found strangled and half-naked in the back of a van on a lonely road near Milngavie on the outskirts of Glasgow. Two weeks earlier, McPhie had been an usher at McGrory's wedding.

Just as police in the Toye case had been confident of a conviction only to be disappointed at the outcome, so were officers now, because once more McPhie walked from the dock, having heard the jury give a not proven verdict. But the number of his enemies was growing. In May 2000, he was driving a van in Glasgow when he became aware that he was being followed. Not realising that he was being chased into a well-worked-out trap, he drove to his home in Maryhill. But as he leapt out and ran to safety, a sniper was waiting on a nearby building, and McPhie died from a single shot to the chest, some saying this was the penalty for falling out with a well-known Glasgow crime clan.

That same month, Sydney Draper staged yet another escape, this time from Spring Hill jail in Buckinghamshire, but was again recaptured. That year also saw the highly publicised arrest of Terry Millman, who had regularly visited Billy in Scotland. Terry was apprehended by police investigating one of the most audacious robberies ever attempted in Britain. A gang had smashed into the Millennium Dome using a JCB and armed with a nail gun, a hammer, smoke bombs and a Catherine wheel firework. Their target was the De Beers Millennium Collection, a handful of diamonds valued at between £200 million and £350 million, including the world's most perfect gem, the Millennium Star. But police had been tipped off, and more than 100 officers, many armed, were waiting.

The gang was caught and it included Terry, who was suffering from terminal cancer of the stomach and lungs. He had joined the raiders knowing he would never benefit but determined to leave a nest egg for his family. In fact, he was so ill that he would never face trial, being freed on compassionate grounds to die in July with his family around him. 'I was completely shattered to hear of Tel's death,' remembers Billy. 'He was the life and soul of the company, never moody, down or rude to anybody. Just a great guy with perfect manners, one of the Frankie Fraser school, where the message was a simple one: "Put up or shut up." Not for them veiled threats. Terry was a real diamond geezer among the paste characters with whom gangland is filled.'

As Terry was dying, Freddie Sewell was finally released, while Billy's old friend Alan Brown was being jailed for another three and a half years at Lewes Crown Court for drugs offences. Reading of that brought back memories of meetings with John Murphy and Jim Aitken, two men Billy respected, but his thoughts were tinged with sadness when he discovered the big Irishman had died in hospital.

Billy's sense of humour had helped him to survive the long years of imprisonment and, as others discovered, it was an asset he retained, although it wasn't always appreciated. In March 2000, drug dealers Gerald Donnelly and Kenneth Murray, from Ayrshire, were whooping it up at the posh Cameron House Hotel on the banks of Loch Lomond. Their scruffy appearance attracted suspicion and someone called the police, who opened up their car and found an astonishing cache of weapons, including a sub-machine pistol, as well as £500,000 worth of heroin and £40,000 in cash. The pair had been so indiscreet that a senior detective tagged them 'Dumb and Dumber'. Billy was with friends when Donnelly's wife rang one of them to pass on the news of her husband's arrest and ask if he could help by picking up a change of clothing for him and Murray and collecting a pit bull terrier from a police pound. The dog had been discovered in the car, apparently protecting the contents of the boot.

'I offered to go along for the drive,' says Billy, 'and we collected the wives, who were understandably distraught, sobbing in the back of the motor. Just to try to settle them, my friend suggested they might get to see their menfolk, but I thought, "Fat chance of that. No way."

'Gerry's wife collected the dog from the police kennels and it sat between the women. By now, the police had refused to let them see their husbands, which made them even more upset. As we drove them home, I had a pipe of hash, which made me feel better, and as I drew in one lungful after another I saw out of the corner of my eye the pit bull staring at me in the rear-view mirror. I blew out hash smoke and said to my friend who was trying to jolly the atmosphere, "Don't you think it's funny that the dog was released without bail? I bet it put its paws up and grassed the guys just so it could get out." Just then, I spotted a roadside sign indicating there was a lay-by half a mile ahead. I said to my friend, "Pull over and I'll do the dog in with your car jack for grassing the guys." My pal pulled into the lay-by and both women screamed, "Don't you dare," and tried protecting the dog with their bodies. I couldn't believe it. They were serious. But then they saw the funny side and we all ended up splitting our sides with laughter. At least the joke cheered the women up.'

So Billy continued to enjoy his freedom, a gift Archie Hall, the murdering Glaswegian butler, would never again experience. He published his autobiography, *A Perfect Gentleman*, in 1999 and died from a stroke in Kingston prison, Portsmouth, in 2002, aged 78. Unlike him, Andy Walker, the army payroll killer, had some good news. His sentence of 30 years was reduced to 27. Billy, meanwhile, was about to find life was getting serious.

Ben Alagha lived under the constant fear of falling out so badly with his intelligence handlers that they would sever their links with him, leaving him vulnerable to deportation. With a view to getting an Irish passport, he asked Billy to arrange a meeting with one of his friends from prison who was living in Ireland. The friend agreed to the request as a special favour to Billy.

Just three and a half months after his release in January 2002, Paul ended up back in prison, recalled after a series of unsubstantiated allegations by Strathclyde Police, including his having been spotted in the vicinity of a suspected drug dealer. He was held at Frankland jail for six weeks before the Home Office threw in the towel in the face of an onslaught from his bright lawyer Lisa French. Paul was then invited by Alagha to spend a few days with him in London. It seemed an act of kindness.

On the night of 5 February 2003, Billy had arranged to meet Paul at the New Morven bar in Springburn, Glasgow. It was the spot where Tony McGovern, a member of the family who had a hand in running the bar, had been shot dead in 2000. Billy had already visited a few pubs in Glasgow in the company of Lance McGuiness. They waited at the New Morven, but when Paul failed to show up returned to Irvine, where the brothers finally caught up with each other.

The following day, a murder hunt began following the discovery of the body of schoolboy Jason Hutchison.

One night in March, Billy and Carol-Anne were at home. She had no fears for the future of her marriage. 'I knew Billy wouldn't bring us trouble. The boys had never been in trouble, and he had warned that if they stepped out of line, he would get somebody to leather them. He said to them, "If either of you do something that gets the jail, I know somebody in every prison and I'll make sure you're taught a lesson that guarantees you never go back again."

'I looked out of the window at eight o'clock that morning and saw the house surrounded by scores of police. Suddenly, they were banging on the front and back doors. Then, without waiting for an answer, they stormed in. Billy hid down the side of the bed. The police asked me, "Where's Billy?" and I said, "No idea. He never came in last night." But about five minutes later they came downstairs holding Billy in handcuffs. I plucked up the nerve to ask him, "How did you get up there?" He just laughed. The police looked at me as if to say, "Liar."

'They kept trying to throw my dog out of the house as they searched everywhere, ripping out drawers and scattering everything we had over the floor. One policeman kept tapping the dog on the head, and I warned him, "Stop doing that or he'll bite." The guy wouldn't listen, with the result that the dog ripped his sleeve. He was furious. I said, "I told you," and a policewoman said, "She did tell you not to do that." The boys and I were taken to the police station, where I insisted on continuing the interview without a break because I knew that meant the police couldn't have one either. They were raging because they missed their lunch and tea breaks. We were there for 12 hours.'

Having been charged with murder, Billy awaited his trial. He heard that Donald Forbes was again back in prison, given

12 years for a drugs offence. Like Archie Hall, Donald would never again taste freedom. Rab Carruthers had been released in 2003 but a year later was found dead in his Glasgow flat. The news of both men was distressing, but there was worse to come. Billy discovered with horror that he had been betrayed by Ben Alagha.

Billy had befriended and looked after Alagha in Maidstone, but now he told himself that had he known the truth about the portly, balding Iranian, he would have felt safer being cooped up in a cage filled with scorpions. In a signed Statement of Fact made in September 2002, Alagha stated that one of his names, Seyed, indicated that he was directly descended from the Prophet Muhammad. On his maternal side, he was related to the Qajar family who ruled Persia for 200 years until they were overthrown in 1924. His father's grandfather, the Agha, was the Grand Ayatollah and head of the Muslims in Persia before it became Iran. He had been educated in Iran and India, studying political science and law.

After graduating, he started work as an analyst in the anti-terrorist and counter-intelligence division of SAVAK, the secret service. From there, he saw service as a legal adviser to the then Persian rulers. With their overthrow in 1979, he decided it was time to save his hide and leave. He settled in Britain, bringing with him a talent for deceit and fraud. In 1982, he was jailed for seven years for handing a glass containing Lemsip cold cure to a twenty-five-year-old secretary after spiking it with a drug that left her defenceless when he raped her. That offence was the equivalent of a death sentence, because it was accompanied by a deportation order, meaning that when his time in prison was over he would be sent back to Iran, where the mullahs, led by Ayatollah Khomeini, were waiting to take revenge on SAVAK operatives.

A year later, Alagha was given 20 years for his part in an arms sting, in the same case in which Dogan Arif was acquitted. It was while serving that sentence that he had met Billy and through him Paul. As the years drifted past and freedom neared, so did the likelihood of his dangling at the end of a rope hanging from the jib of a crane in Tehran. Alagha set about saving himself by becoming a spy. In a Statement of Fact, he stated that he began working for law-enforcement agencies in the hope that it would help him to avoid deportation to Iran, where he feared he would face execution. He passed on information to drugs squad officers from Scotland Yard, who answered his request for a meeting, resulting in a number of dealers being jailed. In June 1994, he volunteered to work for the National Criminal Intelligence Service and was recruited by customs investigators. His betrayals seemed effectively to give him immunity from deportation.

Throughout, Alagha had kept in touch with the Ferris brothers. Paul had occasionally visited him while he was in prison, a fact the Iranian passed on to the handlers in the intelligence service. Paul had no reason to suspect he was anything other than the genuine article. Alagha had been married to Kim, the daughter of wealthy businessman Henry Suttee, with whom Paul was later jailed. Although the couple had split up, Henry still trusted his son-in-law.

In 1997, Alagha had been exposed in the *News of the World* during an investigation into shady arms deals. The newspaper described him as 'the Doc' and 'a merchant of death' after he agreed to sell undercover reporters 46,500 landmines. He claimed, when confronted, that a letter on headed notepaper and sent from the house where he was staying in Epsom was 'a forgery'.

Having given Billy a job and helped Paul out with accommodation in London, the spy would make use of the friendships with the brothers that those seemingly good deeds had reinforced. In a codicil to his Statement of Fact, he said that he told his security-service handlers what he knew of Paul's activities and agreed to try to learn what the younger of the Ferris brothers was planning. He claimed he was not keen to spy on Paul, but in the end did, again in the hope of avoiding possible deportation. As a result, for the next two months he passed on information about the activities and ideas of Paul and his close associates. The intelligence he provided encouraged police to step up their monitoring of the younger Ferris's movements.

There was worse to come, as Billy was to learn shortly before the start of the murder trial. Alagha had made a statement in September 2003 claiming that Billy had told him he knew who had attacked Carol-Anne and implicating the brothers in a revenge attack.

Appalled by the extent of Alagha's treachery, Billy contacted his friend in Ireland, telling him what the Iranian had done and warning him that Alagha might be setting him and his associates up. 'Thanks, Billy. I'll sever all connections with this rat,' his friend told him.

The deceit of a man whom Billy had thought was a friend was one of a thousand thoughts that raced through his brain as he waited for the jury to return a verdict. When it came, it was a shock and disappointment not only to him and his family but to those who had defended him. He was found guilty of murder and sentenced to life, with a recommendation by the trial judge that he stay in prison until he was 75.

An attempt to have that figure reduced was unsuccessful and he is now preparing an appeal against his conviction, a process that could take several years. One avenue being explored is the suggestion that, as a result of the information given by Alagha, Paul would have been under surveillance at the time of the murder by police interested in the suggestion of his further involvement in a gun plot. Security experts have confirmed to the brothers that details of his movements would have been logged. Both Billy and Paul are adamant that such records would provide clear evidence of Billy's innocence in the killing of Jason, but efforts to have these details made available have drawn a blank.

In prison, Billy has much to think on, not least the behaviour of Alagha. 'When I met him at Maidstone in the mid-1980s, my initial impression was of a man filled with sincerity, but I would learn that his integrity was just gold-plated. At the time I was in prison with him, and for years afterwards, I never believed that he of all people would stoop as low as he did. But then the lesson to learn quickest in jail is to be surprised by nothing.'

Billy continued to hear of the comings and goings of old friends and enemies. In 2006, luck was on the side of Walter Douglas, the Tartan Pimpernel, when he was arrested in Ibiza with a fake passport. He was still wanted in Holland, but an international warrant for his arrest had expired and had not been renewed, with the result that he was freed. Not so fortunate was Stan Carnall, whose friends had helped Billy after his recapture in Blackpool. In 2006, following his release on licence, Stan was officially warned by police on Merseyside that they had come across information to the effect that his life was in danger. He armed himself with a gun after police refused to offer him protection, and two days later, following a tip from the Scottish Drug Enforcement Agency, his home was raided, the weapon was found and he was sent to prison for another six years.

The following year came news of Jake Devine. He had been handed an extra three years for his part in the riots at Peterhead and in 1993 made a claim at the Court of Session in Edinburgh for £30,000 damages in compensation for injuries he said he suffered when the SAS stormed the prison. Devine told the court that after freeing the hostage, soldiers seized him in an attic and after telling him, 'You're going for a spin, pal', threw him 12 ft to the floor and then down a series of flights of stairs. He lost his action and, in July 2007, his life, when he was murdered in Glasgow's Cowlair Park.

In April 2008, Donald Forbes died in prison. The following month, John Bowden went on the run from Noranside open jail. He was recaptured after a ten-hour siege at a farmhouse near Clydebank and had six months added to his sentence. Billy's sympathies were with him, but he felt satisfaction on hearing a story about William Lobban, who would never lose his terror of being on the receiving end of retribution over his role in the killing of Joe Hanlon and Bobby Glover. In September 2008, on the seventeenth anniversary of their execution, two undertakers arrived at a hotel in the Highlands where Lobban had been hiding out. They were carrying a coffin, saying a Mr Glover had sent them.

Lobban had lost a leg through illness, a fact on which Billy seized with relish. 'He used to dress up as a woman to disguise himself. The talk is that he is now known as Peggy because he only has one leg. The joke is that a pair of nylons lasts him twice as long.'

Before the year was out, justice had caught up with John Haase when a jury convicted him and Paul Bennett of perverting the course of justice. Haase was jailed for 22 years and Bennett for 20.

33

MA

IN HER NEAT HOME CLOSE to the seaside, Jenny Ferris is surrounded by photographs of her family. One has a prominent place on the wall of her living room. It is a picture of her sons, taken in Frankland prison during a visit there by Billy to see Paul. It is easy to see they are brothers. But Jenny does not hesitate when asked about them: 'Totally different. Paul thinks about things. William is outspoken. He just opens his mouth and comes out with comments whether the listener likes them or not. And he has an amazing sense of humour. Even Paul can get quite embarrassed at some of the things he says.'

The many years Billy has spent in jail, where social niceties are not exactly strictly observed, almost certainly account for both his candour and the fact his mother also sees him as 'a very private person who, if he had something worrying him, wouldn't tell anyone but would keep it to himself'. That private nature was demonstrated by his long reluctance to discuss the motive for the murder of Alan Thompson, a reticence that caused him to spend many more years behind bars than would be normal in such a case. At the same time, only a man who has known prison can attest to openness or friendliness sometimes being interpreted there as weakness, a potentially dangerous characteristic.

Once released, Billy's enthusiasm for wanting those around him to share in the joy of freedom could sometimes be difficult to appreciate. Jenny remembers having a Chinese meal with her son and Carol-Anne, of whom she is particularly fond. 'William was ordering for us and laughing like a hyena. He laughed so much that two prison officers who simply happened to be in the same restaurant heard the noise. One apparently said, "If I didn't know better, I'd say that was Billy Ferris." The other replied, "It can't be. He can't be in here." But he was, and Billy spotted the pair of them. He brought them over to our table, and I could have crawled underneath with embarrassment as they talked about things that happened when he was in prison. Neighbours of one of my daughters were at another table and could hear everything that was said.

'His driving is terrible, because he's so busy talking and laughing he doesn't concentrate. Once, he arranged to pick me up and I dreaded this. I had never been in a motor with him before, but I'd heard what he was like. There was a knock at the door, and there stood William. He said, "You won't believe this, but my motor has packed up down the street," and he gave me such a strange look when I said, "Thank God."

'When the time came to go home, William called a taxi, and when it arrived he asked the driver if he was on social security and paying tax. The man asked why he wanted to know, and William told him, "Because I don't want you taking my ma up the road and being stopped and getting into trouble with her in your car." Some people would have been offended, but the driver took it in good spirit. He even rang his controller and got him to confirm that he wasn't claiming social security. Even so, William insisted on photographing the number plate.

'At home with Carol-Anne, he would sit in the garden sunbathing and having a drink and inviting anybody who passed to join him. I don't know how he has managed to hold himself together after spending so much time in prison.'

Now, in jail again, he telephones her every day, but Jenny finds it too distressing to visit her eldest boy. And mother and son do not write to one another. The last time she sent him a birthday card, the message read 'Hope you have a lovely day'. He called her to ask, 'How can I have a lovely day in prison?' So birthday cards are out, too, but to make up for that Carol-Anne sends him three.

Like her sons, Jenny has scant respect for the police. 'When William was in prison before, they would continually come to our house looking for Paul. We tried telling them he didn't live with us, but they ignored that. They would still come in and search until I was fed up. When Willie was alive, someone burned out our car outside the house. It was left at the front door and the police said they didn't want it moved, even though it was an eyesore. They realised Willie knew who had done it and were angry because he wouldn't shop the people responsible. Eventually, a friendly policeman arranged for somebody to tow it away, but when his superiors found out what he had done, he was rapped over the knuckles for helping us.

'The police gave us a terrible time. The month after Willie died, I had a heart attack and was in hospital. When I came out, I didn't want to stay on my own and so went to live with one of my daughters, leaving my house empty. The police were aware Paul wasn't there, but that didn't stop them smashing my door in. A neighbour told them that there was nobody there and that she had a key and would let them in, but they ignored her. She telephoned to tell me about the damage. The police then said they had made the door secure and a padlock had been fitted. But when we went to ask for the key, they claimed they didn't know where it was. They just said it was up to us to work out how to get back into our house.'

Jenny is convinced the authorities determined long ago to keep the brothers apart. But one occasion when they were positively happy for her sons to be together was during a spell when Billy had been transferred to Barlinnie and discovered Paul was there serving an 18-month sentence. Paul remembers what happened. 'The two of us ended up in the same cell in A Hall after I asked if we could share, and the prison officers were quite happy with that arrangement. But Billy took the piss. One day, he said he was feeling ill with flu and didn't want to go to work. I passed this on to the senior officer, and the following morning he again said he was too ill. The routine was that I'd get up in the morning, go and fetch Billy his breakfast, take it to our cell, then when I'd finished work I'd fetch his dinner and take it up also, and do the same with his supper.

'On the third day of his illness, I happened to be called over to see a social worker, and on the way I heard the sound of Billy laughing. His laughter is kind of infectious. Once you hear it, you don't forget it. I thought, "I'm saying nothing about this. I'm glad he's feeling better." After the meeting with the social worker, I went back to work as normal, and when it was time to go back to the cell I expected Billy to be his sprightly self again. But, lo and behold, he was under the sheets on the bed. The normal ration was two blankets, but Billy had six because he'd said he was feeling cold. I asked how his flu was. He told me he was feeling slightly better and asked me to fetch his meal. I ended up pulling out a weapon, saying, "How sharp do you think this is?" and taking a swipe at the blankets. Billy jumped right out of the bed shouting, "You daft bastard, you nearly cut me." He had all his clothes on. I just said, "I'm glad you're feeling better, Billy."

'How would I sum up Billy? He is a mixture of many emotions, an emotional roller coaster. Sometimes you want to hug him, sometimes you want to roll about with him, sometimes you want to lamp him and sometimes you don't even know what you're laughing at, it's just that he's laughing. Billy is probably an enigma. You ask yourself whether somebody who has been shut up in prison for that length of time can come out without being mentally scarred. I don't think anybody can. When you're coming out of prison and trying to re-engage with society, after losing the biggest part of your youth, do you allow for mood swings? Based on my own experience, which is on a much smaller scale, the answer has to be of course you must.

'He has retained his amazing sense of humour. When I was put back inside, he got in touch, his usual upbeat self, and told me, "Just our fucking luck this happened, isn't it? Now I've got to come down and visit you." His humour is one of the strengths that will see him through this new battle to prove his innocence. Because, be in no doubt, he is innocent of this murder. I'm sure the prosecution have concluded, in cases where people have been found not guilty, "Well, obviously the jury didn't understand the case." Surely, in cases where someone is convicted, the defence is equally entitled to argue that same conclusion. We will exhaust every single avenue, because my brother is in a position where he might never get out.'

Carol-Anne has never doubted her husband's innocence, despite the devastation the case has brought to her life and that of her family. Her opinion of the police has been soured. 'Because of the way they acted on the day Billy was arrested, I don't like most of them now. For the first time, I saw how they act towards people who have done nothing wrong. My reaction then, and it's still my view, is that they tried everything to put Billy back in jail to keep him and Paul apart.

'Some people cannot understand why I stand by Billy. Billy has told me, "I don't want you to be a jail widow. Go and live your life. Do what you want." But I'm not interested in doing that. I realise Billy will be away for a long time, but I'm not going anywhere. He's not a gangster and if he's asked to describe his feelings after spending so much of his life living around men from the underworld, he will simply say, "The underworld is an illusion. The only underworld is the subway."'

Unless he can win an appeal against his latest conviction, Billy will have to remain in prison until 2025, meaning five decades of his life will have been spent behind bars. When he is released, he will be 75. Carol-Anne will be waiting.

The Happy Dust Gang:
How Sex, Scandal and Deceit
Founded a Drugs Empire

● ● ● ● ● ● ● ● ● ● ● ● ● ● ●

ISBN: 9781845962616

£7.99

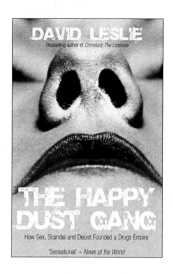

Charlie, snow, toot, white: cocaine goes by many different names. But in Glasgow in the early 1980s, they called it Happy Dust.

At no-holds-barred parties of the glamorous and wealthy, cocaine was the new aphrodisiac. A few lines of Charlie and a humdrum party could become an orgy.

Hot from the forests of Colombia, Charlie flooded onto the streets of Glasgow and was passed along the line to the cocktail set, highly paid sports stars and yuppies desperate for kicks and thrills. Behind it all was a man they called the Parachutist.

But all too soon, the party was over. People became too greedy and the Parachutist was double-crossed. Some of the gang did shady deals with detectives in hotel rooms; others flew to seek shelter in the sun, their reputations destroyed but not their fortunes.

The good times might have been over for the Happy Dust Gang, but their legacy lives on to this day.

Crimelord: The Licensee –
The True Story of Tam McGraw

● ● ● ● ● ● ● ● ● ● ● ● ● ● ● ●

ISBN: 9781845961664

£7.99

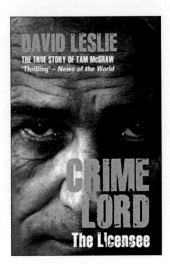

Crimelord is the gripping life story of elusive multimillionaire gangster Tam McGraw. A notorious criminal kingpin, McGraw rose from extreme poverty in the East End of Glasgow to become one of Scotland's wealthiest men.

When hash started to flood into Scotland from the late 1980s onwards, suspicion centred on McGraw, leader of the infamous Barlanark Team. After a two-year surveillance operation, police discovered the drug had been hidden in buses carrying young footballers and deprived Glasgow families on free holidays abroad. It was a scam reminiscent of the movie *The Italian Job*, only this time Scots kids had been sitting on hash worth over £40 million. Police claimed McGraw was the financier and mastermind but in 1998 a jury declared him innocent while other suspects were jailed.

As McGraw refused to discuss his life publicly, his remarkable tale is told through friends, fellow crooks and the occasional rival. It is an outrageous, often hilarious, true gangster story.

The Gangster's Wife:
An Empire Built on Cards

● ● ● ● ● ● ● ● ● ● ● ● ● ● ●

ISBN: 9781845964313

£9.99

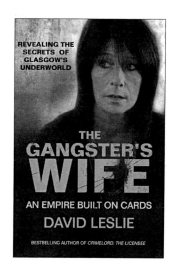

For four decades, Margaret 'Mags' McGraw was a keeper of secrets. Her husband, Tam, the notorious gangster known as 'The Licensee', amassed a fortune by leading a safe-cracking gang before masterminding a spectacular £50-million drugs racket.

Mags was a devotee of Tarot cards and fortune telling, so when Tam and his associates wondered whether luck would be with them, it was to her that they turned. But Mags discovered that the cards gave signs that warned of much more than years in prison cells: they predicted death. Not only did she live with the awful knowledge that her friends would perish violently, but her cards also foretold when they would die.

Furthermore, she learned that her own husband was also doomed to a fate that was unexpected by everyone but her. Tam died in the arms of the wife he called his 'rock' while her secret lover frantically tried to save him.

In *The Gangster's Wife*, Mags reveals her gripping life story, from being a London clippie through often hilarious days running an ice-cream van during the infamous Glasgow Ice Cream Wars to managing a notorious bar, being agony aunt to the toughest criminals around, hiding a secret love and sharing a life with The Licensee.